PIONEERS OF CHILD PSYCHOANALYSIS

For Cesar
with warmest best
wishes

Beatriz Markman
2014

PIONEERS OF CHILD PSYCHOANALYSIS
Influential Theories and Practices in Healthy Child Development

Beatriz Markman Reubins

Edited by
Marc Stephan Reubins

KARNAC

First published in 2014 by
Karnac Books Ltd
118 Finchley Road
London NW3 5HT

British Library Cataloguing in Publication Data

A C.I.P. for this book is available from the British Library

ISBN-13: 978-1-78049-170-7

Typeset by V Publishing Solutions Pvt Ltd., Chennai, India

Printed in Great Britain

www.karnacbooks.com

To my husband Marc and daughter Gabriella

CONTENTS

ACKNOWLEDGEMENTS

I would like to express my deepest gratitude to Dr Harold Blum, Dr R. Horacio Etchegoyen, Dr Eugene Halpert, and Dr Marc Reubins, all of whom I greatly admire, for agreeing to read my book. They guided me with their knowledge and intelligence.

I appreciate the help of Dr Harold Blum for reading Freud's chapter and assisting me with his illuminating ideas, and Dr Halpert for his valuable commentaries.

I am very grateful to Dr R. Horacio Etchegoyen for spending time with me and giving me valuable ideas to complete the chapter on Melanie Klein.

I offer so many thanks to my dear friend and Winnicott expert, Dr Raquel Goldstein, for her time and thoughtful commentaries on the Winnicott chapter.

I would also like to thank my dear friend and colleague, Dr Andres Rascovsky, past president of the Argentine Psychoanalytic Association, for giving me his father's book *Filicide*, which allowed me to include Arnaldo Rascovsky's own important ideas about filicide.

I am very grateful to my husband Marc, a child psychoanalyst, who helped me with many valuable ideas, especially for his suggestion of adding a chapter dedicated to influential child psychoanalytic thinkers around the world, and for agreeing to be the editor of the book. He warmly supported me throughout this process even though this meant time taken away from his own work.

I would like to thank my colleague Dr John Christman, who spent time looking through the book and helped me both with suggestions on the fluidity of the language and with valuable comments about the content of the book. Also, many thanks to Dr Daniel Cohen for his thoughtful review.

And my very special thanks and gratitude to my wonderful daughter Gabriella for her time in reading the book, and in helping me to be sure that my English was fluent and accurate. She not only gave me her welcome thoughts on language, but also provided valuable observations, concepts, and ideas. Best of all, her personal creativity is reflected in my use of one of her paintings on the cover of my book.

I would like to thank all my patients who, over my more than forty years of practice, inspired me to learn and research, leading me to the study of these great thinkers.

I also would like to thank my editor, Rod Tweedy, who from the beginning and throughout the publication process answered all my questions, and was always there for me.

I am grateful to these people and to the many others who have given me the opportunity to voice my knowledge and my ideas about the importance of child-rearing.

Beatriz Markman Reubins, MD, received her medical degree from Buenos Aires Medical School of the University of Buenos Aires. She is a licensed clinical psychologist, also from the University of Buenos Aires. She trained in child, adolescent, and adult psychiatry at North Shore University Hospital on Long Island, New York, and is a child, adolescent, and adult psychoanalytic graduate from the Argentina Psychoanalytic Association. She has been an Assistant Professor in Psychopathology at the University of Buenos Aires. She is currently an Associate Attending at NorthShoreLIJ Hospital, where she teaches psychoanalysis and supervises psychiatric residents and child psychiatric fellows. She is in full private practice working with children, adolescents, and adults at her private office in Old Westbury, Long Island, New York.

Dr Markman Reubins is a member of the Argentine Psychoanalytic Association, the International Psychoanalytic Society, and past President of the Long Island Psychoanalytic Society in New York. She is also a member of CAPA (China–American Psychoanalytic Alliance), and is a supervising psychoanalist in China.

She is married to Marc Reubins, MD, child, adolescent, and adult psychiatrist and psychoanalyst. She has one daughter, Gabriella Juliet Reubins, who is also a physician.

Marc Stephan Reubins, MD, received his medical degree from the Chicago Medical School. He trained in adult psychiatry at the Hillside Medical Center of Long Island Jewish Hospital where he was Chief Resident in his last year. He then trained at the Albert Einstein Medical Center in Child and Adolescent Psychiatry. He was a research fellow in Forensic Psychiatry at the New York University School of Medicine. He is certified by the American Board of Medical Specialists in adult, adolescent, and child psychiatry. He is a graduate of the New York Psychoanalytic Institute.

Dr Reubins is a member of the American Psychoanalytic Association, the International Psychoanalytic Society, and past President of the Long Island Psychoanalytic Society in New York.

He is married to Beatriz Markman Reubins, MD, and is the father of Gabriella Juliet Reubins, MD.

PROLOGUE

*Harold Blum**

This volume provides a lucid and engaging introduction to Freud and the wellsprings of psychoanalytic theory.

Following a brief biography of the founder of psychoanalysis, Freud's life within his family, his friends, and disciples are artfully elaborated. The human, complex aspects of Freud's personality are further revealed in his attitude towards dissidents, drop-outs, and antagonists of psychoanalysis. The basic concepts, and the paradigmatic interpretation of dreams, seamlessly appear in a chronological sequence.

Beatriz Markman Reubins accomplishes an illuminating integration that simultaneously stimulates further enquiry and investigation. The volume will open new vistas, and inspire the reader to delve more deeply into the history and development of psychoanalysis. It is especially recommended for those who want to enlarge their knowledge of Freud, and of his early followers, the pioneers who fostered and enriched the evolution of psychoanalytic thought and practice.

---

*Former Editor, *Journal of the American Psychoanalytic Association*
Vice-President, International Psychoanalytic Association

FOREWORD

R. Horacio Etchegoyen*

Many books and articles have been published on child psychoanalysis in the past, and I am pleased to address one of the few that spans a broad overview of this discipline. In addition to the book's comprehensive discussion of pioneers, it has the merit of doing so with depth and equanimity.

The author begins with Freud's great discoveries by reviewing the structural and topographic theories in Chapter One, and exploring his various articles on child psychology with special attention to the analysis of "Little Hans" in Chapter Two.

In Chapter Three, the author carefully examines the life and work of Anna Freud, stressing her unique contributions to the concept of defence mechanisms. In this vein, Anna followed the ideas of her father but also added other defence mechanisms such as idealisation, altruism, and identification with the aggressor, which Ferenczi had postulated just a few years earlier.

*Former President, International Psychoanalytic Association
Former President, Buenos Aires Psychoanalytic Association

In "Normality and Pathology in Childhood", Anna Freud, as highlighted by the author, suggested the fertile and original idea of developmental lines, which follows the trajectory of childhood growth under emotional maturation in terms of the interaction of the ego with the id, the superego, and the external world with regard to the development of libidinal and aggressive impulses. Anna Freud also described the evolution from childhood dependence to the organisation of self and object relations. The author is careful to point out that the multiple developmental lines do not always develop simultaneously, a reality that may not be pathological. Dr Markman Reubins recalls her impressions when she visited Anna Freud's Hampstead Clinic (today, the Anna Freud Centre) and her idea to write this book was born. The chapter concludes with a clear exposition of Anna's technical approach to the treatment of children.

As the discussion of Anna Freud was thorough and rigorous, so we find the well-balanced approach to Melanie Klein in Chapter Four. After exploring Klein's family life and marriage with Arthur Klein, the author traces Klein's life from Budapest, where she met Sándor Ferenczi, her analyst and teacher for many years, and it was through his influence that she was encouraged to treat children. It was in Budapest that Klein started with child therapy, when she analysed her son Eric. From Budapest, Klein went to Berlin, invited by Karl Abraham, her second analyst. It was there that she developed her play technique to analyse children. Finally, she went to London, where she elaborated her main theory. The author creatively interweaves growth, technique, and practice with Klein's personal history.

Dr Markman Reubins strives to present the ideas of Melanie Klein and Anna Freud through linking their disputes and discussions in a manner that highlights the evolution of their common growth. The chapter ends by contrasting and comparing the technical ideas of Melanie Klein and Anna Freud.

No less attention is given to another pioneer of child psychoanalysis, Donald Woods Winnicott, in Chapter Five. Here, we see the early history of this great psychoanalyst described in detail, highlighting his contacts with other well-known analysts. Winnicott described the role of the environment on children's development and developed ideas about some children's antisocial tendencies.

Melanie Klein's ideas were a great influence on Winnicott's thinking, but gradually he developed his own, although he always considered her a great analyst and a genius. He shared with her the decisive influence of the child's early life and his relationship with the mother. Like other analysts who greatly appreciate Klein but reserve the right to disagree with her, Winnicott was one of the leaders of the Independent Group, which also included Ronald Fairbairn, Michael Balint, John Bowlby, Adam Limentani, and others equally prominent.

In her thorough description of the theoretical development of Winnicott, Markman Reubins highlights his understanding of child development from the beginning as more accurately characterised as unintegration than disassociation or death instinct. The mother's role was crucial for Winnicott; he thought that maternal care was not sufficiently appreciated by Klein. There is a bridge between the internal and external, an area that he called the "transitional space". On this concept depends the development of the true self or of a false self, and the nature of this development is connected with a good-enough mother, or holding environment. After her careful description of Winnicott's ideas, the author explains how he understood the therapeutic process, the dialectic between interpretation and holding in a unique play experience between two people.

In Chapter Six, the author describes her own treatment of a five-year-old girl, using this to illustrate how the three previous authors might understand and treat the case. This is a highly instructive exercise that I am sure the reader will deeply enjoy and appreciate.

In the following chapters, Seven to Nine, Beatriz Markman Reubins studies, with the same care as for the previous authors, the other major child psychoanalytic pioneers around the world.

In the Conclusions, the author outlines her belief that studying these theories will open the path, to understanding them, seeing the similarities and the differences. Despite the differences, Beatriz points out that all the theories have a common denominator, and that is the importance of the child's early experiences, particularly the mother–infant relationship, and also including the value of the father and social environment as well as the child's own personality development.

All these psychoanalytic thinkers of early development recognise that it is not easy for parents to meet all the needs of their children, and the author points out that sometimes parents do not know the impact on their babies when they go away for days or weeks, leaving their infant with strangers. Too few parents recognise what these scholars teach us, that early abandonment by parents and leaving the children in the hands of strangers can provoke unseen and later negative, possibly even pathological, development. The author concludes that her hope is to transmit this profoundly important legacy to psychoanalysts and to parents.

This book is a rigorous and well-balanced, enthusiastic study which will take the reader through a rich and varied world of psychoanalytic work. The author clearly put great effort into writing this book, and the reader will certainly find it rewarding.

Buenos Aires

PREFACE

My motivation for writing this book began in my mind when I met Anna Freud at her Hampstead Clinic in London in 1974. I saw her in action while she was moderating a case presentation at their weekly case conference. I found Anna Freud's thought, charisma, strong personality, and piercing eyes deeply illuminating, and this experience marked the beginning of my interest in researching the different ways of approaching psychoanalytic theory and technical work with children. After the conference, I spoke with her and expressed my desire to return to her clinic for more discussion; she warmly welcomed me and invited me to return.

On that second day, I met with Mrs Mason, the psychoanalyst who had presented the case at the conference, and I had the opportunity to see the offices and discuss some of my cases with her. After being there the second time, my mind was opened to other ways of practising child psychoanalysis.

I had come to England with a background rooted in Kleinian theory and technique. During my psychoanalytic training at the Argentine Psychoanalytic Association (APA), Kleinian theory was strongly applied not only to child analysis but also to adults.

I wondered: What is the truth? Who is right? Both Kleinian and Freudian theories work with children, although they have different clinical and theoretical approaches. As time went by, and I studied, experienced, and exposed myself to different theories, I concluded that all of them have made great contributions in the field of child psychoanalysis. And I discovered with fascination other psychoanalysts' desires to learn, research, and create. From Anna Freud all the way to John Bowlby, each left us with an enormous legacy from which we now benefit in our current thinking and work.

As I began to teach psychiatric residents and child psychiatric fellows at North Shore LIJ Hospital, in New York, I was interested in cultivating their curiosity in theory and technique so that they would be able to apply it to their clinical work.

André Green (1927–2012), a well-known French psychoanalyst, first proposed the need to integrate the Freudian model with the post-Freudian model in order to create another model, one that provides a common ground for our understanding and practice. With a wider knowledge of theory, everybody would be able to understand how emotional and physical constancy in the early life of the baby build the basis for future psychological health in the child, adolescent, and adult.

My goal and major interest in writing this book is to expose emerging professionals in the field of psychoanalysis to theories of human development, paying particular attention to the importance of infant experiences and how these experiences affect future adult behaviour.

In doing so, I hope to help analysts to be "good-enough" mothers-therapist to their children-patients, as Winnicott conceptualised it.

The theories illustrated in this book can also serve as a series of blueprints to guide parents through the process of child-rearing so that their own children may avoid future pathology.

Dr Charles Brenner, a well-known American psychoanalyst, said that with the knowledge of different theories we have to take what is useful and disregard, temporarily or for ever, what is not useful in our practices (Brenner, personal communication, 1980).

INTRODUCTION

In creating the innovative theory and technique of psychoanalysis to address psychopathology, Sigmund Freud planted the seed for opening other areas where his discovery could be applied. One of the most important ones was the introduction of his theory to child psychoanalysis. Since his time, many thinkers have discovered, researched, and expanded theories of child development and psychoanalysis.

After spending years practising adult and child psychoanalysis and researching the parent–child dynamic, I am still surprised that so many people do not have a clear idea of the risks and consequences of leaving their young children in the care of strangers at the beginning of life, and how profoundly this can affect their future development. As therapists, we can help children with psychopathology, but another of our important tasks is to educate parents and future parents about risk factors in the development of the child.

This book describes the lives and theories of the pioneer child psychoanalysts who created the field of child psychoanalysis and contributed to the understanding of child development. Through observation and research, the psychoanalysts discussed in this book have also made great progress in helping other analysts understand the dynamics and pathology arising in the development of children, and to help understand or forestall their future behaviour and pathologies. In turn, this process also enlightens us in our understanding of adult patients, who, through their symptoms, express their unresolved childhood difficulties, conflicts, and anxieties.

The biographies of the men and women who developed these pioneering theories and techniques serve as a gateway to historic moments in the field of developmental psychology as well as providing a lens through which to observe the minds of highly motivated and creative individuals. The main concepts of each pioneer have been summarised with the intent to highlight how they understood and conceptualised their own observations of the behaviour of children and parents. Ultimately, I hope that, through learning more about these authors and the context in which they evolved the field, clinicians will be inspired to create and further their own understanding, leading to the enrichment of their theoretical and clinical work.

Thank you to Karnac Books for giving me the opportunity to achieve my goals.

CHAPTER ONE

Sigmund Freud

Volumes have been written concerning the subject of Freud's life and work. In this chapter, the focus is narrowed to Freud's immediate family, his parents, siblings, children, and grandchildren. The history of the Vienna Psychoanalytic Society, Freud's circle of friends and the pioneers of what became the International Psychoanalytic Society, is also highlighted.

Freud and his siblings

Sigmund Freud was born on 6 May 1856, in the Moravian town of Freiberg (now known as Příbor, in the Czech Republic), during the era of the Austrian Empire. His parents were of Jewish Galitzian descent. His father, Jacob Freud (1815–1896), was born in Tysmenitz, Galitzia, a part of the Austro-Hungarian Empire. In 1886, at the age of forty-one, Jacob married his second (or possibly third) wife and Sigmund Freud's mother, Amalia Malka Nathansohn, a woman twenty-one years her husband's junior. Sigmund was their first child.

Jacob Freud had two children from his first marriage to Sally Kanner (1829–1852), Emanuel (1833–1914) and Philipp (1836–1911). Both children were born in Tysmenitz in Galitzia. It is not known and questionable whether Jacob had a second wife, Rebecca, who died after three years of marriage (1852–1855).

Jacob Freud's older son, Emanuel, married Marie in the city of Freiberg; they had two children, Johann (1855–1919) and Pauline (1855–1944). Johann and Sigmund were very close in age, and during their early childhood they played together, but lost touch after the emigration of Emanuel and his family to Manchester, England, in 1860. In Manchester, Emanuel and Marie had two more children, Bertha (1866–1940) and Samuel (1870–1945). Jacob Freud's second son, Phillip, married Bloomah Frankel and they had two children, Pauline (1873–1951) and Morris (1875–1938).

Sigmund Freud kept in touch with his British half-siblings and their families through regular correspondence with Samuel, and the two men eventually met for the first time in London in 1938, one year before Freud's death.

Jacob Freud had eight children with his wife Amalia Nathansohn. Sigmund, whose birth name was Sigismund Schlomo, was the first born, in 1856; he changed his name to Sigmund in 1877, when he was twenty-one.

Freud's siblings
Sigmund (Freiberg, 6 May 1856–London, 23 September 1939) Julius (Freiberg, October 1857–Freiberg, 15 April 1858) Anna (Freiberg, 31 December 1858–New York, 11 March 1955) Rosa (Vienna, 21 March 1860, deported 23 September 1942) Mitzi (Vienna, 22 March 1861, deported 23 September 1942) Dolfi (Vienna, 23 July 1862, deported 23 September 1942) Pauline (Vienna, 3 May 1864, deported 23 September 1942) Alexander Gotthold Ephraim (Vienna, 19 April 1866–Canada, 23 April 1943).

Freud's younger brother, Julius, died in infancy (1858) when Sigmund was a toddler. His first sister Anna was born in Freiberg in 1858, and was the only sister who survived the Nazi occupation. Anna married Ely Bernays (1860–1921), who was Sigmund Freud's brother-in-law. In 1892, the Bernayses moved to the United States and settled in New York. They had four daughters and a son, Edward Bernays (1891–1995), who became well known in the area of public relations and advertising. Their daughters were Judith, Lucy, Hella, and Martha.

Freud's second and favourite sister, Regine Debora (Rosa) (1860–1942) married a medical doctor, Heinrich Graf (1852–1908). They had a son, Hermann (1897–1917), who was killed in the First World War, and a daughter, Cacilie (1899–1922), who committed suicide after an unhappy love affair.

Freud's sister Maria (Mitzi) married her cousin Moritz Freud. They had three daughters, Margarete, Lily, Martha, and a son, Theodor, who died at the age of twenty-three after a drowning accident.

Freud's sister, Esther Adolfine (Dolfi), never married and remained in the family home to care for her parents until their deaths, while his fifth sister, Pauline Regine (Paula), married Valentine Winternitz (1859–1900). The couple emigrated to the United States where their daughter, Rose Beatrice, was born in 1896. After the death of her husband, Paula and her daughter Rosi returned to Europe. When Rosi was seventeen, she developed psychological problems; ten years later, she became pregnant and married Ernst Waldinger, a poet. It was an unhappy relationship, and in 1931 she suffered a relapse and emigrated to the United States, where in 1946 she entered analysis with Paul Federn in New York.

Freud's youngest brother, Alexander, married Sophie Sabine Schreiber, and the couple had one son, Harry (1909–1968). Alexander was intelligent and hard-working and became a specialist in transportation at the Vienna Chamber of Commerce. As the Second World War approached, Alexander lost his business, and in March 1938 he and his family escaped the Nazis by moving to Switzerland. In September, they emigrated to London, joining his son Harry; later, he and his wife immigrated to Canada, where he died in 1943.

Their father, Jacob Freud, died on 23 October 1896, at the age of eighty-one; their mother, Martha Freud, died in 1930 when she was ninety-four. Both parents died in Vienna.

At the time of the Nazi persecution, Sigmund Freud pleaded to Marie Bonaparte to get permission for his sisters to leave Vienna, but it was not possible, and his four younger sisters were murdered by the Nazis, including Adolfine (Dolfi) Freud who was killed in the Treblinka concentration camp.

Freud in Vienna

In 1859, when Sigmund Freud was four years old, the Freud family moved from Freiberg to Vienna following an economic crisis that ruined his father's wool business, and Sigmund lived in Vienna until his forced immigration to London in 1938.

Freud attended medical school at Vienna University in 1873 at the age of seventeen. He was brilliant, always ahead of his class, and graduated in March 1881. He was excellent at his research, which concentrated on neurophysiology in Brucke's laboratory, and in 1883 he joined Theodor Meynert's service in the psychiatric hospital. After spending a short time as a resident in neurology and director of a children's ward in Berlin, he returned to Vienna in 1886.

Freud and his children

In September of 1886, Freud married Martha Bernays (1861–1951), whom he loved immensely. In November 1895, Minna Bernays, Martha's sister, lost her fiancé Ignaz Schoenberg, a close friend of Freud's, to pulmonary tuberculosis. Minna moved in with the Freuds and lived with them until the end of her life.

Freud and Martha had six children and eight grandchildren. Only Anna, the youngest child, followed in her father's footsteps and became a psychoanalyst.

Freud's children
Mathilde (Vienna, 1887–London, 1978)
Jean Martin (Vienna, 1889–London, 1976)
Oliver (Vienna, 1891–United States, 1969)
Ernst (Vienna, 1892–London, 1970)
Sophie (Vienna, 1893–Vienna, 1920)
Anna (Vienna, 1895–London, 1982).

Freud's oldest daughter Mathilde married Robert Hollitscher in 1909. The couple did not have children, and in 1938, during Nazi persecution, she left Vienna to settle in London.

Freud's eldest son, Jean Martin, was named in honour of the great French clinician Jean Martin Charcot. Martin served as a lieutenant in the Austrian Artillery from 1914 to 1915, but from 1915 to 1919 was held prisoner in Genoa, Italy, until his release at the age of twenty-five.

On his return to Vienna, he became a lawyer, ultimately working in a bank and managing Freud's finances and his accounts.

Martin met his wife, Ernestine Drucker (1896–1980), in Vienna, and they married on 7 December 1919. The couple had two children, Anton Walter (1921) and Myriam Sophie (1924). After the Nazi occupation in 1938, the couple fled from Austria to France. They separated but never divorced, and Ernestine remained in France with their daughter while Martin left for London. She and their daughter Sophie escaped France in 1940 by way of Morocco, where they boarded a ship for the United States. There, Ernestine began a speech pathology practice and remained in the United States until her death in 1980. Martin's life in London was difficult. He held several different jobs for short periods. His last job was in a smoke shop near the British Museum. In 1958, against his sister Anna's advice, he published his memoirs, *Sigmund Freud: Man and Father*, which is still in print.

Oliver Freud was also born in Vienna, during the same year the Freuds moved to their new home, Berggasse 19, which has become the current location of the Freud Museum. In 1909, Oliver attended the Vienna Polytechnic, graduating with a degree in civil engineering in 1915. During the Second World War and until December 1916, he was put to work building barracks and tunnels; after this assignment, he was made an officer in an engineering regiment. Oliver married for the first time in December 1915, but was divorced by September 1916; in 1921, he began analysis with Franz Alexander.

He later married Henny Fuchs (1892–1971), and the couple had one daughter, Eva Mathilde, who was born on 3 September 1924. Oliver lived and worked in Berlin until Hitler came to power in 1933. At the time of the persecution, he fled to France. Later, Oliver and his wife emigrated to the United States, while their daughter Eva remained in France with her fiancé. Eva died of influenza in 1944. Oliver died in 1969.

Ernst Ludwig was born in 1892. He began his studies in Vienna in 1911 and graduated in 1919, in a tumultuous political time. In Munich, he met Lucy, his future wife, who was the daughter of a wealthy family from Berlin and a student of art history. In 1920, they moved to Berlin and married. Ernst developed a successful architectural career in Berlin, where the couple had three children: Stephan Gabriel; Lucian (1922–2011), the internationally recognised painter; and Clement (1924–2009), who became a writer. In 1933, with the rise of National Socialism and the related murder of one of his wife's family members, Ernst and his family fled to London; by November, he and his family were settled there, where he became a partner in an architectural firm and built his own clientele. Many psychoanalysts asked him to build and update their offices, and he succeeded in establishing himself for a second time. He died in 1970 in London.

Sophie married Max Halberstadt and had three children. She died during the Spanish influenza epidemic in 1920.

Freud's youngest daughter, Anna, was born in 1895 in Vienna, and died in 1982 in London after a notable psychoanalytic career. She never married.

The Freud family lived at Bergasse 19 in Vienna until they immigrated to London in 1938, just as Vienna was becoming an increasingly dangerous place for Jews. Not long afterwards, Sigmund Freud died of cancer of the mouth and jaw, a disease he had suffered from for the last twenty years of his life. He died at the age of eighty-three, in London, on 23 September 1939. Martha Bernays Freud died in London on 2 November 1951; her sister, Minna Bernays, had died there earlier, 13 February 1941.

Freud and his friends: the Wednesday meetings

Sigmund Freud was an intense and passionate man, especially when it came to his wife Martha, his family, his children, his friends, and his psychoanalytic discoveries. As he was developing ideas in search of an explanation for the mental health and symptoms of his patients, he shared his discoveries with his best friends, also physicians, with whom he exchanged numerous letters containing his ideas regarding himself and his patients. One of his closest friends was Wilhelm Fliess, a German-Jewish physician.

Freud successfully treated William Stekel, a physician and psychologist, who suggested to him in 1902 that he should begin a group to discuss various issues related to his ideas. This was the beginning of the Wednesday meetings, at that time called the "Wednesday's Psychological Meetings". Every week, a group of men (later three women were included) met at Freud's home at Berggasse 19. The founding men in the group included Alfred Adler, Wilhelm Stekel, Paul Federn, Isidor Sadger, Edward Hitschmann, Max Kahane, Rudolph Reitter, and Otto Rank, with Freud present for each meeting.

The men came from a range of medical backgrounds. Alfred Adler (1870–1937) was a medical doctor, and specialised in ophthalmology at the beginning of his career. Wilhelm Stekel (1868–1940) was a medical doctor. Paul Federn (1871–1937) was a medical doctor who first met Freud in 1902 and remained loyal to him until he died. Isidor Sadger (1867–1942), a medical doctor, was an important pioneer who remained a member of the group until it ended in 1938. He was respected for his work in the area of the perversions. Edward Hitschmann (1871–1958) was a medical doctor who specialised in internal medicine. He joined the group in 1905, making him one of the last remaining members of the group, always loyal to Freud. He then emigrated to the United States and settled in Boston, Massachusetts. Max Kahane (1856–1923), another medical doctor, was one of the first members of the group, while Rudolph Reitter (1865–1917) was a well-known medical doctor when he joined the group in 1902. Otto Rank (1884–1939) was a good friend and one of Freud's favourite members, until Rank left the group.

Over the years, the Wednesday meetings boasted many other members.

Some Wednesday meeting members

Fritz Wittels, MD, joined the group in 1907, became a psychoanalyst and settle in New York in 1932. He was a member of the New York Psychoanalytic Society.

Rudolf von Urbantschitoch, MD, joined the group in 1909, psychiatrist and psychologist was interested in human sexuality. He became a psychoanalyst and settle in Carmel, California in 1936.

Maximilian Steiner, MD, specialised in dermatology.

Erdwin Hollerung, MD, specialised in surgery.

Albert Jochim, MD, director of a well-known sanatorium in Vienna.

David Bach, PhD, was a music critic.

Philipp Frey, a teacher and writer.

Hugo Heller, a publisher who also owned a bookshop where the intellectuals of the time used to gathered for discussions.

Max Graf, PhD, an Austrian author, critic, writer, and music expert who was also a close friend of Freud. He was the father of Herbert Graf, the boy in Freud's famous case known as "Little Hans".

Adolf Hautler, a philosopher.

Alfred Meisl, MD, specialised in internal medicine in Gumpendorf, a Vienna suburb.

Alfred Bass, MD, specialised in general medicine in Vienna.

Guido Brecher, MD, was a physician at the spas of Bad Ganstein and Merano.

Adolf Deutsch, MD, specialised in physiotherapy.

Unfortunately, no record exists of the meetings held between 1902 and 1906. In 1908, what had been the Wednesday meetings formally became the Vienna Psychoanalytic Society, for whose membership participation and attendance were obligatory. While still meeting on Wednesday, in 1910 the society's gatherings moved from Freud's home to the Medical Society building and, from then on, attendance and participation were not obligatory.

All the members were interested in psychology, and were seeking new ideas to help them understand the behaviour and the pathology of the human being. Freud's ideas were fascinating and innovative, but not everybody agreed with them. Within the medical community, certain groups rejected him, and for some time Freud felt lonely and isolated. Some of them criticised him, hated him, and ostracised him. Freud suffered tremendously because he was a social man who loved people. It was after Freud's disappointment in his isolation that he turned to the Wednesday meetings as a place for discussion and intellectual stimulation.

The Wednesday gatherings included a heterogeneous group of intellectual physicians, educators, and writers. They discussed a wide range of issues, such as clinical cases, books and articles, biology, psychology, sociology, mythology, religion, art, literature, education, and criminology.

Adler was the first to emphasise the importance of aggression at the psychological level. Freud valued this idea and further developed the concept in 1915 in his paper "Instincts and Their Vicissitudes", further elaborating his ideas in 1920 in *Beyond the Pleasure Principle*. As a member of the group, Adler began to slowly and systematically promote his ideas, which eventually contradicted Freud's basic concepts. However, Freud was tolerant and named Adler president of the society, a position that he held until his participation in the group ended.

Also close to Freud was Carl Gustav Jung, another physician who lived in Switzerland. Freud was very fond of him, and while Jung was not a member of the Wednesday group, he visited it occasionally, and Freud nominated him president of the International Psychoanalytic Society. Later, Jung developed his own ideas and the two men separated.

Over the years, some members left the group, but most of them remained until its end in 1938 when Hitler invaded Austria, after which Jewish doctors were not allowed to belong to the psychoanalytic group. The last members who remained were Federn, Hitschmann, and Sadger.

It is important to mention that there were three women who were invited to participate in the Wednesday group: Hermine Hug-Hellmuth, the pioneer of child psychoanalysis, whom Freud named the representative of child psychoanalysis; Sabina Spielrein, the Russian psychoanalyst, who was also considered one of the first child analysts, and who dedicated her life to the study and development of child analysis; and Margarete Hilferding, an Austrian woman who taught and was also an individual psychologist, she was the first woman admitted to the Wednesday Psychoanalytic Society. She died in 1942, during her transport to an extermination camp. Freud's openness and acceptance of women's intellectual capacities is demonstrated by his inclusion of these three women in the Wednesday group. Given that these were times when women were not considered to be thinkers, this was a bold move on Freud's part, and marked a considerable step towards the places that women would go in the field of psychoanalysis in the future.

Freud's friends and dissidents

Freud had seven physician friends who developed their own ideas, separated from him, and became dissidents: Wilhelm Fliess, Alfred Adler, Wilhelm Stekel, Carl Jung, Otto Rank, Wilhelm Reich, and Sándor Ferenczi.

Wilhelm Fliess

Wilhelm Fliess (1858–1928) was a German-Jewish medical doctor who specialised in otolaryngology and practised in Berlin. It was at Dr Joseph Breuer's suggestion that Fliess attended Sigmund Freud's conferences in 1887 in Vienna, where the men established a strong and intense friendship. Their correspondence and meetings became an important part of the history and development of psychoanalytic theory. Their exchange of letters took place from 1887 to 1904; it was a time when Freud was making many fundamental discoveries of psychoanalytic concepts.

Sigmund Freud's letters to Fliess, his closest friend at that time, contained some of his most productive investigations as a psychoanalyst. It was Fliess who suggested to Freud the importance of jokes as useful material for psychoanalytical researching. Fliess, however, developed an unusual theory that there was a connection between the nose and the genitals, one he called the "reflex nasal neurosis". It has been suggested that their friendship disintegrated in 1904 because Fliess believed that Freud had used one of his own theories, periodicity theory, to develop one of his own concepts.

> It was Fliess who first suggested to Freud the principle of innate bisexuality, which builds upon the finding that each sex contains rudimentary anatomical representations of the opposite sex. Freud, at the urging of Fliess, developed the principle in psychological direction by claiming that both male and female elements are represented in the unconscious.
>
> (Glosskurth, 1991, p. 8)

Freud and Fliess argued fiercely at their last meeting in August 1900, and their friendship became a competitive rivalry. Freud ordered the destruction of the correspondence, but Marie Bonaparte was able to purchase the letters to Fliess and refused to allow them to be destroyed, but most of Fliess's letters to Freud have not survived. Fliess died in Berlin, on 13 October 1928, at the age of seventy.

Alfred Adler

Alfred W. Adler (1870–1937) was born in Austria. He was only sixty-seven at the time of his death. An ophthalmologist, Adler became interested in psychoanalytic ideas, later becoming a psychotherapist and the founder of the School of Individual Psychology. After reading a criticism of Freud, he was compelled to write a defence. Once Freud learned about the letter, he wrote to Adler and invited him to be one of the inaugural members of the Viennese Psychoanalytic Society. Freud and Adler were good friends for ten years until Adler became the first of others to come to break from Freud's theories, and he resigned his presidency in 1911.

Adler was not interested in the unconscious or spirituality. He emphasised the social aspect of the neurosis; he believed that the need for social relationships is present from the start.

He believed that we have to consider the future, our expectations, rather than the past, to explain neurotic behaviour. He thought that Freud was too concerned with the past.

Adler rejected the sexual aetiology of neurosis, and regarded neurosis as being caused by feelings of inferiority, believing that that inferiority feelings are the source of all human striving.

In Adler's theory, masculinity represents strength and power, and he spoke of the *masculine protest* in both men and women. He described the inferiority complex and the development of *overcompensation* as a coping mechanism for whatever the subject feels inferior about. In addition to seeing the masculine protest as a way for understanding neurosis, Adler also believed that social forces must have a part in analytic explanations.

Adler's therapeutic approach was directed to work with the individual, leading the patient to uncover misperceptions, values, and assumptions. The task of the therapist was to help the patient with awareness and insight of his errors, and re-orient him towards a more useful way of living.

Adler established several child guidance clinics in Austria geared to help under privilege children with emotional problems, these clinics were closed by the nazi government due to his Jewish heritage. He emigrated to the United States where he began a professorship at the Long Island College of Medicine. Adler died on 1937 from a heart attack while on a lecture tour in Aberdeen, Scotland.

Wilhelm Stekel

Wilhelm Stekel (1868–1940) was born in Bukovina, Austria-Hungary, and died in London at the age of seventy-two. Stekel broke with Freud in November 1912, after Adler and shortly before Carl Jung. An innovator in the area of technique rather than theory, Stekel developed a form of short-term therapy called *active analysis*, which has much in common with some modern forms of counselling and therapy. Stekel thought that current conflicts are as important as conflicts from the past.

Carl Jung

Carl Gustav Jung (1875–1961) was a Swiss psychologist and psychiatrist who developed analytical psychology. Jung proposed and organised the concepts of the extraverted and introverted personality, archetypes, and the collective unconscious. Born in Kesswil, Switzerland, Jung died in Zurich at the age of eighty-six. He married Emma Jung (1903–1955) and had five children.

Jung's fascination with medicine and spirituality led him to the field of psychiatry. From early in his career, he knew about Freud's psychoanalytic theories, and finally in 1907 the two met and spent time together discussing psychoanalytic issues.

The contact with Freud had a great impact on Jung's later theories. Initially, Freud viewed him as somebody who would follow his ideas, and thus named Jung president of the International Psychoanalytic Society. The friendship began to dissolve, however, as Jung developed his own ideas that diverged from Freud's views. The complete break came in 1912, with the publication of his new interpretation of the nature of the libido in his paper "The Psychology of the Unconscious", and it was clear that his increasingly independent ideas had come to a point of irreparable rupture with Freud's.

To Jung, the primal libido was an undifferentiated energy and universal life urge. He rejected the idea of sexuality in the oral phase, stating that the oral stage had a neutral quality, and therefore libido in the oral stage was hunger, not sexual. He observed that there were similarities between neurotic people and primitive people. His speculation was that there was a hereditary portion of the mind that contained the imprints of ancestral experience. He called these "archetypes", imprints that appear in associations, phantasies, drawings, and dreams. Jung identified the most common archetypes as *animus*, the ideal mate for the female psyche, and the *anima*, the ideal mate for the male psyche. He also described a collective unconscious that contains the archetypes, and divided the human psyche into the *persona* (a superficial social mask) and the *ego* (the deeper part of the psyche, partly conscious and partly unconscious).

Otto Rank

Otto Rosenfeld, who as a young man changed his name to Otto Rank (1884–1939), was born in Vienna, and died in New York at the age of fifty-five. A psychoanalyst, writer, and teacher, Rank was a young student when he joined Freud's inner circle of the Viennese followers and was one of Freud's closest colleagues for twenty years.

Around 1920, he began to experiment with short-term therapy, with activity and passivity in the analytic situation, and also with changes at the technical level. The break between Rank and Freud developed over time. Rank first moved to Paris and later to New York. The most devastating attack to Freud's thought came with the 1920 publication of Rank's *The Trauma of Birth*, when he introduced the idea that the experience of birth is the source of all anxiety. The controversy then intensified further upon Rank's idea for a new technical approach, which he termed "non-directive" or "client-centered" therapy.

Wilhelm Reich

Wilhelm Reich (1897–1957) was born in Austria-Hungary and died in Lewisburg, Pennsylvania, at the age of sixty. After graduating from the University of Vienna in 1922 with a medical degree, Reich studied neuropsychology and became a psychoanalyst, a member of the second generation of Freud psychoanalysts, and one of the most radical figures in the history of psychiatry. He was very productive and wrote numerous books and articles. Reich broke from Freud in 1932 after a controversy over the existence of the death instinct and, in particular, the causation of masochism.

Sándor Ferenczi

Sándor Ferenczi (1873–1933) was a psychoanalyst and close friend of Freud. Born in Miskolc, Austria-Hungary, he died in Budapest when he was fifty-nine years old. Ferenczi first met Freud in 1908, and was president of the International Psychoanalytic Association from 1918 to 1919. In his work, Ferenczi encouraged acting out, giving love, and admitting mistakes to patients. He also permitted himself on occasion to get emotionally involved with the patient, about which Freud was highly critical. Ferenczi's emphasis on love, warmth, and permissiveness provoked a reaction in Freud's psychoanalytic circles. Both Freud and Ferenczi distanced themselves from each other but never completely severed the relationship.

Freud's main theoretical concepts

In order to provide the foundation upon which subsequent psychoanalytic theories developed, this section discusses some of Freud's main concepts. Freud's main concepts not only guide us in the treatment of children but also open critical theoretical perspectives on the understanding of adult pathology.

Freud knew how important it was to prevent mental illness through the understanding of childhood sexuality; however, he realised that he would not be able to extend his theory and technique into the field of child development in his lifetime. He encouraged Anna, his youngest daughter, to further explore his discoveries and to create and extend the field of child psychoanalysis. However, when Freud was consulted by one of his friends about his five-year-old son, whom we now know as "Little Hans", Freud recognised this as an opportunity to observe the sexual impulses and wishes of a child directly, although he had already been exploring these through his treatment of adults.

Believing that infantile sexuality is a common property of all human beings, a part of the human constitution, even if, in the case of neurotics, an exaggerated or distorted one, Freud encouraged his pupils and friends to collect observations of the sexual life of children, an issue that had been overlooked and denied in the past.

The first people who approached Freud to express their interest in child psychoanalysis were Sabine Spielrein and Hermine Hug-Hellmuth. Hermine Hug-Hellmuth founded Vienna Child Guidance, and participated in Freud's classes, conferences, and international meetings. When Anna Freud expressed her desire to follow the psychoanalytic profession, Freud stimulated her to be in contact with Hermine, and they worked together. Later, Anna developed her own discoveries and clinical practice, thus making a significant contribution to the field of child psychoanalysis.

The seduction theory

The seduction theory was Freud's early hypothesis for the source of symptoms of hysteria and obsessional neurosis. Freud based this theory on a number of his patients whose distress, he claimed, was rooted in trauma from their childhood social environment. He initially thought that the symptoms of hysteria and obsessional neurosis were caused by repressed memories of actual infantile sexual abuse in early childhood, mostly before the age of four. To this, he added his belief that the root of all neurosis was the premature introduction of sexuality into the experience of a young child. The repressed memories would manifest themselves later in life in the form of symptomatic neurosis.

Years later, he abandoned this theory, and in 1897 Freud explained that the impulses, phantasies, and conflicts that he claimed to have uncovered beneath the neurotic symptoms of his patients were in fact related to the mind of the child itself, which he referred to as the theory of infantile sexuality.

The topographic theory: the unconscious, the preconscious, and the conscious

In Chapter Seven of *The Interpretations of Dreams* (1900a), Freud constructed a general model of the mind and its workings. In this major book, he proposed a topographical model of the psychical apparatus. Freud explained mental functioning in both normal and pathological states, based on his clinical observations on dreams and his study of neurosis. For the first time, he defined the unconscious, preconscious, and conscious. Between the unconscious and the preconscious appears what he called *censorship*, the forerunner of the concept of the super-ego, which controls what is allowed to move between unconscious, preconscious, and conscious.

Freud stated that dreams allow us to reach another part of the psychological apparatus beyond consciousness. He described the existence of the preconscious (Pcs.) processes, which can reach consciousness in certain conditions. Furthermore, he described a system behind the preconscious that he called the unconscious (Ucs.) processes, which have no access to the conscious except through the preconscious. Famously, too, Freud stated that dreams are the *via reggia* (royal path) to the unconscious.

Primary process and secondary process

Freud gave the names *primary process* and *secondary process* to two kinds of processes of excitation, or modes of energy discharge. The two are opposed yet complementary modes of functioning within the psychic apparatus. Psychical life is entirely regulated by the equilibrium between these two types of processes, which vary between subjects and at different points in time in their development.

The primary process is an unconscious, irrational mode of mental functioning, involving free energy, used to relieve tension caused and activated by the drives at the service of the pleasure principle; this energy is discharged immediately. The primary process follows the laws of the unconscious: it is atemporal (time does not exist), and contradiction does not exist (love and hate can coexist).

The secondary process is a conscious, rational mode of mental functioning and intervenes as a system of control and regulation in the service of the reality principle. This bound energy is more willing to defer its discharge. Discharge is only partially blocked and accumulates.

The reality principle, working through the ego, controls behaviour to meet the conditions imposed by external reality; under its influence, the free energy of the pleasure principle becomes bound energy.

The structural theory: id, ego, superego

Freud first discussed the structural model in 1920 in his essay *Beyond the Pleasure Principle* and more fully elaborated it in 1923 in his theory of the psychic apparatus in his paper *The Ego and the Id*. The structural theory described the organisation of the mind into three theoretical systems: the id, ego, and superego.

Id

The id is the unorganised part of the personality structure that contains a human's basic instinctual drives. The id contains the libido, which is the primary source of instinctual force that is unresponsive to the demands of reality. The id acts according to the pleasure principle, seeking to avoid pain or displeasure, and being aroused by increases in instinctual tension.

Freud said that the infant is all id at birth and that from the id, the ego begins to differentiate through the defence mechanisms of projection and introjection. The id operates under the pleasure principle, meaning that it has no regard for reality, constraints, or consequences. Sexual fantasies and dreams are purely id.

Ego

Freud described the ego for the first time in his 1895 book *Studies on Hysteria*, as a conscious ego, but it was only in his 1923 book *The Ego and the Id* that he described the unconscious interactions between ego, id, and superego in a person's mind.

The ego balances the drives of the id against the reality of the world and can delay or discharge various impulses of the id that lead to release tension. The ego tries to avoid displeasure and pain, is governed by the reality principle, and acts as a moderating influence on the pleasure principle. In sum, the ego moderates the pressures of the id, the demands of the superego, and the impact of the external world. The person distinguishes between perceptions coming from the outside and hallucinations or memories coming from within the self.

The operation of all these structures is essential in the development of the ego, superego, ego-ideal, character formation, and identity.

Superego

Freud described the superego as the heir of the Oedipus complex. It functions like a censor in relationship to the ego, appearing to develop through the internalisation of parental demands and prohibition. Freud developed the concept of superego from combining his earlier views on two of its aspects, the ego-ideal and the moral conscience. The ego-ideal appears after the second year of life, after primary identification. The child displaces to the ego-ideal his narcissistic love. The ego-ideal appears before the formation of the superego, and is later integrated with the moral conscience during the dissolution of the Oedipus complex to become the superego entity.

Freud's idea is that superego formation comes from a successful identification with the parental agency, and that it also takes on the influence of those who will represent the parents, such as educators, teachers, and people chosen as ideal models. The superego aims for perfection, and belongs to the aspect of the personality that is not entirely unconscious, including ego-ideals and spiritual goals. It can be conceptualised as a type of conscience that punishes misbehaviour with feelings of guilt. While the id wants instant self-gratification, the superego controls our sense of right and wrong and guilt, which helps us to adjust to society. Freud's theory conceptualised the superego as a symbolic internalisation of the father figure and cultural regulations. The superego acts as the moral conscience.

In Freud's work *Civilisation and Its Discontents* (1930a), he discussed the concept of a "cultural superego". Freud suggested that the demands of the superego coincide with the precepts of the prevailing cultural superego. Furthermore, he believed that the two processes, the cultural development of the group and the cultural development of the individual, would be always intertwined.

Conflict

Freud described conflict as the expression of opposite internal demands, such as opposite wishes and representations. The conflict can be manifested, for example, between a desire and a moral demand, or between two contradictory feelings. It can also be latent, expressing itself in a distorted way at the manifest level, or be translated into symptoms. Psychoanalysis considers conflict as part of human nature, and there are different kinds of conflicts, conflicts between desire and defence mechanisms, conflicts between the instincts, and Oedipal conflict, where not only do opposite desires exist, but also desire to face the forbidden, as in the Oedipus conflict.

For Freud, the opposition between self-preservation and the sexual instincts is the source of the conflicts that emerge in the transference neurosis. Conflict results from the fact that sexual drives, which can obtain satisfaction through phantasy and follow the pleasure–unpleasure principle, appear to go against the reality principle, represented by the self-preservation instincts, which cannot obtain satisfaction other than through a real object.

Oedipus conflict and penis envy

The Oedipus conflict appeared for the first time in the last edition of *Three Essays on the Theory of Sexuality* (Freud, 1905d). Freud discovered the Oedipus complex in his self-analysis, and later stated that it emerges in the course of child development and constitutes the central organiser of mental life. He associated this conflict with the myth of Oedipus. It is around the Oedipus conflict that the individual's sexual identity is structured. For Freud, it is a universal. It is not limited to normal development but also lies at the heart of psychopathology, forming the nuclear concept of the neuroses.

Freud described the positive, direct Oedipus complex. The boy's first object of affection is the mother, whom he desires to possess. At the age of three to five, the love for his mother brings rivalry with his father, whom he begins to hate. He then fears that the father will castrate him, deprive him of his penis, in response to the incestuous wishes he feels for his mother and hate for his father. Under the impact of the anxiety aroused by the threat of castration, the boy gives up the idea of fulfilling his incestuous sexual wishes for his mother, and enters into the latency period.

Later on, Freud began to understand that female development is different from that of the male. The young girl has to change her object of desire, moving from the love of her mother towards the love of her father, but through a different pathway. Freud believed that girls' psychosexual development is crucially influenced by penis envy, for which the desire to have a baby with her father is a substitute.

In talking about penis envy, it is essential to understand the cultural organisation of Freud's time, when women had a very different role in society. For the most part, they were expected only to be housewives, teachers, or governesses, and thus did not have access to the same education as men (Harold Blum, personal communication, 2012).

The patients Freud observed were women suffering from the cultural limitations of their time. In his early writings, he considered the seduction theory, in which child abuse and seduction were considered to explain the development of the symptoms present in hysteria and obsessional neurosis. Freud considered seduction trauma essential to psychopathology from about 1895 to 1900. A few years later, he took phantasy into consideration, as well as the psychological processes that would be more determinant of women's suffering.

In his 1923 paper *The Ego and the Id*, Freud developed the concept of mental and psychic bisexuality. He added the concept of the negative Oedipus complex, whereby the boy wishes to be like his mother. This passive feminine wish, which the boy feels towards his father, leads him to relinquish his heterosexual desires for his mother as well as his masculine identification with the paternal rival.

Instinct theory

Freud believed that people are driven by two conflictive desires: the *libido*, described as a mental energy, and the *death drive*. The death drive, or death instinct, was elaborated in his 1920 paper *Beyond the Pleasure Principle*.

The term "instinct" was originally used in psychoanalysis to express the concept of the forces motivating human behaviour. Later, these forces were described as instinctual drives. Freud said that the instinct is a dynamic pressure with a source, an aim, and an object. Models of instinctual drives are the need for food and the search for sexual satisfaction, which are present in all human beings. The aim is satisfaction, and the object is variable; it may be external, someone close to the person, or part of the person's body, yet the specific object is incidental and can be replaced.

Freud said that the object might be changed any number of times in the course of the vicissitudes which the instinct undergoes during its existence. An instinct arises from a somatic process, which occurs in an organ or part of the body, and the stimulus created by the instinct has a mental representation. Freud noted that the mental apparatus is governed by the pleasure–unpleasure principle and that its workings are regulated automatically by feelings belonging to the pleasure–unpleasure series.

Freud proposed to group instincts under an ego or self-preservative instinct or the sexual instinct. At the beginning of life, the sexual instincts are attached to the instincts of self-preservation, which provide them with an organic source, direction, and object. It is only when the external object is abandoned that the sexual drives become independent, as, for example, in the pleasure an infant receives from suckling the mother's breast (object). In the beginning, the satisfaction is linked to feeding; however, later, the pleasure of suckling will detach itself from feeding and can be satisfied through phantasy, so that the sexual instinct becomes independent from the self-preservation instinct.

Freud developed the concept of the vicissitudes of the sexual drives, saying that the sexual drive can undergo the following vicissitudes: (1) reversal into its opposite, as in, for example, sadism-masochism, voyeurism-exhibitionism, love and hate (connected with ambivalence); (2) turning round upon the subject's own self; and (3) repression or sublimation.

Libido

Libido refers to a person's sexual drive energy or desire for sexual activity. The sexual drive usually has biological, psychological, and social components. Libido was recognised early by Freud as a dynamic force that gives rise to internal conflict in the course of mental development. The other major forces were the self-preserving interests of the individual and the aggressive drives. The libido can cathect both the intrapsychic representation of objects (object libido) or the self (narcissism): in other words, sexual energy is a link to the mental representation of the object, or the self.

The death instinct

In the 1920 paper *Beyond the Pleasure Principle*, Freud described the death drive, the drive towards death, self-destruction, and the return to the inorganic. The death drive is also referred to as Thanatos in post-Freudian thinking, complementing Eros, the life instinct. Freud said that there is an opposition between the ego or death instincts and the sexual or life instincts.

Psychosexual development

In 1905, Freud published *Three Essays on the Theory of Sexuality*, a paper that is often considered to be Freud's second most important work after *The Interpretations of Dreams*. In 1887, while in the course of his self-analysis, Freud came to the conclusion that sexual impulses were present very early in life in all children and that they were manifested in adulthood upon the appearance of a trigger factor.

In the 1915 edition, he added the idea of an organisation of the libido in successive stages, each of which corresponds to the primary erotogenic zone, describing the oral stage, the anal stage, and the genital stage. In 1923, he added the phallic stage of organisation, locating it between the anal and genital stages. The phallic stage includes the discovery of the penis in boys and the clitoris in girls. The development of sexuality thus followed a path from the pregenital (oral, anal, and phallic) to the genital organisation, which began at puberty.

Freud indicated that it is through repression that development advances from one stage to the next stage; shame, disgust, and morality are important in restraining instinct within the limits of normality. Freud said that neurosis is based on sexual instinctual forces and the energy of the neurosis, and that its consequences in adult sexual life are expressed in symptoms. The symptoms constitute the repressed sexual activity of the patient.

During latency, the sexual impulses turn away from sexual aims and are directed towards other ends in the form of cultural achievements. Freud called this process *sublimation*. He added that occasionally the sexual drive might break through during latency.

In summary, the sequence of psychosexual development, according to Freud's theory, is: autoerotism—narcissism; oral stage; anal stage; phallic stage; genital stage.

The *oral stage* lasts from birth to about eighteen months; the focus of pleasure is the mouth, and sucking and biting are the preferred activities. The *anal stage* lasts from about eighteen months to three or four years old. Here the focus of pleasure is the anus, and holding in and letting go are enjoyable. The term of the *phallic stage* varies from three to seven years old, and in it the focus of pleasure is the genitalia; masturbation is common.

The *latent or latency stage* can begin at between the ages of five and seven years and last until puberty or around twelve years old. Freud believed that during this stage, the sexual impulse was suppressed in the service of learning. While most children seem to be calm, sexually, during their latent school years, some of them might be quite busy masturbating and playing "doctor".

The *genital stage* begins at puberty and represents the resurgence of the sex drive in adolescence, and includes the more specific focus of pleasure through sexual intercourse. Freud believed that masturbation, oral sex, and homosexuality in adults were immature sexual activities, aberrations of normal sexual activity. Today, they are socially acceptable in sexual adulthood.

Autoerotism—narcissism

In his 1914 paper *Introduction to Narcissism*, Freud used the terms "autoerotism" and "narcissism" with little distinction. The word "narcissism" was brought into psychoanalysis from the Greek myth of Narcissus. Narcissus fell in love with his own image reflected in a pool of water. His desire to kiss what he did not know was his own image made him fall into the water and drown, and he was then changed into a flower, the narcissus. The connection between this myth and the psychological state is that narcissism is used to designate self-love.

Freud used this term for the first time in 1910 to describe the object choice of homosexuals, choosing somebody similar to themselves, taking themselves as the sexual object. Shortly after this statement, Freud also described narcissism as an intermediate stage in the child psychosexual development, between autoeroticism and a more advanced stage of object-love.

Freud stated that the libido is primarily sexual in nature. He described an early form of narcissism that he called *primary narcissism*, whereby infants take themselves as their love-object and feel that the world revolves around them, before going on to choose some external object. As development progresses, the child is capable of loving other people separate from himself. Freud added that the sexual cathexis on the individual's own body is found in the course of normal psychosexual development, but that it can also be psychopathological later in life.

According to Freud, *secondary narcissism* occurs when the libido withdraws from objects outside the self, and returns back to the ego. In normal development, secondary narcissism lays the foundation for self-esteem and coexists with object-love. For Freud, while both primary and secondary narcissism emerge in normal human development, problems in the transition from one to the other can lead to pathological narcissistic disorders in adulthood.

Freud then described two types of object choice: (1) *anaclitic object choice* is made when the object is loved with the recognition that it is different from the self. In contrast, (2) *narcissistic object choice* is based on the love that the individual has for himself and will lead the person to choose someone similar to himself.

Fixation—regression—detention

According to Freud, libido can suffer in different ways in its progress through the different stages of psychosexual development; libido can be fixated in one stage, can regress to a previous stage, and/or can stop in one of three stages:

1. *Fixation*: This deviation from normal sexual life, which later in life will lead to neurosis and perversion, is established from early sexual experiences in childhood. Freud described different causes of fixation: constitutional, an increased pertinacity of early impression, and stimulation of the sexual instinct by external influences. Fixation can occur following either frustration or excessive gratification in one particular phase of psychosexual development.
2. *Regression*: Regression is the reversion to immature patterns of behaviour, and describes a regression to a previous stage of psychosexual development.
3. *Detention*: The libido does not advance through the process of sexual development and stays in one particular stage.

Transference—countertransference

Freud first studied the concept of transference in 1891–1892, when he became aware of this phenomenon in using hypnosis with one of his female patients, who, upon awakening from the hypnotic trance, threw her arms around him. Freud realised that this deep emotion was a reproduction of repressed experiences, mostly from childhood, now displayed in the analytic situation, where the analyst becomes the substitute for an important person in the childhood of the patient.

He realised that a conscious perception in the present could be distorted by unconscious wishes, as day residue was in dreams. When "Dora" walked out of Freud's office, the strength of this behaviour and emotion opened up a new theoretical concept called *transference*. During 1905 to 1925, this became another important concept he integrated into his theory.

In sum, *transference* is a phenomenon characterised by unconscious redirection of feelings and desires, especially of those unconsciously retained from childhood, towards a new person, specifically the analyst in the setting of treatment.

In his 1914 paper "Remembering, Repeating and Working Through", Freud emphasised the repetitive dimension of transference, and showed that the greater the patient's resistance, the greater the tendency to repeat the core problem situation through enactment rather than through remembering would be. He called this transference *transference neurosis*, and described it as an artificial illness that is generated in and by the analytic situation. He further described two kinds of transference: the *positive*, based on affectionate feelings; and *negative*, based on hostile feelings.

Freud observed that cure comes with the analysis of the compulsion to repeat, turning it into a motive for remembering in the setting of the transference. In his paper "Observation on Transference-Love" (1915a), Freud wrote that transference love is a form of resistance that opposes the development of the transference, and that through the psychoanalytic treatment it is important to uncover the unconscious origins of the resistance.

Countertransference describes the state that occurs when a patient induces emotions in the analyst and when a therapist becomes emotionally entangled with the patient. These feelings have to be acknowledged and overcome by the analyst. Countertransference appears in the therapist as the result of the patient's influence on the therapist's unconscious feelings. Freud said that if these feelings are not overcome, they present an obstacle to the process of the transference. For this reason, Freud demanded that all analysts be aware of their countertransference and control it, which can be done through a personal experience of analysis, followed by self-analysis.

Melanie Klein stated that the countertransference helped her personally, but not her patients.

Dreams

In his book *The Interpretations of Dreams* (1900a), Freud developed his discovery of the symbolism of dreams, saying that dreams are the royal road to the knowledge of the unconscious activities of the mind. He explained that the state of sleep makes dream formation possible by reducing the psychological internal censorship.

Freud described the dream as a psychic world whose goal is a wish fulfilment, although it is not recognisable as a wish, because its peculiarities and absurdities are due to the influence of the psychic censorship active during dream formation. Freud thus postulated that dreams are a form of *unconscious wish-fulfilment*.

Through the analysis of his own dreams, he discovered that dreams have a *manifest content* and a *latent content*. The meaning of a dream would be uncovered through the dreamer's free associations. It was in Chapter Seven of *The Interpretation of Dreams* that the concepts of the conscious and unconscious were first described.

Freud described a number of unconscious mechanisms that lead to the organisation of the dream, as follows:

1. *Condensation*: Through the mechanism of condensation, several elements, such as images and thoughts belonging to different chains of association, come together into a single one.
2. *Displacement*: Displacement describes the substitution by incidental thought of the more meaningful dream-thoughts that conceal the wish-fulfilment.
3. *Representability*: Through this mechanism, the dream thoughts are transformed into images.
4. *Secondary revision of the dream, and dramatisation*: The secondary revision of the dream appears on awakening, when the dream content is presented to the dreamer in a more coherent and intelligible manner.
5. *Dramatisation*: Dramatisation is the process of transforming the thought into a situation.

Other aspects to consider in the interpretation of dreams are:

6. *Residues of the previous day*: The dreamer always involves events that occurred the previous day to develop the dream scenario.
7. *The role of censorship*: During sleep, there is a relaxation of censorship, but it is not completely eliminated. Freud considered dreams as the guardians of sleep, but to perform this function, the repressed elements have to be hidden. Dream censorship applies to repressed infantile sexual wishes. Latent content relates to the fulfilment of erotic wishes.
8. *The role of symbols*: Through censorship, symbols enable the dreamer to strip the dream of its sexual representations. There are two kinds of symbols: the universal ones, and those connected with the dreamer's life. It is important when we analyse a dream to look for the patient's associations with each of the symbols in the manifest content.

Dreamwork
With regard to dreamwork, Freud first took careful notes of the dream material as it appeared to the dreamer upon awakening. He broke down every aspect of the dream and noted the associations that emerged spontaneously in relation to every fragment of the dream. Taking into account this material, he asked for further associations and made connections between the different sequences, building the possible interpretations of the dream. His main thesis was that dreams are the expression of the fulfilment of a frustrated wish, and that thanks to the analytic work, the wish-fulfilment would be discovered.

Freud compared dreams with jokes. Jokes have a verbal expression and also a thought behind them. He said that there is sense behind joking nonsense, and that it is this sense that makes the nonsense into a joke. He then described the *innocent* joke, which is an end in itself, and the *tendentious* joke, which is at the service of an intention related to all kinds of motives, including **hostility** (aggressiveness, satire, cynicism), **obscenity** (with the aim of exposing), **bawdiness** (sexual matters), and **scepticism** (the worst of all motives). Through the joke, these tendencies are satisfied, and that satisfaction is a source of pleasure. The purpose of jokes is to obtain pleasure, not only with the techniques employed but in going back to infantile unconscious desires.

Complemental series

In his 1905 work *Three Essays on the Theory of Sexuality*, Freud described three main aspects of hereditary and environmental factors involved in the development of the neurosis.

1. *Biological*: Constitutional factors and hereditary dispositions;
2. *Phylogenetic* (experiences of early childhood): Those infantile impressions and sexual-life developments in early childhood that Freud considered would lead to repression and regression; and
3. *Psychological*: Triggers of the illness, including adult experience as accidental experiences, which later appear as traumatic experiences.

Freud called the first two aspects, biological and phylogenetic, "Serie Dispositional", referring to the constitutional factors and experiences of early childhood.

Defence mechanisms

Freud first introduced the concept of defence in his 1894 papers "The Neuro-Psychoses of Defence" and "The Aetiology of Hysteria", in which he described the struggles between the ego and the painful ideas and affects that the patient found intolerable.

Later, in his book *Inhibitions, Symptoms and Anxiety* (1926d), he introduced the term "repression". He described the need of the ego to protect itself from the demands coming from the id, the superego, and the external world. Repression was one of many defence mechanisms, but it was essential in the development of the neurosis. Freud noted that repression is the most useful mechanism but also the most dangerous, because it can so significantly impoverish the functioning of the ego. He also described repression as the basis of compromise formation and the neurosis.

Freud also described a number of different defence mechanisms throughout his work, including suppression, denial, repression, regression, reactive formation, isolation, undoing, projection, introjection, turning into himself, transformation to the opposite, sublimation, and displacement, as described below.

Suppression is the voluntary and conscious form of repression Freud proposed in 1892. It is the conscious process of pushing unwanted, anxiety-provoking thoughts, memories, emotions, phantasies, and desires out of awareness. This defence is different from repression and denial because it is conscious rather than unconscious.

Repression is an unconscious mechanism employed by the ego to keep disturbing or threatening thoughts from becoming conscious. The repressed material can emerge in the form of neurotic symptoms or can be integrated in normal sexuality. When censorship is less strong, the repressed infantile scenarios can appear in the patient's dreams.

Freud said (1915) that the essence of repression lies simply in turning something away and keeping it at a distance from the conscious. Repression became the main defence mechanism when Freud introduced the distinction between conscious and unconscious. Through the mechanism of repression, the rejecting or blocking of unacceptable ideas or impulses takes place in order to prevent them from entering consciousness.

Dissociation is another psychological state in which thoughts, emotions, sensations, or memories are separated from the rest of the psyche. Dissociative identity disorder is often associated with severe and prolonged childhood trauma, such as neglect or emotional or sexual abuse, and it develops as a way to cope with an overwhelming situation that is too painful or violent to assimilate into one's conscious self. The person literally "goes away" in his or her head to flee from the anxiety-producing experience from which there is no physical escape. This dissociative process allows traumatic feelings and memories to be psychologically separated from so that the person can function as if the trauma had not occurred. While in one mental state, the patient has access to traumatic autobiographical memories with emotional responses to them, as in the case of rape, in the other state, the person claims not to recall nothing related to the rape. This defensive use of dissociation prevails long after the traumatic experiences have ended.

Projection is the unconscious act of attributing one's own thoughts, feelings, or motives to another person. Thoughts more commonly projected to another are those that would cause guilt, such as aggressive and sexual phantasies or thoughts.

Introjection occurs when a person adopts the thoughts or traits of another person and makes them their own. For example, the lost person can be internalised in the process of mourning. However, a person perceived as a bad or hostile object can also be internalised, giving the patient the illusion that the object is controlled by him.

Denial involves eliminating external events from awareness. It is a primitive defence, and may operate either independently or, more commonly, in combination with other mechanisms. The person in denial is faced with a fact that is too uncomfortable to accept and instead rejects it, insisting that it is not true despite overwhelming evidence to the contrary.

Displacement is the redirection of an impulse (usually aggressive) onto a substitute target. Displacement can allow one element to serve as a symbolic substitute for another. It can also be the act of placing the feelings of one person onto another who in some way appears similar to the original object.

Isolation is when the person disengages from the emotional content of a painful experience, or separates an idea from its associated affect in order to avoid emotional disturbance.

With the mechanism of *undoing*, the person neutralises one behaviour with another in order to unconsciously ignore the element or action that contains unwanted emotions.

Rationalisation is the cognitive distortion of the facts in order to make an event or an impulse less threatening. It can often be a fairly conscious matter of making excuses, which may come easily. Rationalisation supplies a logical or rational reason (justification) as opposed to the real reason.

Regression is the act of returning to a previous stage of development or functioning, in order to avoid the conflicts and tensions associated with one's present level of development.

With *reaction formation*, the person behaves in a way opposite to how he or she thinks or feels. Reaction formation can involve conscious feelings that are the opposite of unconscious ones; for example, love–hate, shame–disgust, and moralising can be reaction formations against sexuality.

Through *sublimation*, sexual energy is deflected into socially or culturally accepted acts. It can be complete, as in the case of the artistic disposition, or partial, where perversion is mixed with the aims of an individual. On the other hand, sexual energy can be suppressed by reaction formation and continue throughout the person's life.

Points of fixation and mechanisms of defence

Freud described the mechanisms of defence that appear in each stage of psychosexual development. During the *oral stage*, the prevalent mechanisms are projection, introjection, and denial. In the *anal stage*, reaction formation and undoing can occur. In the *phallic stage*, the main mechanism is repression.

Otto Fenichel's theory on psychosexual development and defences

In his 1932 book *Psychoanalytic Theory of the Neurosis*, Otto Fenichel elaborated on the concept of these stages by describing the defence mechanisms at the time of the libido fixation in each of them. In his view, when the libido is fixed at the beginning of the oral stage, the prevalent defence mechanisms are regression to the stage of narcissism, introversion (turning to fantasies), and omnipotence, leading to schizophrenia.

Fenichel said that when the libido is fixed in the later oral phase, it will develop the defence mechanisms of narcissistic regression, omnipotence, introjection, and denial, leading to depression and mania. In mania, the omnipotence of primary narcissism will be prevalent. When the fixation is in the anal stage, the prevalent defence mechanisms are regression, repression, undoing, isolation, and reaction formation. This leads to symptoms of obsessional neurosis, of order, frugality, obstination, compulsions, obsessions, and stubbornness. With fixation in the phallic stage, repression is the prevalent mechanism of the hysteria. There are two types of hysteria: phobia and conversion. In phobia, the defence mechanisms are repression, regression, displacement, and projection. In conversion hysteria, defences include repression, regression, identification, introjection, and conversion into the body.

Identification

Freud used the term "identification" in an 1896 letter to Fliess, writing in explanation of a patient's symptom, a woman with agoraphobia who identified with a prostitute walking in the street. The following year, in another letter to Fliess, Freud wrote about another patient with an hysteric spasm who identified with a dead person. Later on, in discussing his patient Dora, Freud said that she identified with her mother and Mrs K, two women loved by her father. Her father was both lover and repressor, which explained Dora's unconscious love feelings about her father.

In 1900, in *The Interpretations of Dreams*, Freud said that the process of identification is essential in the development of the ego, superego,

ego-ideal, character formation, and identity. In 1917, the concept appeared in "Mourning and Melancholia". It was in 1921, in Chapter Seven, "Identification", of *Group Psychology and the Analysis of the Ego*, when Freud specified that identification could happen with only a trait of the person-object. Freud described the mechanism of identification as the process of internalisation of objects or persons as the final result of this process.

Concepts connected with identification

The concepts that are connected with the process of identification are: incorporation (oral), assimilation (oral), introjection, ejection, projection, internalisation (superego), imitation, and identity (structured over time and experiences).

Chronologically, the concept of identification develops from *hysteric identification* to *primary* and *secondary identification*.

In hysteric identification, the formation of symptoms through identification depends on the repressed unconscious phantasies. In the case of the patient with agoraphobia and her identification with a prostitute; the patient with spasms and her identification with the dead; and other patients who have phantasies with regard to the servants, the common denominator is that the identifications are developed from a sexual or aggressive impulse repressed in the unconscious. Freud said that the symptom is the realisation of a repressed desire; the symptom is the auto-satisfaction, namely masturbation. Freud also said that dreams are the realisation of a desire.

In the process of mourning of a parent, Freud described the presence of two types of identification, (1) *self-reproach*, which Freud said is directed towards the loved object, which through identification is directed to the patient's own ego; and (2) *self-punishment*, which is the introjection of the forbidden parental figure and the identification of the ego with the abandoned object. The anger over object loss is transformed into anger towards ego loss. The hysteric attack is punishment for the deadly desire towards the hated parent who has abandoned the patient by dying.

Freud described different modalities in hysteric identification, including identification with the object loved, with the person who was loved, and with a repressive object, as well as self-punishment for a forbidden sexual desire, and for desiring the object without libidinal cathexis. These identifications can be superposed with identification as defence mechanism to avoid the expression of the instinctive impulses.

Primary identification

Freud introduced the key concept of primary identification in the evolution of his thinking. He developed this concept in several of his papers, including "Mourning and Melancholia" (1917e); *From the History of an Infantile Neurosis* (The Wolf Man) (1918b); *Group Psychology and the Analysis of the Ego* (1921c); and *The Ego and the Id* (1923b).

Freud described the concept of primary identification as being related to both psychosexual development, where primary identification appears during the phallic phase in connection with narcissism, and to the relationship with the object, whether objectal or anobjectal, prior to the election of the Oedipal object. Freud also ascribed primary identification to an identification with the father. At about the same time or later, the libidinal charge to the object, the mother, begins.

Secondary identification

Freud described secondary identification in *Totem and Taboo* (1913), "Mourning and Melancholia" (1917e), and *The Ego and the Id* (1923b). The secondary identification with the parents is the normal evolution of the Oedipus complex.

Infantile amnesia

Freud described the infantile amnesia of childhood as extending from birth to the age of six or eight years. The infant is capable of expressing pain and joy in a human fashion, as well as love, jealousy, and other passionate feelings. While in adulthood, we have no recollection of it, nevertheless in examining patients we also know that even when we have forgotten, these infantile affects left deep traces in our minds and had strong effects on later development.

Infantile amnesia simply withholds the earlier impressions from consciousness due to repression. Freud compared infantile amnesia with hysterical amnesia. He wondered if hysterical amnesia could be related to the sexual impulses from childhood. He explained that hysterical amnesia, which occurs at the bidding of repression, is only clear thinking about the possession of a store of memory-traces that have been withdrawn from consciousness. Freud believed that infantile amnesia was responsible for the fact that in the past sexuality was never considered to occur in childhood.

Symptom formation

Freud said that the symptom, as the dream, is the realisation of a repressed desire. The symptom is thus the auto-satisfaction of that desire. He added that the symptom, like the dream, is a compromise formation through which a wish struggles to achieve fulfilment. In one letter to Fliess, Freud said that a symptom arises where the repressed and the repressing thought can come together in the wish-fulfilment.

Like the images in a dream, the symptom was overdetermined, and its formation relied on the processes of condensation and displacement. However, symptom formation is different from dreamwork. In dreams, images appear; symptoms are more closely related to bodily expressions, as in hysterical conversion. Symptom formation expresses mental processes and types of behaviour that were repetitive and isolated, and which were not integrated into the rest of the personality. Moreover, the patient perceives that they are pathological and that they are not character traits. Symptoms can lead the patient to seek treatment.

Theories of anxiety

Freud's first theory of anxiety was that it was based in the unsatisfied libido, which achieves discharge by being transformed into anxiety. Later, when Freud was seventy years old, he proposed a new hypothesis as to the origins of anxiety. From 1926, with the publication of *Inhibitions, Symptoms and Anxiety*, Freud's idea of the origins of anxiety had more to do with the mind, understanding that anxiety is an affect experienced by the ego whenever the ego is faced with danger, which implies fear of separation from or loss of the object.

Freud's later thesis is based on the distinction between various kinds of anxiety. These include *real danger*, as when the person is facing a dangerous situation; *automatic anxiety*, as when facing a traumatic situation which triggers anxiety; *signal anxiety* (in threat of danger), when facing a situation where the ego is able to respond to the threat of impending danger, such as fear of loss of the object.

Initially, Freud believed that repression provokes anxiety; later, he changed his mind and determined that *anxiety provokes repression*. To avoid anxiety, the ego develops defences and symptoms. Freud thought that the ego was the actual seat of anxiety, and he gave up his earlier view that the cathectic energy of the repressed impulse was automatically turned into anxiety. In his later studies of anxiety, when he studied phobias and obsessional-compulsive disorder, he developed the concept that anxiety occurs when the person faces the danger of loss or separation. Freud disagreed with Rank, who connected anxiety to the experience of birth.

Throughout the course of child development, the content of the dangerous situation changes. In the phallic stage, fear of losing the maternal object is transformed into castration anxiety. Later, castration anxiety develops into moral and social anxiety, anxiety with respect to the superego, and the fear of losing the love of the superego. Freud pointed out that all these childhood anxiety situations can persist side by side in later life, causing the ego to react to them with anxiety. Castration anxiety is not the only reason for the development of neurosis. Women have castration complexes but not castration anxiety. For women, the dangerous situation is not the fear of loss of the object, but really the loss of the object's love.

Hypnosis and free association

In 1886, Freud began practising medicine, with a specialty in neurology, treating patients with both physical and so-called "nervous disorders". He said that his therapeutic arsenal contained only two weapons, hypnotism and electrotherapy. At first, like Breuer, Freud hypnotised his patients, encouraging them to tell their stories while under a hypnotic trance. But hypnosis wasn't helping them. People would have momentary cures under hypnosis and then lapse right back into their illness again. Later, Freud asked his patients to say whatever crossed their minds. This method he called *free association*, a process that one of his patients described as the "talking cure".

Repetition compulsion

Freud used this concept for the first time in the article of 1914 *Remembering, Repeating and Working-Through*. He noted that the patient does not remember anything of what he has forgotten and repressed, he acts it out without knowing that he is repeating it. He reproduces past experiences in his behaviour, not his memory. This compulsion to repeat past experiences in the context of the relationship with the doctor is the essence of the transference that is always present early in treatment. Hopefully, it is less intense at the end of treatment and can be understood as the patient's route to remembering.

Freud was interested in the relationship between this compulsion to repeat and the transference and resistance. He said that through the process of therapy, the patient returns to an earlier situation, transforming the past unconscious experiences into conscious ones. He explained that there are special experiences that occur very early in childhood, and that were not understood at the time. This material can only be reached by dreams. Because Freud concluded that the patient acts out what he cannot remember, anything that was repressed, and therefore that he has "forgotten". He repeats without knowing that he is repeating. For the patient, the repetition of the action is his only way of remembering. Thus the patient repeats instead of remembering, and repeats under the conditions of resistance. Understanding for resistance the unconscious action of the patient to protect repressive buried material, such as drives, intense feelings, phantasies and behavior patterns surface to conciousness. Freud wondered what it is that the patient actually repeats. His answer was that the patient repeats his unconscious experiences, his inhibitions, attitudes, pathological character traits, and symptoms that move from the unconscious to the patient's manifest personality. This illness is brought out piece by piece by our therapeutic work, which consists of tracing it back to the past. According to Freud, the main instrument for curing the patient's compulsion to repeat and for turning it into a motive for remembering lies in our work with transference. This will lead us to awaken to the memories after the resistance has been overcome.

"Mourning and Melancholia"

In his 1917 paper "Mourning and Melancholia", Freud compared melancholia with the normal process of mourning. He described *mourning* as a reaction to the loss of a loved person, or to the loss of an abstraction that has taken the place of one, such as one's country, liberty, or an ideal. Reality testing shows that the loved object no longer exists; therefore, there is the demand to withdraw the entire libido from its attachments to that object. This process has to be done slowly; each one of the memories and expectations in which the libido is bound to the object must be brought up and hypercathected. Detachment of the libido is then accomplished. When the work of mourning is completed, the ego becomes free and uninhibited again. At that time, the ego is ready to find another object to replace the loss.

Freud described the clinical reaction in mourning and melancholia as follows:

> The distinguishing mental features of melancholia are a profoundly painful dejection, cessation of interest in the outside world, loss of the capacity to love, inhibition of all activity, and a lowering of the self-regarding feelings to a degree that finds utterance in self-reproaches and self-reviling, and culminates in a delusional expectation of punishment.

> (Freud, 1917e, p. 244)

It is important to note that the description of both mourning and melancholia is the same, with the exception that in mourning the disturbance of self-regard does not exist. Freud remarked that in melancholia there are also reactions to the loss of a loved object. The object has not perhaps actually died, but has been lost as an object of love, yet one cannot see clearly what it is that has been lost. Freud said that melancholia is related to an object loss that is withdrawn from consciousness, in contrast to mourning, in which there is nothing about the loss that is unconscious.

In melancholia, while the patient experiences a severe diminution in his self-regard, it is the ego itself that is impoverished. The patient represents his ego to us as worthless, incapable of any achievement, and morally despicable. He reproaches himself, vilifies himself, and expects to be punished. The dissatisfaction with the ego on moral grounds is the most outstanding feature. Freud observed that this self-reproach is directed to the loved object internalised in the patient's own ego by the mechanism of identification.

Freud's explanation of the dynamics of this process was that in the past there had been an object choice, but the relationship was shattered; it was not a normal withdrawal of the libido from this object. It was not displaced to another object; it was withdrawn into the ego, and was thus an identification of the ego with the abandoned object. The object loss was transformed into an ego loss. The disposition to become melancholic lies in the predominance of the narcissistic type of object choice. The most remarkable characteristic of melancholia is its tendency to change into mania, a state opposite of melancholia in its symptoms.

CHAPTER TWO

Freud's papers concerning child psychoanalysis

F reud, through his many publications related to child analysis, was an early influence in the development of child analytic thinking. He was able to be in close contact with symptomatic children and applied his theory to them, keenly aware of the importance of having direct observation of the child to corroborate what he was discovering in his adult patients.

The following papers represent Freud's thoughts on the children he observed. Among them is "Little Hans", the five-year-old son of one of his close friends, and another is about the eighteen-month-old boy who was the son of one of his daughters.

- "Symptomatic and Chance Actions", in *The Psychopathology of Everyday Life* (*SE* 6, 1901b, pp. 191–216)
- *Three Essays on the Theory of Sexuality* (*SE* 7, 1905d, pp. 135–243)
- *Analysis of a Phobia in a Five-Year-Old Boy, "Little Hans"* (*SE* 10, 1909b, pp. 5–149); A biography of "Little Hans"
- "Reflections on Schoolboy Psychology" (*SE* 13, 1914f, p. 241)
- "Children's Dreams" (*SE* 15, 1914, p. 126)

- "Associations of a Four-Year-Old Child" (*SE 18*, 1920d, p. 266)
- *Beyond the Pleasure Principle* (*SE 18*, 1920g, pp. 7–64).

"Symptomatic and Chance Actions" (1901)

In his 1901 book *The Psychopathology of Everyday Life*, Freud dedicated a section to the explanation of "symptomatic and chance actions". These apparently insignificant occurrences, with no clear explanation, both play a part in symptoms and give expression to something that the person has otherwise not suspected.

Freud observed that such symptomatic and chance actions can either occur habitually, regularly under certain conditions, or occur only sporadically or rarely. He added that symbolism plays a greater role in the childhood of normal people than he had thought earlier. Furthermore, Freud said that the symptomatic acts that can be observed in healthy and sick people are important to take into account in the analytic process. After describing numerous clinical examples, Freud concluded that such symptomatic acts often offer the best understanding of peoples' intimate mental lives.

Regarding the symptomatic acts that occur sporadically, he notes that because these actions are unintentional, they inevitably become the source of misunderstandings in human interaction: the person does not hold himself responsible for these actions. Freud concluded that while we find a freedom to self-express through words and forms, it is behind the form where a glimpse of a deeper meaning may be had. The images and expressions of people generally have significance behind them, often unintentional.

Three Essays on the Theory of Sexuality *(1905)*

One of Freud's three most important works, *Three Essays on the Theory of Sexuality*, shares this rank with *The Interpretations of Dreams* (1900a) and *Studies on Hysteria* (1895d) because one of his most important discoveries was that the causative factors of hysteria derive from childhood, an idea he began to develop in 1896. Freud said that what is normal during the psychosexual development of a child can become abnormal in adult life.

The elements of *Three Essays of the Theory of Sexuality* were presented in the following order: (1) the sexual aberrations; (2) infantile sexuality; and (3) transformations of puberty.

First essay: sexual aberrations

In this essay, Freud introduced two technical terms, *sexual object* and *sexual aim*. His observation was that sexual deviations occur both in respect to the sexual object and to the sexual aim. Freud connected sexual aberrations to infantile sexuality, indicating that what is normal in childhood can become perversion in adulthood, in the form of fixations on the stages that come before the realisation of the primacy of the genitals and the satisfaction of the instinct as a reproductive act.

Deviations in regard to the sexual object

With regard to deviations from the sexual object, Freud described *inversion* and *bisexuality*. He described *inversion* as taking place when the object choice of a man is another man, and the object choice of woman is another woman. In bisexuality, Freud explained that certain degrees of anatomical hermaphroditism occur normally, and that in every normal male or female traces of the apparatus of the opposite sex are found. This will persist without function in rudimentary organs or become modified into a unisexual one, leaving behind only a few traces of the sex that has become atrophied. In 1886, Krafft-Ebing said that every individual's bisexual disposition endows him with masculine and feminine brain centres, as well as somatic organs of sex; these centres develop only at puberty.

The person's final attitude towards the choice of sexual object will be decided after puberty, and, according to Freud, there are many factors that can influence this choice, including those of a constitutional nature.

Deviation as a consequence of fixations of preliminary sexual aims

In considering this cause of perversions, Freud indicated that this happens in two forms: actively and passively. These include such perversions as *voyeurism, exhibitionism, sadism,* and *masochism.*

Scoptophilia (voyeurism, exhibitionism)

Scoptophilia is a term that describes "the pleasure of looking", but we "look" through two senses: touch and sight. Freud said that touching is common and necessary among human beings before the normal sexual aim can be reached. The same is true for the sense of sight, with seeing being an activity derived from touching. Scoptophilia becomes a perversion if it is restricted to looking only at the genitals instead of its preparatory phase in the normal sexual aim. The same is true in exhibitionism, the act in which a person exhibits his or her own genitalia, or in order to have a reciprocal view of the genitals of the other person, as in voyeurism.

Sadism—masochism

Freud said that sadism and masochism are the most frequent and significant of all perversions. Sadism is the aggressive component of the sexual instinct that becomes independent; it describes the desire to inflict pain upon the sexual object. The pleasure an inflicted one receives from pain is known as masochism.

The sexuality of most male human beings contains elements of aggressiveness, a desire to dominate the object. Sadism would correspond to an aggressive component of the sexual instinct, a component that becomes independent and intense. Perversion is when the satisfaction is entirely conditioned on the humiliation and maltreatment of the object. Similarly, in masochism the perversion occurs when the physical or mental pain and suffering that are received from the sexual object are the only source of sexual satisfaction.

Sadism and masochism are the most common among perversions because the contrast between activity and passivity behind them is one of the universal characteristics of sexual life. What is important to note is that the most remarkable feature of these perversions is that their active and passive forms are habitually found to occur together in the same individual. The active and passive forms coexist, although one can be more predominant. Sadism coexists with masochism and vice versa.

In the stages of normal sexual development, shame, disgust, and horror or pain come biologically determined. Because of feelings of disgust or shame, for instance, a child will give up the pleasurable act of thumb-sucking or excreting in a nappy.

According to Freud, neurosis is based on instinctual sexual forces. The symptoms are created on the basis of the normal and abnormal sexual activity of the neurotic patient. Freud defined the *perverse* as occurring when the instinct is expressed directly in the phantasy and action without being conscious. Symptoms are formed, in part, at the cost of abnormal sexuality. Freud said, "Neuroses are the negative of perversions". In the neurosis, the sexual instincts are repressed; in the perversions they are acted out (Freud, 1905d, p. 165).

Freud said that the unconscious mental life of all neurotics (without exception) shows inverted impulses, that is, the fixation of their libido towards persons of their own sex. Every active perversion is accompanied by its passive counterpart, as in the case of sadomasochism. Freud ended this section by saying that the sexuality of neurotics has remained in, or been brought back to, an infantile state.

When Freud described the *polymorphously perverse disposition*, he said that under the influence of seduction children can become polymorphously perverse, and can be led into all possible kinds of sexual irregularities.

Second essay: infantile sexuality

Freud considered that infantile sexuality was neglected and ignored, and little consideration was given to the existence of a sexual instinct in childhood. He warned about the difference between sexual and genital, saying that the sexual instinct has a course of development from the beginning of life (from early childhood until six or eight years old) and has different sources. He believed that the reason that infantile sexuality was not recognised was that, later on, the person does not have any recollection of such experiences and phantasies but only weak and fragmentary memories.

Freud described *infantile amnesia* (from the beginning of childhood until six or eight years of age), which he paralleled with hysterical amnesia. Through the examination of patients, he said that the childhood impressions that have been forgotten have an important influence on our minds and will have an impact in later development. He believed that it is due to the repression of infantile sexuality that sexual phantasies are forgotten.

The period of sexual latency in childhood and its interruptions

Freud wrote that he was certain that the germs of sexual impulses are already present in the newborn and develop over time. The sexual life of children usually emerges and is accessible to observation by the third or fourth year of life. This is the period during which mental forces are built up and later interfere with the course of the sexual instinct and restrict its flow. Freud explained that *sexual inhibitions* occur when the flow of the sexual instinct is restricted by disgust, feelings of shame, and the claims of aesthetic and moral ideals. He recognised that education also has a role in this instinctual flow, but notes that its development is organically determined and fixed by heredity, and can occasionally occur without education. Freud said that in the beginning of the period of sexual latency of childhood, when the child starts school education, the sexual impulses move from those of sexual aims to those of cultural achievement, a process he called *sublimation*.

During the years of childhood, sexual impulses cannot be utilised since the reproductive functions have been deferred. On the other hand, in and of themselves these impulses would seem to be perverse, because they arouse unpleasurable feelings of shame or guilt. These are mental forces and reactive impulses that suppress the sexual impulses, which Freud called interruptions of the latency period of the sexual impulses; although the sexual instincts can begin to emerge during latency, they finally emerge strongly in puberty.

Freud said that, from time to time, a fragmentary manifestation of sexuality that has evaded sublimation may break through, or some sexual activity may persist through the duration of the latency period until the sexual instinct emerges with greater intensity at puberty.

Manifestations of infantile sexuality

Infantile sexuality is seen in thumb-sucking, a grasping instinct, and rubbing. Thumb-sucking (or sensual sucking) appears in early infancy and may continue into maturity, or even persist for a lifetime. In connection with thumb-sucking, a grasping instinct may appear and manifest itself as a simultaneous rhythmic tugging at earlobes or catching hold of some part of another person (as a rule, the ear) for the same satisfactory purpose. Many children go from sucking to masturbation.

The important feature of masturbation is that the instinct is not directed towards other people, but towards the child's own body. The behaviour is *auto-erotic*; it is the child's first and most vital activity, connected with the infant's suckling his mother's breast, or as a substitute for it, and this activity familiarises the child with pleasure. In early sexual activity, the pleasure is attached to functions serving the purpose of self-preservation. Sexual activity and self-preservation become independent of one another later in development.

Freud described three characteristics of infantile sexual manifestation: (1) at its origin, it attaches itself to one of the vital somatic functions; (2) it has as yet no sexual object; and (3) it is auto-erotic, and its sexual aim is dominated by an erotogenic zone. These characteristics will be found to apply equally to most of the other activities involving the infantile sexual instincts.

The sexual aim of infantile sexuality

The sexual aim achieves its satisfaction through the stimulation of the erotogenic zone. The satisfaction must have been previously experienced, for instance suckling the mother's breast, and Freud thinks that experience is of biological nature. During psychosexual development, there are specific erotogenic zones, and the aim of sexuality is pleasurable feeling more than the quality of the stimulus.

The example of thumb-sucking shows the importance of the erotogenic zone in infantile sexuality. Freud described the characteristics of erotogenic zones as arising in the part of the skin or mucous membrane in which stimuli of a certain sort evoke a feeling of pleasure possessing a particular quality, a rhythmic character. A pleasurable feeling does in fact possess a specific quality.

Masturbatory sexual manifestations

Freud understood that the nature of the instinct arises from a single one of the erotogenic zones—the labial, anal, and genital—although there are distinctions between one zone and another concerning the satisfaction of the instinct.

The labial zone encompasses the area of the mouth, which will be satisfied by the breast, and the activity of sucking; this will later be replaced as the infant develops by other muscular actions according to the position and nature of the other zones, other stages of psychosexual development.

It is during the anal phase that anal zone symptoms, such as intestinal disturbances, such as constipation, stool-holding, and intestinal catarrhs, can be seen, which can later provoke symptoms of neurosis. Actual masturbatory stimulation of the anal zone by means of the finger, provoked by a centrally determined or peripherally maintained sensation of itching, is rare among older children. Faeces are treated as a part of the body and can have symbolic representations in the future, from such forms as gifts to babies and money.

During the genital phase, sexual activities are focused around the erotogenic genital zone, which is part of the sexual organs; these are the beginning of "normal" sexual life. Micturition, touching, or putting the legs together can all be expressions of activities aimed at sexual satisfaction.

Freud distinguished three phases of infantile masturbation:

1. The *first phase* appears in *early infancy* and disappears after a short time, but may persist until puberty.
2. The *second phase* begins at about four years of age. After infancy and before the age of four, the genital sexual instinct usually appears and persists for a while until suppressed. It is different in every case. Normally, infantile amnesia leaves no memory of infantile sexual activity, but this activity can leave behind deep, unconscious impressions in the subject's memory that may determine whether the subject will be healthy or neurotic after puberty. Symptoms can arise from the repressed sexual activity.
3. The *third phase*, or pubertal phase, occurs during puberty. Early sexual excitation from infancy can return, for example as tickling that is relieved by masturbation, or nocturnal tension as relieved by nocturnal emissions of the adult years. Freud described nocturnal enuresis as nocturnal emissions.

Component instincts

Freud called *component instincts* the various aspects of infantile sexual activity that lead to genital maturity. We could say that, in perversions, the sexual drive breaks up into various parts, called component instincts, while in normal sexuality the component instincts come together and work towards genital maturity.

Infantile sexual activity involves the predominance of erotogenic zones and other people as sexual objects. Even when repression of the impulses occurs, the desire persists, becoming a tormenting compulsion with the formation of symptoms.

Small children do not have shame, they expose their bodies and genitals without a thought, as part of their childish nature. The counterpart is their curiosity about seeing other people's genitals. In childhood, the cruel component of the sexual instinct is independent, and appears before the genital phase. The capacity for pity develops relatively late. What is normal in children can have the quality of perverse symptoms later, such as voyeurism.

Sexual research in childhood

Freud described the child's thoughts, curiosity about, and desire of explanation for their questions at different stages of development. These include the following.

- *Instinct of knowledge*: When the sexual life of children reaches its first peak, between three and five years old, the signs of research and quest for knowledge begin. Becoming *curious* is a subliminal way to use the energy of scoptophilia.
- *The riddle of the Sphinx (Theban Sphinx)*: At this time of development, the main first question is: Where do babies come from? The boy thinks that everybody is born with a penis, and girls think that they have lost theirs.
- *Castration complex and penis envy*: These terms describe a conviction that is maintained by boys. Girls think that they had a penis and lost it through castration. The girls recognise that they have a different sex organ and feel envy towards the penis.
- *Theories of birth*: Children have a wealth of sexual theories; however, Freud uncovered one widespread belief: that babies come from eating something special and are born through the bowel, like discharging faeces. Additionally, babies are thought to come from the breast or the navel. All of these ideas are repressed.
- *Sadistic view of sexual intercourse*: Children interpret intercourse as an act of subjugation in a sadistic sense.

Typical failure of infantile sexual researches

Children are capable of understanding sexual issues, but are not aware of the fertilising role of semen and the existence of the mother's orifice. Their sexual research in these early years of childhood is always carried out in solitude. It constitutes a first step towards taking an independent attitude in the world, and implies a high degree of alienation on the part of the child from the people in his environment, who formerly enjoyed his complete confidence.

Phases of development of the sexual organisation

Freud described phases of the sexual infantile organisation as follows:

1. *Autoerotism*: The characteristic of infantile sexual life is essentially autoerotic with regard to the sexual object.
2. *Pregenital organisation*: In his description of psychosexual development, Freud divided phases according to age, erotogenic zone, and defence mechanisms; as discussed above, he also developed the concepts of the oral, anal, and genital phases.
3. *Ambivalence*: The concept of ambivalence (a term coined by Bleuler, who brought us "love–hate") is characterised by the opposing pairs of instincts, which are developed to an equal extent.
4. *Diphasic choice of object*: Freud described the choice of object in two periods; the *first period* occurs between two and five years of age, followed by latency; the *second period* appears during puberty and determines the final outcome of sexual object choices in the person's life.

Sources of infantile sexuality

Freud described situations that would trigger sexual excitement. These include:

1. *Mechanical excitation and/or muscular activity*. (Freud also wondered about the connection between physical activity and sexuality, as, for example, in wrestling.)
2. *Affective processes*: In these processes, tension and fear can be stimuli for sexual excitement.
3. *Intellectual work*: Intellectual strain produces excitation in some young people as well as in adults.

Third essay: the transformations of puberty

Freud wrote that during puberty, there are two processes working together to form a complicated apparatus. The first is the manifest growth of the external genitalia; the second is the development of the internal genitalia needed to discharge sexual products and procreate. This apparatus can be set in motion by stimuli from the external world, erotogenic zones, organically from the interior, and by mental life, which results in sexual excitement. It is during puberty that the sharp distinction between masculine and feminine is established.

Finding the object

In early life, sexual satisfaction is linked to nourishment, as the sexual object is the mother's breast, outside the infant's body. Freud said that too much or too little nourishment from the mother can lead to the libido's fixation on the oral stage. He added that the child suckling his mother's breast becomes the prototype of every relation of love.

The sexual object during early infancy

A mother who takes care of and loves the baby treats him as a substitute for a complete sexual object. This affection rouses her child's sexual instinct and prepares him for his later intensity. The mother fulfils her task in teaching the child to love. Neurosis can appear if the baby later demands too much from his parents' love. Parents can provoke neurosis with excessive caresses or the opposite; that is, too much gratification or frustration can lead to fixation in the libido.

Infantile anxiety

Children are dependent on the people who look after them. *Anxiety in children is an expression of the feeling of the loss of the person they love.* The fear of the dark is related to not seeing the parent physically. A neurotic adult behaves like a child, is insecure, and fears to be alone and away from someone he loves.

The barrier against incest

The individual struggles with the temptation of incest during this development. The barrier is a cultural demand made by society. Phantasies in puberty derive from the phantasies during infantile sexuality, which were forgotten due to infantile amnesia, but that remain embedded in the unconscious and are important in the context of many symptoms.

Object choice

Between the ages of two and five, the choice of an object is considered. This phase is an important precursor to the final sexual organisation. The nature of this childhood sexual manifestation is predominantly masturbatory. In adulthood, all the sources of sexual excitation will come together under the primacy of the genital zones and the process of finding an object.

Factors interfering with development

Freud said that the order in which the sexual impulses appear is phylogenetically determined, so there is a period of time that they are active before they can become repressed. This period will vary according to the duration of the presence of the impulses that can produce an impact in the normal development of the sexual and psychological organisation of the child. He then described factors that will interfere with normal development as follows:

1. *Fixation*: Fixation can occur in the early stages of sexual development. The causes of fixation may include constitutional ones, frustration, or excessive gratification.
2. *Constitution and heredity*: We should consider the impact of factors related to the biological constitution and the hereditary factors.
3. *Repression*: The repressed material does not disappear, and it can emerge in the form of symptoms, or can be integrated in normal sexuality.
4. *Sublimation*: Sublimation can be complete or partial. It is complete when the socially unacceptable ideals or desires are consciously put to use in other fields, such as in innovations or the arts. It is partial when the alternate behaviours of an individual are exhibited but the perversion is still present.
5. *Suppression*: Suppression can happen as a result of reaction formation and may continue throughout the person's life.
6. *Accidental experiences*: Later traumatic experiences can affect the sexual development.

Analysis of a Phobia in a Five-Year-Old Boy,
"Little Hans" (1909)

Freud did not work directly with Little Hans in this case history. Having had contact with the child only one time, Freud worked by corresponding with Hans's father, who was familiar with Freud's theories. When Hans's father shared with Freud his concern about his child, Freud suggested to the father a possible line of therapeutic questioning that the father could try with Hans. Afterwards, he reported back to Freud what had taken place.

Hans was a five-year-old boy who feared that horses in the street would bite him. This fear seemed somehow connected with having been frightened by a large penis (represented by the penis of a horse). It is important to note that transportation in the early twentieth century was by horse-drawn carriages. By 1909, Freud's ideas about the Oedipus complex were well established, and Freud interpreted this case along the lines of this theory.

Freud and the father together tried to understand what the boy was experiencing, and they undertook the challenge of resolving his phobia of horses. Hans's parents agreed to raise their child with only the minimal coercion necessary for maintaining good behaviour. According to Freud, Hans's parents described him as a cheerful, good-natured, and lively little boy; the experiment of letting him grow up and express himself without being intimidated went on satisfactorily (Freud, 1909b, p. 103).

At the time, the family lived close to a busy coach inn. Therefore, Hans was frightened to leave his house because there were many horses right outside his door. He said he was frightened the horses would fall down and make noises with their feet. On one occasion, during a walk with his nanny, Little Hans saw a horse collapse, make noises, and die in the street. The one and only time Hans visited with Freud, he said that he did not like white horses with black bits around the mouth. Freud believed that the horse was a symbol for his father, and the black bits were a moustache. After the interview, the father recorded an exchange with Hans when the boy said to the father "Daddy, don't trot away from me".

Over the next few weeks, Hans's phobia gradually began to improve. After several exchanges between Freud and the father, Freud concluded that the boy was afraid that his father would castrate him for desiring his mother.

Freud described how Hans had a lively interest in sexual matters, curiosity about his "widdler" (penis) and the widdlers of others, his parents, and his baby sister Hanna, who was born when Hans was three-and-a-half years old. Freud described in the discussion section of the case study that Hans repeatedly expressed to his father and his mother his regret that he had never yet seen their widdlers, and it was probably the need for making a comparison which impelled him to do this. Hans had observed that large animals had widdlers that were correspondingly larger than his. Hans consequently suspected that the same was true of his parents, and was anxious to confirm this. Freud added that Little Hans's sexual constitution, the genital zone, was the one among his erotogenic zones which give him more pleasure. He experienced similar pleasure through micturition and evacuation of the bowels.

Freud said, "Hans really was a little Oedipus who wanted to have his father 'out of his way', to get rid of him, so that he might be alone with his beautiful mother and sleep with her" (Freud, 1909b, p. 111).

The most important influence upon the course of Hans's psycho-sexual development was the birth of his baby sister, which accentuated his relations with his parents and gave him some insoluble problems to consider. His first attitude was hostility, followed by affection towards Hanna.

Both Freud and the boy's father tried to present Hans with his unconscious wishes, his love for his mother, and his resentment of the father and sister for getting in his way. The core of the treatment of Hans's phobia was to bring out the boy's awareness of his unconscious wishes.

Hans did not initially recover from his phobias after his personal meeting with Freud. Before Hans made a full recovery, his father had to work with him for many months, bringing his conflicted feelings of hostility and anxiety into the open within a supportive environment.

When Little Hans was nineteen, he appeared at Freud's consulting room after he read his case history. He told Freud that he was perfectly well, and suffered from no troubles or inhibitions. His emotional life had successfully endured difficult times with his parents' divorce and each of them had remarried. He was living on his own and was on good terms with both of his parents. He added that, in reading his case history, he did not recognise himself and could not remember anything. Nevertheless, after reading his case, he was able to analyse his dreams and peacefully return to his sleep.

A biography of "Little Hans"

Little Hans, whose real name was Herbert Graf, was born in Vienna on 10 April 1904, and died in Geneva on 5 April 1973, at the age of sixty-nine. He was the son of Max Graf (1873–1958), an Austrian author, critic, musicologist, and member of Sigmund Freud's circle of friends. Max Graf also participated in Wednesday meetings at Freud's residence.

Herbert Graf became a famous opera director. In 1930, he directed the world première of Schonberg's *Von Leute auf Morgen* ("From Today to Tomorrow"), and he was director of the Opera School at the Hoch Conservatory from 1930 to 1933.

When the Nazis took over power, he was forced to leave his position and emigrated to the United States, where he became a successful and popular opera producer at the New York Metropolitan Opera. In the late 1950s, he returned to Europe and directed at London's Royal Opera House and Covent Garden. In 1959, he returned to New York, and in 1960 he settled in Switzerland, working at the Zurich Opera, before he moved to Geneva, where he died in 1973. He was the author of three books: *The Opera and Its Future in America* (1941), *Opera for the People* (1951), and *Producing Opera for America* (1961).

"Some Reflections on Schoolboy Psychology" (1914)

In this short essay, Freud described his belief that the nature and quality of a child's relationships with people later in life are established in the first six years of the child's life. These elements can develop and transform in different ways, but these years are at the base of the child's experiences. The main people in the child's early life are his parents and siblings.

Later on, the people whom he will encounter are substitute figures for these first objects of his feelings. Freud also included other significant people, like nurses and/or other caretakers from early childhood, who can also play a major role in future relationships. Freud called them the *imagos* of father, mother, siblings, and others.

Freud reinforced the importance of the father, whom the little boy is bound to by love and admiration. In early childhood, the father is the most powerful, the kindest, and the wisest creature in the world. Later on, as the child faces the Oedipal phase, the father becomes a model to imitate, but also to eliminate, in order to take his place. This leads to the feeling of ambivalence.

As the child develops, the father is no longer the mightiest, wisest, and richest of beings, and the child learns to criticise him and estimate his place in society, therefore detaching himself from his father, and thus entering a new stage. The growing boy also comes in contact with his teachers, other men who become substitute fathers. The young person transfers on to these substitutes the respect and expectations, and treats them as the father was treated at home.

"Children's Dreams" (1914)

When Freud focused on the dreams of small children, he found that they were short, clear, coherent, easy to understand, and unambiguous. He stated that dream distortion sets in early in childhood. Dreams dreamt by children between the ages of five and eight have been reported to bear all the characteristics of later dreams. But dreams of younger children up to the age of five have characteristics described as "infantile dreams".

Through the study of dreams of young children, Freud said that the dream is a reaction of the child's mental life, as he sleeps, to the experience of the previous day. These children's dreams are intelligible, completely valid mental acts. They are without any dream distortion and do not require interpretative activity. Here, the manifest and latent contents coincide, although we might recognise a small piece of dream distortion. A child's dream is a reaction to an experience of the previous day or a longing, a wish that has not been dealt with. The dream produces a direct, undisguised fulfilment of that wish.

For young children, the dream is a reaction to a psychical stimulus. These dreams are not disturbers, but guardians of sleep that get rid of sleep disturbances.

The dream represents the wish fulfilled as a hallucinatory experience. It is the transformation of a thought into an experience. Freud compared the dream with a *parapraxis*, or "Freudian slip". A parapraxis is an error in speech, memory, or physical action caused by unconscious sources, a slip of the tongue that reveals a concealed thought or motive. The purpose of sleep and the parapraxis is to satisfy a wish. It is partly achieved and partly abandoned.

A parallel concept is the *daydream*, which is the wish fulfilment of ambitions and erotic desires but through actual thoughts, not hallucinations. Some other dreams are also undistorted; they are generally related to imperative bodily needs, hunger, thirst, or sexual need, and are also wish-fulfilments as a reaction to internal somatic stimuli. Finally, Freud added that adults could also occasionally dream infantile dreams.

"Associations of a Four-Year-Old Child" (1920)

In this paper, Freud wrote about a letter he received from a mother of a four-year-old girl who, in talking about her cousin Emily getting married, said to her mother, "She will have a baby ... because when anyone gets married, a baby always comes." She added that she knows that trees grow in the ground and that God made the world.

The mother seemed to have understood the child's remarks. Freud said that the mother was justified: what the girl was trying to say was, "I know that babies grow inside their mother". Symbolically, she replaced mother with Mother Earth. Furthermore, Freud said that through observations, we know how children make use of symbols. Through the little girl's remarks, he suggested that the mother offer more information to her daughter towards understanding the origin of babies. Freud concluded that the girl thought God makes the world, but "I know that it's all the work of the father" (Freud, 1920d, p. 266).

Beyond the Pleasure Principle (1920)

Here, Freud described his observation of the eighteen-month-old boy who played with a wooden reel with a piece of string tied around it.

> He held the reel by the string and skilfully threw it over the edge of his curtained cot, so that it disappeared into it, at the same time uttering his expressive "o-o-o-o" (gone). He then pulled the reel out of the cot by the string and hailed its reappearance with a joyful "da" (there).
>
> (Freud, 1920g, p. 14)

It was when Freud observed the toddler playing with the reel that he discovered the psychological mechanisms of ludic activity. Freud understood that the child not only played for pleasure but also repeated the painful situations (gone), working through the anxieties experienced by the ego.

Freud's interpretation of this play was that the child was able to accept the absence of his mother without protesting because he was working through his anxiety related to his mother's leaving. When his mother left the room, the child was in a passive situation, so he took an active part in playing the repetitive game, a process that is connected to what Freud described in 1914 as "repetition compulsion".

CHAPTER THREE

Anna Freud

Biography

The youngest daughter of Sigmund and Martha Bernays Freud, Anna Freud was born in Vienna, Austria, on 3 December 1895, and died in London on 8 October 1982 at eighty-six years of age.

Anna had a very close relationship with her father, but not with her mother or her siblings. Anna was emotionally and psychologically attached to her Catholic nursemaid, Josephine Cihlarz, who was hired when Anna was born. Josephine took care of Anna and the younger children, Ernst and Sophie, and remained with the Freud family until Anna completed her first year of elementary school, when she left to marry and have a family of her own. Anna was twenty-nine years old when Josephine died in Vienna, and Anna attended her funeral.

Anna Freud became a teacher in 1914, working as an elementary school teacher from 1917 to 1920. While her professional life was centred on childhood education, her home environment provided unique intellectual stimulation that would shape the rest of her life. Anna was frequently present at psychoanalytic discussions held in her home by her father and his colleagues.

Anna Freud had a unique exposure to the dynamics of psychoanalysis by being treated by her father from 1918 to 1922 (at that time, they were the pioneers of psychoanalysis; at the present time, this practice does not take place any more and is considered contraindicated). Her own psychoanalytic therapy, along with the meetings at her home and her father's encouragement, inspired her to pursue a career in psychoanalysis, particularly in the field of child analysis. She became a member of the Vienna Psychoanalytical Society in 1922, and in 1923 she began her practice in child psychoanalysis with a focus in latency and adolescence.

From 1925 until 1934, she was the secretary of the International Psychoanalytic Association, continued child analysis, and conducted seminars and led conferences on the subject. In 1935, Anna Freud became the director of the Vienna Psychoanalytic Training Institute, and in 1936 she published one of her more important contributions, *The Ego and the Mechanisms of Defence*. This became a founding work of ego psychology and established her reputation as a pioneering theoretician. She maintained a lifelong interest in education, and her extensive contributions in this field are related to aspects of family law, paediatrics, and psychoanalytic psychology, both normal and abnormal.

Her work in Vienna was ended by the Nazi invasion. When she was interrogated for one full day by the Gestapo in 1938 and finally released, it was then that Sigmund Freud decided to leave Vienna and to settle in London. With the help of some of Freud's friends, mainly Princess Marie Bonaparte and Ernest Jones, the Freud family fled to England, escaping the death camps. Because of her father's precarious health, Anna organised and prepared the entire emigration. Once in England, she continued her work while caring for her sick father, who died the following year, in 1939.

At the time of Anna Freud's arrival in London, in 1938, Melanie Klein had been established as a child analyst for nine years. Anna closely followed her father's ideas and developed her own as a continuation of her father's work. After the outbreak of the Second World War and her father's death, in 1941 Anna set up the Hampstead War Nursery for child war victims, where children received foster care, which also gave her the opportunity to observe the effects of deprivation of parental care. After the war, Anna founded an orphanage for concentration camp survivors, the Bulldogs Bank Home, run by her colleagues. Based on these observations, Anna Freud published studies together with Dorothy Burlingham, her best and closest friend, focusing on the stress of parentless children and their ability to find affection and love among their peers.

Anna Freud founded the Hampstead Clinic Therapy Course in 1947, where she gave courses and seminars; then, in 1952, she added the Clinic, where she and her peers continued the care of children. The building was located at 21 Maresfield Gardens, close to her home in Hampstead.

Focusing on research, observation, and treatment of children, Anna established a prominent group of child analysts, which included Erik Erikson, Edith Jacobson, and Margaret Mahler. They noticed that children's symptoms were analogous to the personality disorders found in adults and that these were related to the children's developmental stages.

She created a comprehensive developmental theory and the concept of "developmental lines", which incorporated her father's important drive model. Anna Freud and Melanie Klein clashed and competed to the point where there was a threat of dividing the British Psychoanalytical Society, to which they both belonged. Following the "controversial discussions" between 1942 and 1944, some people followed one and some the other, so two parallel groups were formed within the society in order to try to avoid a split in the institution. The Middle Group was also created, and grew into the Independent Group, to which, with their own theoretical concepts and psychotherapeutic technique, Donald Winnicott, John Bowlby, and others belonged.

Anna Freud became interested in the growth of the ego and in the problems of adaptation, and for a time worked with Heinz Hartmann, one of the founders of ego psychology, before he left Vienna for the United States. However, it is important to note that Anna distanced herself from ego psychology, and based her practice on Freud's structural theories.

Anna Freud and Dorothy Burlingham were close friends, mutually describing their relationship as "the ideal friendship", and Anna was close to Dorothy's children as well.

At the time of Anna Freud's death when she was eighty-six years old, the Hampstead Child Therapy Clinic was renamed the Anna Freud Centre, and her home at 20 Maresfield Gardens became the Freud Museum. This house now holds almost all the contents from the family's Vienna home. The remaining contents were left in Vienna at Berggasse 19, now also known as a Freud Museum, which opened in 1986.

Anna Freud's main theoretical concepts

Anna Freud's major contributions in psychoanalytic theory are: the mechanisms of defence (1936); developmental lines (1965); the diagnostic profile for the assessment of the child (1962); and a technique for the analysis of the child (1965), as discussed below.

Mechanisms of defence

One of Anna Freud's more important books was *The Ego and the Mechanisms of Defence*, first published in German in 1936. Its first English translation quickly followed in 1937. Here she further developed the concept of the ego being connected with the id, the superego, and the external world. We can reach the id, meaning the instincts, the id contents, and its transformations, said Anna, through its derivatives from the unconscious to the preconscious, and conscious. She believed that when the id is calm and satisfied, we cannot reach its contents, and that the same held true for the superego, and that when the ego faces hostile or critical material from the superego, the result is guilt.

In *The Ego and the Mechanism of Defence*, she described the ego and its functions as follows: (1) observation; (2) dealing with the id; (3) dealing with the superego; (4) dealing with the external world (A. Freud, 1936, pp. 5–6).

The id is dominated by the primary process, meaning an unconscious, irrational mental functioning based on the pleasure principle that involves free energy governed by mechanisms such as condensation and displacement. Following the law of the unconscious, the id is atemporal and contains no contradiction. The ego is dominated by the secondary process, a conscious, rational mode of mental functioning, based on the reality principle, which includes bound energy. The reality principle involves conversion of free energy into bound energy. The defence mechanisms are silent, but become evident when they appear in the activity of the ego, as, for example, in the inhibition of play, relationships, and so on. When the repressed material returns (the return of the repressed), a conflict between the impulse and the defences develops, leading to neurosis.

How we can read the unconscious? We can reach the unconscious through the interpretation of dreams, free associations, slips of the tongue (*lapsus linguae*), and transference (of libidinal impulses and of mechanisms of defence). The *analysis of the defences* is important in analytic psychotherapy because the analysis is the liberator of the repressed elements of the id, whose repression leads to the symptoms. In the therapeutic process, the ego of the patient is in alliance with the therapist, allowing the observation of the derivatives of the id; this is the *analyst–ego alliance*. The defence mechanisms are the unconscious activity of the ego.

Anna Freud described the defences as working against the instinct and also against the affects. The ego is in conflict with the id derivatives, the unconscious material that tries to access consciousness and obtain gratification, and also with the affects associated with these instinctual impulses. The first task is to come to terms with these affects.

The affects of love, pain, jealousy, mortification, and mourning accompany sexual (libidinal) wishes. The affects of hatred, anger, and rage accompany the impulses of aggression. In the transference, the ego develops resistance to stop the instinct from appearing to consciousness. The defences are a form of resistance in the therapeutic work. When the defensive manifestations are rigid, they form the character. The analysis of the character traits is painful and difficult for the patient.

Symptom formation

Symptom formation in children can be produced by the stresses and strains that are inherent in development itself. Inhibitions and symptoms commonly appear when a particular phase of growth makes unusually high demands on the child's personality and the parents are unable to handle this appropriately. These symptoms can disappear as soon as the adaptation to the developmental level is achieved.

The role of the ego in the formation of neurotic symptoms consists in the use of specific defence mechanisms when it is confronted with instinctual demand. Anna Freud wrote:

> There is a connection between a particular neurosis and special modes of defence, for example hysteria with repression; obsessional neurosis with isolation and undoing. There is a constant connection between neurosis and defence mechanisms.

> (A. Freud, 1936, p. 34)

In her view, the symptoms appear as the fixation of the defence mechanisms in one stage of development, and can occur as a result of too much gratification or too much deprivation.

Neurosis and defence mechanisms

Anna Freud described defences which are frequent in one particular structure organisation of the diagnostic pathology. Fixation of the libido in different psychosexual stages of development will lead to defences organised around that period. In *hysteria*, the defence that will be prevalent is repression, and somatic symptoms will appear. In *phobia*, the defences will be projection, avoidance, and return of the repressed impulses. In *obsessive neurosis*, we observe mainly regression, isolation, undoing, and reaction formation as defences. In *paranoia*, we find that introjection, identification, and projection will be the main defences.

Sigmund Freud described a number of defence mechanisms throughout his work with patients, including denial, regression, repression, reaction formation, isolation, undoing, projection, introjection, turning against the self, and reversal. Anna Freud added another one: *sublimation*, or *displacement of instinctual aims*, which presupposes the existence of the superego. She wrote: "At that time the ego had ten different methods at its disposal in its conflicts with instinctual representatives and affects" (A. Freud, 1936, p. 44).

Through her own observation with her patients, Anna Freud also added *asceticism, idealism, intellectualisation, identification with the aggressor*, and *altruism*.

- *Asceticism* can be observed when young people reject impulses that are connected with sexuality. During puberty, asceticism could be interpreted as a manifestation of the innate hostility between the ego and the instincts, a hostility that is indiscriminate, primary, and primitive. Young people in this phase seem to fear the quantity more that the quality of their instincts.
- *During puberty*, there is often evidence of a transient attempt to overcharge the contents of the superego. Anna Freud called this the *idealism* of adolescence.
- *Intellectualisation* during puberty is mental activity that is an indication of a tense alertness of the instinctual processes. It involves the translation of the perceived sexual impulses and the new instinctual demands of the person's own id, which threaten to revolutionise their whole lives, into abstract thought.
- *Identification with the aggressor* is a defence of the transformation of passive into active; that is, becoming the person who is feared through introjection of aggression, and directing aggressive acts

towards others. Anna Freud said this is not uncommon in normal development of the superego.

• *Altruism* is the projection of one's own instinctual impulses in favour of other people.

Anna Freud suggested a *chronologic classification*, from the early to the more mature mechanisms, as from introjection and projection, which help to structure the ego, to repression and sublimation, which can only develop later. Regression appears in the early stage.

She felt that the ego has to already be established to develop the mechanisms of introjection and projection. This is different from Melanie Klein's ideas; Klein thought that through the mechanisms of projection and introjection, the already existing ego develops from birth. According to Anna Freud, the defences are born under the pressures of the superego. Furthermore, she mentioned that during treatment, it is important to give attention to the functioning of the superego.

Sources of defence

Anna Freud said: "The instinctual dangers against which the ego defends itself are always the same, but its reasons for feeling a particular irruption of instinct to be dangerous may vary".

(A. Freud, 1936, p. 54). The sources of defences are:

1. *Pressures and fear of the superego*: "The instinct is regarded as dangerous because the superego prohibits its gratification and, if it achieves its aim, it will stir up trouble between the ego and the superego" (A. Freud, 1936, p. 55). The result is *superego anxiety*.
2. *Fears of the external world*: Children suffer from sometimes unnecessary objective anxiety, fear of punishment, if they gratify their instincts. *Objective anxiety* is seen.
3. *Fear of the intensity of the instinct coming from the id*: With fear of the intensity of their own instincts, "defence mechanisms are brought into operation against the instincts, with all the familiar results in the formation of neurosis and neurotic characteristics" (A. Freud, 1936, p. 59). Anxiety here is due to the strength of the instincts.
4. *Interaction between the pleasure principle and reality principles*: The adult ego requires harmony of conflicts, conflicts between opposite tendencies, such as homosexuality and heterosexuality, passivity and

activity. "When instinctual gratification is warded off from one or the other of these two motives, the defence is undertaken in accordance with the reality principle. Its main purpose is to avoid this secondary pain" (A. Freud, 1936, p. 61).

Anna Freud observed that anxiety activates the defensive process. In treatment, it is essential to understand that when we address the defences, anxiety increases. The struggle between the ego and instinctual life generates anxiety. She described three kinds of anxiety: instinctive, objective, and conscious.

The ego tries to avoid pain, and defences are part of the normal process of ego development, but what is normal in childhood can appear as a psychological problem in the future. Anna Freud constantly considered the role of education, saying that being aware of these concepts can help parents and educators intervene in children's development. More ego plasticity and freedom of action will allow the child to develop all forms of sublimation.

With regard to defence mechanisms, she elaborated on repression, reaction formation, sublimation, and projection. Taking into account psychosexual development, the fixation in any of the stages will determine specific behaviour and defences. It is important to remember that fixation occurs when the child faces frustration or excessive gratification; under these conditions, the libido will fixate in that particular stage.

She described the behaviour of the child as a consequence of libido fixation in different stages of psychosexual development. If the fixation is in the oral phase, the child will exhibit voracity, demand, selfishness, clinging, dissatisfaction, fear of being intoxicated, and rejection of some food. If the fixation occurs in the urethral phase, the child will have impulsive behaviour. If the fixation is in the anal phase, the child will express anal tendencies, such as a tendency to order, punctuality, cleanliness, and need to be exact, and also avoiding contact with aggressive impulses. With fixation in the phallic phase, symptoms of shyness or modesty (a reaction formation to exhibitionism) can cause the child to possibly behave like a clown, or express exaggerated masculinity or loud aggression as an expression of castration anxiety. The child can also express boredom as an expression of the repression of masturbatory fantasies and masturbation.

Finally, Anna Freud concluded that the defensive activity of the ego is against both internal and external danger. The defence mechanisms come not only from the ego, they influence an instinctive process, so they are also related to the proprieties of instinct. The return of the repressed that leads to the formation of the compromise formation (symptoms) means a failure in the defensive function, a failure of the ego. The ego is successful when its defensive functions are in place, when it avoids anxiety and pain, and when it assures the person satisfaction through the transformations of instinct that are necessary to achieve a harmony between the id, superego, and the forces of the external world.

Developmental lines

In her book *Normality and Pathology in Childhood* (1965), Anna Freud developed an assessment of normality and pathology in the child and introduced the concept of developmental lines. She used parameters of development to assess the emotional maturity or immaturity of the child, as well as the interaction between the ego and the id and their development levels.

Development of the sexual and aggressive drives

Anna Freud followed the structure of psychosexual development described by Sigmund Freud and the flow of the libido in the different stages of development, beginning with oral, anal, phallic, latency, preadolescence, adolescence, and genital. In the development of the aggressive drive, it is first intertwined with the libidinal drive. In the oral stage, it is expressed in biting, spitting, and devouring. In the anal phase, sadistic torturing, hitting, kicking, destroying, overbearing, and domineering are often exhibited. In the phallic phase, forceful behaviour is common. In adolescence, inconsiderateness, mental cruelty, and dissocial outbursts can often occur.

Throughout development, the chronology of the defence activity and the growth of the moral sense varies. Additionally, intellectual functions are age-related expressions of development. Developmental lines are historical realities that convey a sense of the child's personal achievements or his failures in personality development. Anna Freud initially distinguished several developmental lines.

From dependency to emotional self-reliance and adult object relationship

This developmental line describes the changes at the level of observable mother–child relationships alongside the evolution of internal representations of objects that create templates for later relationships.

> This is the sequence which leads from the newborn's utter dependence on maternal care to the young adult's emotional and material self-reliance, a sequence for which the successive stages of libido development (oral, anal, phallic) merely form the inborn, maturational base.
>
> (A. Freud, 1965, p. 65)

Along this developmental line, the following stages are identified:

1. *The biological unity between the mother–infant couple*: The infant is under the assumption that the mother is a part of him and is under his control, and the mother experiences the baby as psychologically part of her. Separation from the mother in this stage is thought to give rise to separation anxiety.

   > According to Margaret Mahler (1952), the child develops from a state of autism, later becomes symbiotic, and finally enters the separation-individuation phase, with significant danger for developmental disturbances in each individual phase.
   >
   > (A. Freud, 1965, p. 65)

2. *The part-object*: There is a need-fulfilling anaclitic relationship between the child and her object, it is connected with the child's imperative body needs. The child has a naturally fluctuating character, as the need for the object increases with the arousal of drives, but the importance of the object for the child is reduced when satisfaction has been reached. The way that the child is nurtured and satisfied will lead to the formation of an image of a "good and bad mother", more specifically a "good and bad breast", the part-object that Melanie Klein described.

3. *The stage of object constancy*: At this stage, the child achieves a consistent representation of the mother, which can be maintained irrespective of the satisfaction of drives, making the representation of the mother

more stable. The child is able to form reciprocal relationships that can survive disappointments and frustrations.

4. *The ambivalent relationship*: The ambivalent relationship between the pre-Oedipal and the anal-sadistic stage is "characterised by ego attitudes of clinging, torturing, dominating, and controlling the love object" (A. Freud, 1965, p. 65). The toddler's positive and negative feelings are visibly focused on the same person (known as the "terrible twos"). The child is in conflict, wishing both to be independent and to retain the complete devotion of the mother. In this stage, ambivalence is considered to be normal.

5. *Object-centred*: The so-called phallic-Oedipal phase is "characterised by possessiveness of the parent of the opposite sex and jealousy and rivalry with the same-sex parent" (A. Freud, 1965, p. 65). The child becomes aware that there are aspects of the relationship between the parents from which he is excluded.

6. *The latency period*: In the latency period, the urgency of the child's drives is reduced and there is a transfer of libido from parents to peers and others in the child's social environment and the community.

7. *The pre-adolescent before the adolescent revolt*: In this period, there is a regression from the reasonableness of latency children to a demanding, contrary, inconsiderate attitude characteristic of earlier stages, especially towards the part-object, along with need-fulfilling, and ambivalent attitudes or behaviour. This strengthens oral, anal, and phallic drive components, reviving infantile fantasies and intensifying intrapsychic conflict.

8. *Adolescence*: During adolescence, the ego struggles to master the upsurge of sexuality and aggression. "Struggle around denying, reversing, and shedding the tie to the infantile objects, defending aginst pregenitality, and finally establishing genital supremacy with libidinal cathexis transferred to objects of the opposite sex, outside the family" (A. Freud, 1965, p. 66). Two new defence mechanisms, intellectualisation and asceticism, emerge in adolescence to defend the individual from the instinctual demands of the body. The adolescent is preoccupied with her internal struggle to transfer emotional investment from parents to new objects.

9. It is only after object constancy has been reached that the external absence of the object can, at least in part, be substituted for by the presence of an internal image that remains stable, and temporary separations can be lengthened, commensurate with the advances in object constancy.

Some developmental lines towards body independence

Anna Freud followed Sigmund Freud's idea that the ego of the infant begins as a body ego. The infant experiences confusion concerning the limits of the body, and the distinction between the internal and external worlds is based mainly in the subjective experiences of pleasure and unpleasure. Early childhood is dominated by body needs, body impulses, and their derivatives. The satisfaction or dissatisfactions are determined by the environment, with the exception of autoerotic gratifications.

From suckling to rational eating

1. *Being nursed at the breast or bottle, according to a schedule or on demand*: This stage will be regulated by the infant's fluctuations of appetite and intestinal upsets, and also by the mother's attitudes and anxieties regarding feeding. Pleasure suckling appears as a forerunner of interference with feeding. "In the process of weaning from breast or bottle, initiated by the infant or the mother, difficulties with solids can appear; new tastes can be welcomed or rejected" (A. Freud, 1965, p. 70). This stage can lead to oral deprivation and symptoms like difficulties with solids, new tastes, and so on.
2. *Transition from being fed to self-feeding, with or without utensils*: Disagreements with the mother and difficulties of the mother–child relationship can appear at this time.
3. *Self-feeding with the use of spoon, fork, and so on*: Here, the mother–child relationship can be difficult, leading to fights and eating disorders. "Gradual fading out of the equation food–mother in the Oedipal period. During this period, irrational attitudes towards eating are now determined by infantile sexual theories, and phantasies about pregnancy and birth, as well as reaction formations against cannibalism and sadism" (A. Freud, 1965, p. 71). "Gradual fading out of the sexualisation of eating in the latency period, with pleasure in eating retained or increased" (A. Freud, 1965, p. 71).

The experience in this line determines future approaches to food habits in adult life. It is important to consider that whatever attitude dominates the feeding process will also become important in other developmental areas.

From wetting and soiling to bladder and bowel control

According to Anna Freud, this line of development include four phases, as follows:

1. *First phase*: The infant has complete freedom to wet and soil. This phase may last days to two or three years. Toilet training is based on object-relatedness and ego control.
2. *Second phase*: This phase is initiated by a step in maturation, from the oral to the anal phase. In this phase, the body products are highly cathected with libido; they are precious for the child and treated as gifts that are surrendered to the mother as a sign of love. Also, when cathected with aggression, they are weapons of rage, anger, and disappointment that are discharged within the object relationship. In this phase, the child's attitude towards the object world is dominated by ambivalence, as seen in violent swings between love and hate (libido and aggression are not fused to each other). Curiosity is turned towards the inside of the body, and the discovery of pleasure: pleasure in messing, moulding, retaining, emptying, hoarding, possessing, destroying, and so on. Depending on the mother's attitude during this stage, toilet training can be smooth and uneventful or difficult.
3. *Third phase*: In this phase, the child accepts and takes over the mother's and the environment's attitude to cleanliness, and through identification makes them an integral part of his ego and superego demands; the cleanliness will be internalised and the ego defences of repression and reaction formation will contain the urethral and anal wishes.
4. *Fourth phase*: Bladder and bowel control become wholly secure in this phase, as these become a fully neutralised, autonomous ego and superego concern.

From irresponsibility to responsibility in body management

For years, the child's feeding and the evacuation needs remain under external control, and in a gradual manner, the child assumes responsibility for the care of her own body and of protecting it from harm. In the first few months of life, aggression towards the child's own body turns towards the external world. Through her development, the child has more understanding of cause and effect, orientation towards the external world, and control of dangerous wishes in the service of the reality principle. The child voluntarily follows the rules of hygiene and medical necessities.

Other developmental lines

From egocentricity to companionship

The development from egocentricity to companionship also parallels a sequence of behaviours in the relationship of the child with others, as described below:

1. *Selfishness*: "Early in life, the child has a selfish, narcissistically oriented outlook on the object world" (A. Freud, 1965, p. 78).
2. *Children regarded as lifeless objects*: In this stage, other children are likened to lifeless objects, like toys. The child is asocial at this stage.
3. *Children related to as helpmates*: Later on, the child begins to consider seeking helpmates in carrying out a desired task; the duration of the partnership is determined by the task. This stage is the minimum requirement for socialisation in the form of acceptance into a community or into a nursery group.
4. *Children as partners*: In this phase, the child is able to consider other children as partners and objects in their own right. "The child can admire, fear, or compete with whomever he loves or hates. He is able to share possessions on a basis of equality. It is only in this stage that the child becomes equipped for companionship and friendships of any type and duration" (A. Freud, 1965, p. 78).

From the body to the toy and from play to work

1. In the early stages, infant play begins with an activity yielding erotic pleasure, involving the mouth, fingers, vision, and the whole surface of the skin. It is an autoerotic play or play on the mother's body (connected with feeding); there is no distinction between the two of them.
2. The properties of the mother's and the child's body are transferred to some soft substance or object. Winnicott's *transitional object*, which is cathected both with narcissistic and with object libido, is an example.

3. Clinging to one specific transitional object develops further into several symbolic objects, which are cuddled and maltreated, cathected with libido and aggression. The child can express a full range of his ambivalence towards them.

4. Cuddly toys fade out gradually, except at bedtime. In daytime, their place is taken by play material, such as (a) toys that help to develop ego activities; (b) movable toys, providing pleasure in motility; (c) building materials offering opportunities for construction and destruction in line with the ambivalent trends of the anal-sadistic phase; (d) toys serving the expression of masculine and feminine trends and attitudes. In solitary role-playing, these may be Oedipal objects, for staging the various situations of the Oedipus complex in group play.

5. Direct or displaced satisfaction from the play activity itself gives pleasure in the finished product of the activity. Pleasure is experienced in task completion.

6. Ability to play changes into ability to work when other faculties develop, such as: (a) the ability to control, inhibit, or modify the impulses in order to use the materials positively and constructively; (b) the ability to carry out preconceived plans, postpone pleasure, and progress from primitive instinctual to sublimated pleasure, together with neutralisation of the energy employed; (c) the ability to go from the pleasure principle to the reality principle, which is essential for the development of success in work during latency, adolescence, and in maturity.

Other significant activities

Derived from the progression from the body to the toy, and from play to work, Anna Freud said there are other activities that are significant to personality development, including daydreaming, games, and hobbies.

1. *Daydreaming*, including the capacity for phantasy activity, which persists until adolescence and far beyond;

2. *Games*, which require the ability to compete, tolerate frustration, and provide the craved companionship;

3. *Hobbies*, between play and work, these appear for the first time in the beginning of the latency period in the form of collecting, spotting, and interest specialisation, and can persist throughout life.

Correspondence between developmental lines

In clinical terms, to be a harmonious personality, a child would reach appropriate development in every area of maturation. Some children, however, exhibit irregular patterns in their growth, high in some levels and infantile in others. Such imbalance between developmental lines causes problems and poses the question: how much is innate, and how much is due to environmental reasons? The disequilibrium between developmental lines is not necessarily always pathological, however; it can produce variations of normality which we have to assess.

Developmental lines and psychopathology

In conceptualising the developmental lines, Anna Freud was aware that children could not be expected to proceed evenly across all lines. As the forces determining the child's development are external as well as internal and largely outside the child's control, minor "developmental disharmonies" are to be expected. Gross disharmony, however, can predispose the child to severe neurosis, non-neurotic personality disorders, and other psychopathology.

Anna Freud outlined several examples of phase-specific developmental disturbances with reference to the basic lines delineated above. As such, in phase 1, *biological unity between the mother–infant couple*, an infringement of the biological mother–infant tie, for whatever reason (death, addiction, neglect), can lead to separation anxiety. Similarly, a serious failure on the mother's behalf to be reliable, need-fulfilling, and comforting in phase 2, *the relationship with the part object–mother breast*, will cause breakdowns in individuation. Unsatisfactory libidinal relations to unstable love objects during phase 4, *the ambivalent relationship*, will disturb the balanced integration of libido and aggression, which can lead to uncontrollable aggressive behaviour and destructiveness.

The framework of developmental lines has been helpful in allowing us to track "normal" and "abnormal" development and has led to some interesting practical lessons. For example, Anna Freud writes that the clinging attitudes at the toddler stage (phase 4) are the result of pre-Oedipal ambivalence, not of maternal spoiling, as was thought. Further, in the pre-Oedipal period (end of phase 4), parents cannot expect mutuality in object relations, as this belongs to the next phase, and similarly, no child can be fully integrated in school before libido has been transferred from the parents to the community, which happens in phase 6, the latency period.

Developmental lines can also be useful in making predictions as to when particular events will have the greatest impact. For example, Anna lists the later part of phase 6 as one in which reactions to adoption would be particularly severe. This is because all children experience normal disillusionment of their parents, therefore all children feel as if they are in some way "adopted".

Diagnostic profile

Anna Freud developed the concept of the diagnostic profile based on the concept of the developmental lines. This outline of child assessment helps us to have a better idea of the dynamics of the family and the child, as well as the intrapsychic conflicts that lead the child to particular symptoms. The diagnostic profile will be fully described later in this book with the case presentation at the Anna Freud Hampstead Child Therapy Clinic.

Further influences of Anna Freud's work

Anna Freud's theories were important for the discipline of developmental psychology. She encouraged child analysts to understand, from the psychoanalytic point of view, the most central developmental question: what moves development along? Inspired by her work, today's psychoanalysts take a broad view on child development.

Her concept of developmental lines stimulates other child psychoanalysts to pay attention to various fields in which the child develops. Although she did not know about new processes in neurobiology, genetics, and social psychology, her model is still suitable as a basic model of how to understand children and how we can learn more about their development. The lasting contributions of her theories lie in her continued questioning of how mind and body are brought together.

The field of developmental psychology has learned from Anna Freud always to consider that the inner world of the child is constructed in the interaction between biological predisposition and the environment.

Some notes about Anna Freud's child technique

In working with children, Anna Freud proposed an introductory phase in order to establish the alliance with the child. She used the interpretation of dreams, daydreams, and drawings to accomplish this. She did not use much of the child's play as an element of analysis.

Anna Freud observed the child's dreams, saying that the child easily talks about his or her dreams, and that children's dreams are easier to interpret than adults'. She said that children can talk more directly about their dreams, and do not need free association, probably because children dream without any dream-distortion, as based on her own observations and in reference to Sigmund Freud's 1915 paper "Children's Dreams".

Anna Freud only maintained positive transference, sought the cooperation of patients, and asked for their help in order to interpret their dreams. She encouraged the child to talk about his phantasies, dreams, and drawings. If negative transference appeared, she immediately tried to dissolve it, never giving interpretation. The child who enters analysis sees in the analyst a new object and treats her as such, in so far as he has a healthy part to his personality.

For Anna Freud, the analyst's task is to interpret unconscious material. The aim of analysis remains the widening of consciousness, without which ego control cannot be increased. During the process of therapy, she analysed the ego resistance before the id content, and allowed the work of interpretation to move freely between id and ego.

She offered the analyst as a transference object for the revival and interpretation of unconscious phantasies and attitudes, and to analyse impulses and to avoid them being acted out and gratified. She sought to expect tension relief not from catharsis, but from the material being lifted from the level of primary process functioning to secondary thought processes, turning id into ego content.

With regard to transference, later in her life Anna Freud rectified her idea of lack of transference neurosis in children. She recognised this concept, emphasising that it is different than in the adult psychoanalytic process. For her, transference was a means to an end, not a therapeutic measure in itself.

Anna Freud said that the ego of the young child has the developmental task to master both an orientation in the external world, and in the chaotic emotional states that exist within him. Verbalisation is very important, in all ages, and is a prerequisite for secondary-process thinking. Verbalisations of the perception of the external world precede verbalising the content of the internal world, and this promotes reality-testing and ego control over id impulses.

Visiting the Anna Freud Hampstead Child Therapy Clinic

In 1974, when visiting the Anna Freud Hampstead Child Therapy Clinic, I was able to attend a clinical presentation coordinated by Anna Freud, and then returned to the clinic a week later. It was then that I had the opportunity to see the offices and to discuss patients with Mrs Mason, the presenter at the previous week's conference. I was impressed to see that her office had a sink with running water in the corner of the room. In my conversation with Mrs Mason, she explained to me that it was very important to have water available so that the child could express feelings and emotions in every stage of their psychosexual develop-ment. The water could be used as a symbolic representation of uncon-scious objects and conflicts.

I presented one of my patients, a five-year-old boy, who had become extremely aggressive after his mother left him and the family. In the beginning of his treatment, during his sessions, he attacked and kicked me and destroyed the toys in his basket. Mrs Mason said that my main intervention at that time of the treatment should be asking the five-year-old boy to put his feelings into words and to stop the acting out. This worked part of the time, but at other times I had to interrupt the ses-sions. At the end of his treatment, he was able to verbalise his feelings, interact well with me, and repair all of the toys that had been destroyed over the years of his treatment.

More than thirty years later, I had the opportunity to see him and his wife in New York. He was then in his forties, a successful musician cur-rently living in Los Angeles. He remembered one time when he was in my office, leaving the water running from the bathroom sink to the office with the bathroom door locked, after a couple of minutes he opened the door, the water covered the floor and the session had to be interrupted. He clearly remembered my words "Put your feelings in words, put it in words", he did and later he asked his son to do the same.

Model of a case presentation based on the diagnostic profile

I would like to describe the outline of the extensive study of the child who was presented and discussed at the meeting I attended, because the presentation included a useful and lengthy evaluation of the family and the child based on Anna Freud's diagnostic profile concept.

The evaluation and the report included the following:

- *Social history* (the history is compiled from three interviews, two with the mother, and one with the father, psychological evaluation, and school report).
- *Reason for referral* (arrest in development, behaviour problems, anxiety, inhibitions, other symptoms).
- *Impression of the parents* (appearance, information about themselves, their marriage).
- *Description of the child* (at home, at school, and when he was alone, described by the child himself).
- *Personal history of the child* (date of birth, parents' background and education, child medical history, health, developmental milestones and the first year of life, schooling).
- *Description of the sister* (development of the infant, schooling, personality description, emotions and behaviour).
- *Parents' background* (Mother: childhood, her own parents' history, relevant experiences in her life, circumstances around the encounter with her husband). (Father: childhood, his parents' history, relevant experiences in his life, including the time he met his wife).
- *Present family circumstances* (relevant situations in their lives, participation of the grandparents).
- *Possibly significant factors for causation of disturbances.*
- *Possible favourable and stabilising influences.*
- *Initial testing:* Wechsler Intelligence Scale for children.
- *School report* (identifying data, impression of the child, work and behaviour, attitude to academic work, manual and physical skills, relation towards teachers and other children). Further teacher comments or problems.
- *Psychological evaluation and report*: WISC (intelligence), TAT (projectives), reading test, Bender Gestalt, house–tree–person drawing test. Description of the child during the test period. Summary of test results. Test results and observation for every test taken.
- *Overall impression of the child.*

After this thorough pre-interview evaluation, the child *first diagnostic interview* was performed, followed by the *second diagnostic interview*.

Provisional diagnostic profile: statement of the problem, the referral, description of the child, family background (mother and father). Personal child history, health, school. Possible significant factors for causation of disturbance. Possible favourable and stabilising influences. Statement of the problem.

Assessment of development

Drive development

1. libidinal phase development
2. libidinal fixation points, regression, and arrests
3. aggressive manifestations/development
4. libidinal (narcissistic) and aggressive cathexis of self
5. libidinal and aggressive cathexis of objects

Ego development:

1. physical apparatus undermining ego development
2. basic psychological functions (testing)
3. ego identifications
4. ego reactions to danger situations
5. defence organisation
6. secondary interference of defence activity with ego achievements

Superego development

Dynamic and structural assessments (conflicts): Internal conflicts—level of maturity

General characteristics: Frustration tolerance—sublimation potential—the overall attitude to anxiety—progressive developmental forces versus regressive tendencies.

Diagnosis and recommendations

After this extensive diagnostic period, the child and the family were able to start psychoanalytic treatment. The sessions with the child were three times per week and with the parents once a week. Mrs Mason mentioned to me that in general the sessions with the parents are with the mothers, due to the fact that the majority of fathers work during the day.

Publications by Anna Freud

1922–1935   *Introduction to Psychoanalysis: Lectures for Child Analysts and Teachers.*

1936   *The Ego and the Mechanisms of Defence.*

Infants without Families: Reports on the Hampstead Nurseries.

1945–1956   *Indications for Child Analysis and Other Papers.*

1956–1965   *Research at the Hampstead Child Therapy Clinic and Other Papers.*

1965   *Normality and Pathology in Childhood: Assessment of Development.*

1966–1970   *Problems of Psychoanalytic Training, Diagnosis, and the Technique of Therapy.*

Psychoanalytic Psychology of Normal Development, in collaboration with Sophie Dann.

CHAPTER FOUR

Melanie Klein

Biography

Melanie Reizes Klein was born in Vienna, Austria, on 30 March 1882, and died in London on 22 September 1960 at the age of seventy-eight. Her father, Moriz Reizes, was a Jewish doctor of Polish origin who came from a traditional Jewish religious background. Born in Lember, Galitzia (now Lvov, Ukraine), Dr Reizes had an early first marriage which ended in divorce. When he was forty-four, he met Libussa Deutsch, who was then twenty-five. At the time Dr Reizes married Libussa, who was from Warkotz, Slovakia, he was forty-seven.

After the marriage, the couple settled in Deutschkreutz, Hungary (now Bergenland, Austria), but in 1882 they decided to move to Vienna, where Melanie Klein was born. The couple had four children, of whom Melanie was the youngest:

- Emily, born in 1876
- Emmanuel, born in 1877, died in 1902 at age twenty-five from rheumatic heart disease

- Sidonie, born in 1878, died in 1886 at the age of eight years from tuberculosis
- Melanie, born in Vienna in 1882.

Dr Reizes was in his fifties at the time of Melanie's birth. Melanie's mother, Libussa, was young and energetic. This may explain why Melanie felt closer to her mother and more distant from her father; nevertheless, Melanie remembered that her family life was surrounded by love and togetherness, although with three tragic moments: the death of her father, her sister, and her brother Emmanuel. Emmanuel was the "genius" of the family, Emily was her father's favourite, and Sidonie was the best-looking of the children and her mother's favourite.

Her sister Sidonie played an influential role in Melanie's early childhood development. Struck down with tuberculosis, Sidonie spent the last months of her life in bed. She dedicated her time to teaching the little Melanie how to read and write. Through these lessons, Melanie and Sidonie grew quite close. Sidonie ultimately succumbed to her illness when she was eight, and her death was devastating for the young Melanie. After Sidonie's death, Melanie became the favourite of her mother and of an uncle.

Owing to the difficult economic situation at that time in Vienna, her father was unable to work as a medical doctor. Dr Reizes had to buy a dental practice and worked as a dentist. Melanie's mother opened a shop selling pets and plants to help her husband with the expenses of the house. She closed the shop in 1907, perhaps about the time Melanie Klein was five years old, when a wealthy uncle came to live with the family and helped them with their finances.

This was a time of intellectual stimulation in their household as her father and her brother Emmanuel engaged in intellectual discussions centring around authors, poets, and writers. Emmanuel stimulated Melanie's intellectual interests and gave her a sense of having almost a duty to seek achievement.

In her early teenage years, Melanie Klein had a strong aspiration to become a medical doctor like her father. When she was fourteen, she began her studies at the Gymnasium in Vienna with the idea of going to medical school. Her brother Emmanuel supported her decision to become a physician, for this was also his dream. He too began his studies in medicine, but was soon forced to abandon them after being diagnosed with a fatal heart condition. He then shifted his academic interests to literature and travel.

In 1899, when she was seventeen, Melanie was introduced to one of Emmanuel's good friends, Arthur Stephen Klein, who was twenty-one at the time, and they were engaged when Melanie was nineteen. Her engagement with him interfered with her plans for medical school, however, and she changed her focus to history and art, a decision she would later regret.

When she was eighteen years old, in 1900, her father died of pneumonia; only two years later, her brother Emmanuel perished from cardiac rheumatism at the age of twenty-five while visiting Genoa. Melanie was thus in a state of mourning while she was dating Arthur Klein. Arthur had studied chemical engineering in Zurich, and was well educated, well read, and spoke many languages. When Melanie was twenty-one, four years after she and Arthur had met, they married, and they remained married for almost twenty years. The couple frequently travelled due to her husband's profession. They lived in small towns, first in Slovakia, then in Silesia, where she was unhappy, as she missed the intellectual stimulation she had enjoyed in Vienna. Finally, however, her life changed when they settled in Budapest in 1910.

The deaths of her father and the two siblings, especially perhaps that of Emmanuel, contributed to the lasting streak of depression that was part of Melanie's personality. When in 1908 she became very depressed, she travelled to a sanatorium in Switzerland where she remained for two and a half months.

Melanie Klein and her children

Melanie and Arthur had three children: Hans, the eldest, was born in 1907; Melitta, the middle child, was born in 1910; and Eric, the youngest son, was born in 1913. Hans followed his father's footsteps and became an engineer. When his parents divorced, he decided to live with his father in Switzerland. In April of 1934, at the age of twenty-seven, Hans died in a climbing accident.

Melitta became a medical doctor and later on a psychoanalyst; she married an analyst, Dr Walter Schmiderberg, who was fourteen years her senior. The couple moved to the United States but returned to England one year after her mother's death, in 1961. Melitta and her mother had a very competitive and troubled relationship.

Eric, the youngest, remained with his mother after the divorce and later settled in Hungary. He was the only child to became close to his mother, and was with her at the time of her death in London. Eric married and had three children, about whom Melanie Klein exclaimed, "These children are the happiness of my life".

Melanie Klein in Budapest (1918–1921)

When Melanie Klein was twenty-eight, she and her husband moved to Budapest, in line with her husband's work. After living in small towns, the city offered Melanie a more intellectually stimulating environment. It was there that she met Sándor Ferenczi, an outstanding Hungarian analyst who was also well liked by Freud; it was through her connection with Ferenczi that her interest in psychoanalysis began.

When Melanie was thirty, at about the time of her mother's death, she began a psychoanalytic treatment with Ferenczi in Budapest that lasted several years. Influenced by Freud and the growing interest in applying psychoanalytic theory to children in Vienna, Ferenczi encouraged her to consider the possibility of applying psychoanalysis for the treatment of children. When she was thirty-five, following the births of her own children, she grew interested in observing children, especially her own. Her observations of Eric led her to write "The Development of a Child", which was published in 1921.

Klein met Freud in 1918, at the International Psycho-Analytic Congress in Budapest. After meeting Freud, she was further motivated to follow her interest in applying psychoanalytic theory in working with children, and psychoanalysis became her life's passion. By 1919, at thirty-seven, she read the first part of her paper "Development of a Child" (based on her own child, but she called him Fritz in this paper) to the Hungarian Society; the paper was published in 1921 in London. She became a member of the Society in 1919 and established herself as an analyst. In 1920, she attended the Sixth International Psycho-Analytic Congress in the Hague and had the opportunity to meet Karl Abraham, who later invited her to work in Berlin.

After meeting Abraham, she decided to leave Hungary and go to Berlin with her children but without her husband, and by January 1921, her permanent address was the Psychoanalytic Clinic in Berlin. In the same month, her husband left Hungary for Switzerland with Hans. The couple ultimately divorced in 1922; Arthur died in Switzerland in 1939, the year of Freud's death.

Melanie Klein in Berlin (1921–1926)

When she was thirty-seven, she moved to Berlin with Eric, and Melitta attended medical school. Klein continued her psychoanalytic practice in Berlin with children and adults, and Karl Abraham, whom she had met at the International Psycho-Analytic Conference, became her mentor. Two years later, she became a member of the Berlin Society that Abraham had founded. She expanded her professional life, widened her practice, and was given the opportunity to analyse the children of her colleagues.

A few years after the move to Berlin, she began psychoanalytic treatment with Abraham, which lasted fourteen months. Their relationship was a pivotal component of her professional life. Klein had already created "play therapy" as a technique to treat children, and Abraham was very supportive of her work and her ideas. He believed in Klein's theory and technique, and on one occasion commented that the future of child psychoanalysis lay in the analysis of play.

Abraham died in December 1925, and his death marked an important moment in Klein's life. The loss of Abraham left Klein in an intellectual void. However, this spurred her to seek opportunities elsewhere. Abraham had analysed both Melanie Klein and Alix Strachey, an analyst from London who had come to Berlin for her analysis with Abraham, and they became friends. Alix told her husband, James Strachey, an English psychoanalyst (Freud's translator for all his publications), about Klein's ideas, and in turn James shared Klein's ideas with Ernest Jones, who both saved Freud and his family from the death camps and became Freud's most important biographer.

Ernest Jones was already very impressed with Klein's ideas and the innovative play technique she had developed for analysing young children. She first presented these concepts at the International Congress in Salzburg, in 1924, which Ernest Jones attended. Later, she developed these ideas further in her paper, "The Psychological Principles of Early Analysis".

Ernest Jones invited Melanie Klein to come to London to give a course of lectures about child analysis to the members of the British

Psychoanalytical Society in 1925. The course lasted three weeks and was very successful; Klein later credited those three weeks as the best time of her life.

Melanie Klein in London (1926–1960)

Melanie Klein was forty-three when she travelled to London for three weeks on the invitation of Ernest Jones, and on 27 June 1926, she returned with Eric to settle there, where she would remain until her death.

Melanie Klein read her paper on the psychogenesis of manic-depressive states at the British Psychoanalytical Society, a paper similar to the ones she had presented in Vienna and Berlin. In her 1934 paper, she introduced the concept of the *depressive position*. This paper produced a strong impact, evoking both positive and negative reactions in the British Society.

The year 1934 was a painful one in the life of Melanie Klein. While her professional life was gaining success, she suffered two painful events in her personal life. The first was the death of her son Hans, and the second was her deteriorating relationship with her daughter Melitta, who had become a physician-psychoanalyst and worked professionally with her mother. Their personal relationship was troubled and strained. Ultimately, Melitta and her husband moved to the United States in 1945, and mother and daughter would never see each other again.

By 1938, when she was forty-six, many European analysts had began their exodus from Europe owing to the worsening political situation and the German persecution of Jews. Most of the analysts went to the United States and England. In 1938, Germany invaded Austria and the Freuds arrived in London. Their arrival posed a threat to Melanie Klein, who was already established as a prominent child psychoanalytic thinker in the British Society. Anna Freud was also already working with children, and Melanie Klein perceived her arrival as a threat to her position in the Society. Nevertheless, Melanie Klein sent the Freuds a welcoming letter.

When the Second World War was declared in 1939, Klein was afraid to remain in the city and temporarily moved to Cambridge with Susan Isaacs, an analyst who was one of Klein's followers. Freud died in September 1939, only a month following the death of her former husband, Arthur Klein.

Pursuing her work, in 1940 she further elaborated the concept of the depressive position in relationship with mourning, reparation, and creativity. She also described the unconscious life of very young children, expressing her idea that there was a core of psychosis in all of us, a concept that provoked a strong reaction within the members of the Society. The discussions between Anna Freud and Melanie Klein intensified the pre-existing turmoil within the Society, and tension grew.

After a short time in Cambridge, Klein returned to London, only to leave again. This time, Klein moved to Pitlochry, Scotland, where she remained for a year to escape the threat posed by the war. It was there that, from April to August 1941, she performed the analysis of a ten-year-old boy she called Richard, painstakingly detailing every session she had with him, including her interpretations of his drawings, dreams, verbal associations, and play. She would revisit the contents of these sessions during the last period of her life in her 1961 book *Narrative of Child Psycho-Analysis*, which was published posthumously.

From 1942 to 1944, significant controversial discussions took place in the Society. Klein triggered both positive and negative reactions within the membership, and Anna Freud and others resigned from the training committee of the Society. Yet at the same time, the formation of the Kleinian School within the British Society was taking place, making three groups within the Society: Anna Freud's, Melanie Klein's, and the third group, the Middle Group. Later called the Independent Group, this group was made up of analysts who developed their own ideas, among them Donald Winnicott and Ronald Fairbairn, both of whom worked on original ideas as well as incorporating portions of Melanie Klein's theories.

In the Klein Group, Melanie Klein was surrounded by a group of loyal followers, and had a forum where she presented her ongoing research. Susan Isaacs and Joan Riviere worked closely with her, and Hanna Segal, Betty Joseph, Donald Meltzer, Elliott Jaques, Herbert Rosenfeld, Paula Heimann, and Esther Bick were also among those interested in her theories.

The introduction of the concept of *projective identification* enabled the Kleinians to understand from their perspective the pathology of schizophrenia and borderline disorders, which had previously been considered unanalysable.

In 1946, two programmes were established in the British Psychoanalytical Society, Group A (Melanie Klein) and Group B (Anna Freud), with the intent of allowing the Society to continue without splitting. It was effective, but Melanie Klein was concerned about the durability of her ideas following the creation of the separate groups.

In 1948, her book *Contributions to Psycho-Analysis* was published, which included a compilation of her papers from 1921 to 1945. *Developments in Psychoanalysis* was published in 1952. This publication set out a general theory of early development of the mind in the first years of life, and the potential pathological distortions of such development. Klein felt that the theory of drives accounted for the dynamics of anxiety, object relations, and defence mechanisms, and explained these in terms of phantasy.

In 1955, *New Directions in Psycho-Analysis: The Significance of Infant Conflict in the Pattern of Adult Behaviour* was published in Klein's honour and as a gift for her seventieth birthday. In 1957, *Envy and Gratitude and Other Works, 1946–1963* was published, followed, in 1961, by *Narrative of a Child Analysis*. This is an important detailed clinical document of the analysis of Richard, a ten-year-old boy who was in six-times-a-week analysis for a total of ninety-three sessions from April to August 1941. Elliott Jacques helped her organise the extensive clinical material of this analysis.

In 1959, she presented her two papers, "A Note on Depression in the Schizophrenic" and "On the Sense of Loneliness", at the International Meeting in Copenhagen. This was her last attendance at an International Congress. At the time of her death in March 1960, she had three patients in analysis: Clare Winnicott, Donald Meltzer, and Hyatt Williams.

Dr Judith Kestenberg, another pioneer of child psychoanalysis, trained at the Hampstead Clinic in 1945 with Anna Freud. Upon meeting Melanie Klein, she suggested to her that in order to be accepted in the United States, she should say that the baby has feelings that were later phantasies. Klein replied "What is the difference?" (personal communication, 1985).

Clare Winnicott, the wife of Donald Winnicott, stated "I use her ideas all the time, my way". Clare recalled that during one of her sessions with Melanie Klein, she was given a twenty-five-minute interpretation, one that Clare viewed as more of an expression of Kleinian theory than personal meaning. Despite Clare's disappointment with her treatment, she was encouraged by her husband to continue the analysis with Klein in order to be certified as a psychoanalyst; as Winnicott regarded Klein as a genius. Shortly before Klein died, she announced that Clare had completed her analysis, and she was certified to practise.

Melanie Klein died on 22 September 1960 at the age of seventy-eight. Anna Freud was twelve years her junior and at that time sixty-six years old.

Melanie Klein's main theoretical concepts

The first year of life

Melanie Klein's concepts on the importance of the first year of life were ideas that triggered discussions and disagreements within the psychoanalytic community. In her 1952 paper "Some Theoretical Conclusions Regarding the Emotional Life of the Infant", she described extensively this concept. She considered the first year of life as a template for subsequent phases of personality development. Anxiety and the defences against it are central in her theory. Klein stated that in the first year of life the infant develops through stages that she called *positions*. During each position, different qualities of anxieties, defences, and relationships to the object will appear, in accord with the age of the infant.

Klein called the first position the *paranoid-schizoid* and noted that it appears in the first three or four months of life. The predominant anxiety in this period is persecutory anxiety. Both the state of the ego and its objects are characterised by splitting, and the main mechanisms of defence are splitting, denial, projection, introjection, projective identification, idealisation, control, and omnipotence. In this position, the infant relates to the mother's breast as a partial object (split between a good and bad breast).

Klein referred to the second position as the *depressive position*, a development that appears in the second quarter of the first year of life. Here, the predominant anxiety is depressive anxiety, and the mechanisms of defence are reparation or the manic defences, such as splitting, denial, projection, and introjection. In this stage, the infant sees the mother as a whole object, a total object.

Anxiety

Melanie Klein saw anxiety as emerging from aggressive impulses, and the threat of the death instinct towards the ego. The source of the anxiety is the death instinct, the fear of annihilation. Libidinal gratification decreases the anxiety; however, on the other hand, frustration increases the aggression and therefore anxiety increases.

At the beginning of his postnatal life, in the paranoid-schizoid position, the infant experiences persecutory anxiety, both from internal and external sources, with the external source connected to the experience of birth. The experience of birth is felt as an attack inflicted on the infant, and the internal source is connected with the threat to the survival of the organism, which, according to Freud, arises from the death instinct.

Klein described two types of anxieties, persecutory and depressive, according to the positions in which the anxiety arises. In the paranoid-schizoid position, the anxiety is persecutory, as a threat to the ego; while in the depressive position, the anxiety is depressive, as a threat to the love object, through the subject's aggression or fear of abandonment by the object.

In her paper "Some Theoretical Conclusions Regarding the Emotional Life of the Infant" (1952a), Klein also wrote about further development and the modification of anxiety and said that the modification of persecutory and depressed anxiety is part of the infant's development during the first year of life. The vicissitudes of anxiety can only be understood in their interaction with all the other developmental factors, including, for example, physical skills, play activities, speech, intellectual progress, habits of cleanliness, growth of sublimations, and progress in the libidinal organisation. For Klein, anxiety arises from the destructive impulses within the child that evoke danger from the death instinct, the source of the destructive impulses.

Melanie Klein added:

> The libidinal development is thus at every step influenced by anxiety.
>
> For anxiety leads to fixation to pre-genital stages and again and again to regression to them.
>
> (Klein, 1952a, p. 223)

> Love, desires (both aggressive and libidinal), and anxieties are all transferred from the first and unique object, the mother, to other

objects, and as new interests develop they become substitutes for the relation to the primary object.

(Klein, 1952a, p. 224)

Envy

In her 1957 paper "Envy and Gratitude", she described the concepts of envy, jealousy, greed, generosity and gratitude.

Klein connects envy with oral greed. Envy (alternating with feelings of love and gratification) is first directed towards the feeding breast; the object of envy is largely oral, and it is envy of the object that gratifies. Later, the envy of the mother's body and her contents (penis and babies) appears. "Envy is an oral-sadistic and anal-sadistic expression of destructive impulses, operative from the beginning of life, and envy has a constitutional basis" (Klein, 1975, p. 176).

Envy contributes to the infant's difficulties in building up his good object. The infant feels that he was deprived of gratification, and that the breast frustrated him. Envy is directed to one person only, and goes back to the earliest exclusive relation with the mother. Klein wrote that: "Envy is the angry feeling that another person possesses and enjoys something desirable, the envious impulse being to take it away, or to spoil it" (Klein, 1975, p. 181).

Klein also analysed the difference between envy, jealousy, and greed.

> While envy is the angry feeling towards another person (at first the mother), jealousy is based on envy but involves a relationship with at least two people, and is concerned with love of or for another person and the feeling that it was taken away from him or in danger of being taken away. Greed is an impetuous and insatiable craving, exceeding what the subject needs and what the object is able and willing to give.
>
> (Klein, 1975, p. 181)

Envy spoils the capacity for enjoyment, and enjoyment mitigates such destructive impulses as envy and greed. The child's feeling of the harm done by envy causes great anxiety and as a result leads to a feeling of uncertainty about the goodness of the object, which in turn will lead to an increase in greed and destructive impulses.

One of the consequences of excessive envy is an early onset of guilt in an ego that cannot yet bear the guilt. In this case, the object that provokes guilt becomes a persecutor, and the experience will be of persecution and disintegration. Later on in development, when the depressive position arises, the more integrated and stronger the ego is, the greater is the capacity to bear the pain of guilt and develop corresponding defences, mainly the tendency to make reparation to the object. If the infant is unable to develop this capacity, manic mechanisms (the mechanism from the previous paranoid-schizoid position) appear instead and persecutory anxiety arises.

I think that envy is a very important concept to consider during the process of analytic treatment, and we should not underestimate its destructive nature.

Jealousy

Jealousy is connected with envy, but involves a relation to at least two people. It is mainly concerned with the love that the subject feels with the object and that he felt was taken away from him or is in danger of being taken away from him by his rival. A man or a woman feels deprived of the loved person by somebody else.

"Jealousy is based on the suspicion of rivalry with the father (in the boy), who is accused of having taken away the mother's breast and the mother" (Klein, 1975, p. 181). This rivalry marks the early stages of the direct and inverted Oedipus complex, which normally arises concurrently with the depressive position in the second quarter of the first year of life. In the case of the girl, the rivalry is with the mother.

If envy is not excessive, jealousy in the Oedipus complex situation becomes a means of working it through. When jealousy is experienced, hostile feelings are directed not so much against the primal object but rather against the rivals (father or siblings) which brings in an element of distribution. At the same time, when these relations develop, they give rise to feelings of love, and become a new source of gratification. Jealousy is felt to be more acceptable and gives rise to much less guilt than does primary envy, which destroys the first good object.

Greed

> Greed is an impetuous and insatiable craving, exceeding what the
> subject needs and what the object is able and willing to give. At
> the unconscious level, greed aims primarily at completely scooping
> out, sucking dry, and devouring the breast. Greed's aim is destruc-
> tive introjection, while envy not only seeks to rob in this way but
> also to put badness, primarily bad excrements and bad parts of the
> self, into the mother, first of all into her breast, in order to spoil and
> destroy her. In the deepest sense, this means destroying her crea-
> tiveness. In other words, envy is a destructive aspect of projective
> identification starting from the beginning of life. Greed is mainly
> bound up with introjection, envy is bound with projection.
>
> (Klein, 1975, p. 181)

Gratitude

Klein said that: "In the course of the infant's development, the relation
to the mother's breast becomes the foundation for devotion to people,
values, and causes, and thus some of the love which was originally
experienced for the primal object is absorbed" (Klein, 1975, p. 187).

A major derivative of the capacity for love is the feeling of gratitude.
Gratitude is essential in building up the relation to the good object and
also underlies the appreciation of goodness in others and in oneself. It
is rooted in the emotions and attitudes that arise in the earliest stages of
infancy when, for the baby, the mother is the one and only object. *The
early bond is the basis for all later relations with one loved person.* According
to Klein, the intensity of envy and the capacity for love have a strong
innate component. The capacity to fully enjoy the first relation to the
breast forms the foundation for experiencing pleasure from various
sources.

Gratitude is closely linked to trust in good figures. The infant's
capacity to invest the first external object with libido leads to the establishment of a good object, which loves and protects the self and is loved
and protected by the self. This is the basis for trust in one's goodness.
The more gratification at the breast, and the more enjoyment and gratitude is felt, the more there is a wish to return pleasure. This recurrent
experience makes possible gratitude on the deepest level and plays an
important role in the capacity to make reparation, and sublimations.

Gratitude is also closely bound up with generosity. When a good object is assimilated, the person becomes able to share its gifts with others and to develop the ability to give.

(Klein, 1975, p. 189)

Phantasy

Susan Isaacs (1885–1948), a British psychoanalyst and member of the British Psychoanalytical Society, was deeply influenced by Melanie Klein's views on the importance of phantasy and play in young children. In her paper "The Nature and Function of Phantasy" (1943), she said that phantasy could be considered the mental expression of instincts. Since instincts operate from birth, crude phantasy life can be assumed as existing from birth. Phantasy forming is a function of the ego.

Susan Isaacs concludes:

1. Phantasies are the primary content of unconscious mental processes.
2. Unconscious phantasies are primarily about bodies and represent instinctual aims towards objects.
3. Early in development, phantasies are elaborated into defences, as well as wish fulfilment and anxiety contents. They become the psychic representatives of libidinal and destructive instincts.
4. Freud's postulated "hallucinatory wish-fulfilment" and his "primary identification", "introjection", and "projection" are the basis of the phantasy life.
5. Phantasies become elaborated through external experience and are capable of expression, but they do not depend upon such experience for their existence.
6. Phantasies are not dependent upon words, although they may, under certain conditions, be capable of expression in words.
7. The earliest phantasies are experienced in sensations, later they take the form of plastic images and dramatic representations.
8. Phantasies have both psychic and bodily effects.
9. Unconscious phantasies form the operative link between instincts and mechanisms.

10. Adaptation to reality and reality-thinking require the support of concurrent unconscious phantasies.
11. Unconscious phantasies exert a continuous influence throughout life, both in normal and neurotic people.

(Isaacs, in Klein, 1952b, p. 67)

For example, the phantasy of the *combined couple*: the mother containing the father's penis or the whole father. The father containing the mother's breast or the whole mother, or the parents fused inseparably in sexual intercourse. Or the phantasy of the woman with a penis.

Concepts of the ego and superego

Ego

According to Melanie Klein, the ego exists from the beginning of postnatal life in a rudimentary form and lacking coherence. From birth, an ego experiences anxiety, uses defence mechanisms, and forms primitive object relations in phantasy and reality.

Klein believed that this ego is different from that in a six-month-old well-integrated infant, and is also different from the ego of the older child and the adult. The early ego is unorganised and labile, in a state of constant flux, and its degree of integration varies from day to day. This early ego is similar to the unconscious part of the ego postulated by Freud. The threat of annihilation by the death instinct within is, in her view, the primordial anxiety, and it is the ego that, in the service of the life instinct, deflects that threat outward. Klein regarded this process as the prime activity of the ego.

Integration is based on a strongly rooted good object that forms the core of the ego. Klein observed that a certain amount of splitting is essential for integration in order to preserve the good object and later on to enable the ego to synthesise the two aspects of it, the good and the bad. The mitigation of hatred by love can thus come about and the depressive position be worked through. Therefore, when the identification with a good and whole object is more securely established, it leads to ego strength and enables the ego to preserve its own identity and goodness. During the paranoid-schizoid position, the interaction between the processes of introjection and projection, and re-introjection and re-projection, determines the ego development.

Superego

During the paranoid-schizoid position, the two aspects of the perception of the mother's breast (good and bad breast), the ideal breast and the dangerous devouring breast, are introjected and form the core of the superego.

Identification

In her 1955 paper "On Identification", Klein introduced the concept of *projective identification*, which is complementary to the introjective processes. She referred to Freud's paper, "Mourning and Melancholia", saying that the discovery of introjection and identification was central in psychoanalytic theory. She said that from the beginning of the infant's life, introjection and projection interact constantly. This interaction builds up the internal world and shapes the picture of external reality.

Klein wrote:

> This inner world is the product of the infant's own impulses, emotions and phantasies. It is of course profoundly influenced by his good and bad experiences from external sources. But at the same time the inner world influences his perception of the external world in a way that is no less decisive for his development.
>
> (Klein, 1975, pp. 141–142)

The projective mechanism underlying empathy is familiar in everyday life. The term "projective identification" is related to those processes that form part of the paranoid-schizoid position.

> Projective identification is bound up with developmental processes arising during the first three or four months of life (paranoid-schizoid), when splitting is at its height and persecutory anxiety predominates. At that time the ego is still largely unintegrated and is liable to split itself, its emotions, and its internal and external objects. Splitting is also one of the main defences against persecutory anxiety. Other defences arising in that stage are idealisation, denial, and the omnipotent control of internal and external objects. Both identification and projection imply a combination of splitting off parts of the self and projecting them onto another person.

In normal development, during the second quarter of the first year, persecutory anxiety diminishes and depressive anxiety comes to the fore, as a result of the ego's greater capacity to integrate itself and to synthesise its objects.

(Klein, 1975, p. 143)

She added that:

internalisation is important for projective processes, in particular that the good internalised breast acts as a focal point in the ego from which good feelings can be projected onto external objects.

(Klein, 1975, pp. 143–144)

The tendency towards integration, which occurs at the same time as splitting, is a dominant feature of mental life even during infancy. Melanie Klein said that identification is the stage before symbol-formation and that it leads to the evolution of speech and sublimation. Klein added that, through her analytic experience, she believed that the process of introjection and projection in later life repeats, in some measure, the pattern of the earliest introjections and projections; the external world is again and again taken in and put back out, re-introjected and re-projected.

Early Oedipus conflict

In the middle of the first year, the infant enters the early stages of the direct and inverted Oedipus complex, called the early Oedipus complex. Because the Oedipus complex implies envy, rivalry, and jealousy, a new anxiety situation arises. There are also changes in the infant's libidinal organisation, from the phantasy of mother containing father's penis or the whole father, to father containing the mother's breast or the whole mother, and the parents fused inseparably in sexual intercourse, the *combined parents*. This moves gradually to a more realistic perception of the parents.

In her 1928 paper "Early Stages of the Oedipus Conflict", Klein said that the

Oedipus tendencies are released as a consequence of the frustration that the child experiences at weaning, and that this appears at the end of the first and the beginning of the second year of life. The infant receives reinforcement through anal frustrations undergone during training in cleanliness. Another determining influence upon the mental processes of the infant is the anatomical difference between the sexes.

(Klein, 1948, p. 202)

Klein concluded that her ideas on the Oedipus conflict did not contradict Freud's in this area, and felt that the only change was that she dated these processes earlier in development.

The early stages of the Oedipus conflict are largely dominated by pregenital phases of development and are earlier than the genital phase. They are active earlier, but only during the third, fourth, and fifth years of life do they become recognisable. At this age, the Oedipus complex and the formation of the superego reach their climax.

Klein's conceptualisation of dynamic development in the infant's first year of life

In her 1952 article "Some Theoretical Conclusions Regarding the Emotional Life of the Infant", Melanie Klein conceptualised the dynamics of the first year of life, which she considered essential in the infant's development, describing two positions, the paranoid-schizoid and the depressive position; for each, she emphasised the development of specific anxieties, defences, and object relations.

The paranoid-schizoid position

The paranoid-schizoid position appears in the first three to four months of the infant's life; it is focused more on aggression than self and other destructiveness. The main anxiety is persecutory, and the defences that the infant develops to deal with this anxiety are splitting, projective identification, idealisation, denial, control, omnipotence, projection, and introjection.

Klein said that from the beginning of life the infant experiences anxiety, both from internal sources (fear of annihilation) and from external ones (experience of birth as the first external cause). One of her basic concepts is that, at the beginning of life, the infant relates to the mother as a part-object, the breast, for both oral-libidinal and oral-destructive impulses are directed towards the mother's breast.

There is always an interaction between libidinal and aggressive impulses, corresponding to the presence of the life and death instincts. There should be an optimal balance in periods of freedom from hunger and tension. When this balance is disturbed, aggressive impulses are reinforced. An alteration in the balance gives rise to the emotion of *greed*, which is first and foremost of an oral nature. With the increase of greed, there is an increase of frustration. In children with a strong *innate aggressive* component, persecutory anxiety, frustration, and greed are easily aroused, and this contributes to the infant's difficulties in tolerating privation and in dealing with anxiety. The experiences of gratification and frustration are stimuli for libidinal and destructive impulses, for love and hatred. The breast is good or bad according to the experiences of gratification or frustration.

In this period, the ego lacks integration, and there is a *splitting* process within the ego and in relation to the object. The mechanisms of projection and introjection contribute to the twofold relation to the first object, the mother–breast. The infant projects his love impulses and attributes them to the gratifying, good breast. He also projects his destructive impulses outwards and attributes them to the frustrating, bad breast. At the same time, by introjection, a good breast and a bad breast are established internally. The perception of the object is distorted in the infant's mind by his phantasies, which are bound up with the projection of his impulses onto the object.

These are the first introjected objects, and they form the core of the superego and later on are gradually integrated to the ego.

There is an interaction between the projection of the oral-destructive qualities of the infant's own impulses when he is in states of frustration, and hatred. He attacks the breast and annihilates it. He then feels that the breast will attack him in the same way in retaliation. As the urethral and anal-sadistic impulses gain in strength, the attack can have the form of using the urine and explosive faeces. These phantasies will give rise to the fear of internal and external persecutors, primarily of the retaliating bad breast. Greed also influences these phantasies. The infant experiences the fear of the object's greed, which may threaten him in a persecutory manner. He will experience the phantasy that the bad breast will devour him in the same greedy way he desires to devour the breast.

This interaction is mainly focused on the feeding relationship with the mother, represented by the breast. There are other aspects of the mother that also play an important role in the interaction with the infant.

The gratification and love that the infant receives counteract the persecutory anxiety, even counteract the feelings of loss and persecution aroused by the experience of birth, and increases the trust in the good object.

Klein said that:

> It is characteristic of the emotions of the very young infant that they are of an extreme and powerful nature. The frustrating (bad) object is felt to be a terrifying persecutor, the good breast tends to turn into the "ideal" breast which should fulfill the greedy desire for unlimited, immediate and everlasting gratification.
>
> (Klein, 1952b, pp. 201–202)

The infant develops defence mechanisms to protect himself from frustration and danger from terrifying and persecutory objects. One of these mechanisms is *idealisation*. This idealised breast is always available and gratifying, and forms the corollary of the persecuting breast, the idealisation is a defence against the persecutory anxiety.

> The idealised breast forms the corollary of the persecuting breast; and in so far as idealisation is derived from the need to be protected from persecuting objects, it is a method of defence against anxiety.
>
> (Klein, 1952b, p. 202)

Another mechanism of defence that develops in this period, in order to deal with the frustration of the object, is the *omnipotent control* of the internal and external object.

The *mechanism of denial*, together with the feeling of omnipotence, give the infant the feeling of protection and avoidance of the frustration from the object, the breast. The early ego employs the mechanism of annihilation to split off aspects of the object in a situation of hallucinatory persecution.

Persecutory anxiety influences these processes; when it is less strong, splitting is less intense, and the ego is more able to integrate itself and synthesise the feelings towards the object.

During this period, states of disintegration of the object (splitting of the object, bad and good breast) and of the ego (feeling that the ego is in pieces) alternate with the state of integration of the ego and synthesis of the object.

Melanie Klein said that external factors play a vital part from the beginning of life. Bad experiences are stimuli to persecutory fear that reinforces schizoid mechanisms and the tendency of the ego to split itself and the object. On the other hand, every good experience strengthens the trust in the good object and makes the integration of the ego and synthesis of the object possible.

The infantile depressive position

In the second quarter of the first year of life, the synthesis between feelings of love and destructive impulses towards one and the same object, the breast, give rise to *depressive anxiety*, *guilt*, and the urge of *reparation* to the injured loved object, so the good breast appears. The focus in this stage is love. This is the beginning of the *depressive position*.

At this time, *ambivalence* appears; what it was towards the part-object, the breast, later will be towards the whole object. This forming interaction between libido and aggression would correspond to a particular state of fusion between the two instincts.

Constitutional factors are essential for the ego strength and capacity to bear tension, anxiety, and frustration tolerance. Furthermore, external circumstances are very influential. Frustration or gratification predominate in the infant's relation to the breast and affects ego integration.

Projection plays a role in the vicissitudes of the paranoid anxiety as oral-sadistic impulses are bound up with greed, with the phantasy of emptying the mother's body of all her good and desirable contents.

Later, anal-sadistic impulses appear, with the phantasy to fill the mother's body with bad substances and parts of the self that are split off and projected into her.

The ego takes control of the object-mother and makes it into an extension of the self. The object-mother becomes a representative of the ego, and these processes are described as:

- identification by projection, or projective identification;
- identification by introjection, or introjective identification.

"Identification by introjection and identification by projection appear to be complementary processes" (Klein, 1952b, p. 207). Projection and introjection interact from the beginning of life.

> There is a constant interaction between persecutory fear relating to the internal and external worlds, projective identification plays a vital part in the process. Projection of love-feelings leads to finding a good object in the future. The introjection of a good object stimulates the projection of good feelings, the re-introjection of this object leads to good internal objects, and the reduction of the persecutory anxiety.
>
> (Klein, 1952b, pp. 207–208)

With the progress of ego integration, the ego synthesises feeling of love and destructive impulses towards one object, namely the mother's breast at first. As the range of perception increases and widens in the infant's mind, it opens to the concept of the mother as a whole and unique person.

Ego development is determined by the interactions between the processes of introjection and projection; re-introjection and re-projection.

The alternating processes of disintegration and integration develop gradually as a more integrated ego, with greater capacity to deal with the persecutory anxiety. The infant's relation to the breast (part-object) changes gradually into a relation with the mother as a whole person. As the ego sustains anxiety, these defences change, and the sense of reality increases. Destructive impulses and persecutory anxiety decrease in power; depressive anxiety gains in strength and becomes predominant.

The beginning of this position is marked by the recognition of the mother as a whole person and is characterised by a relationship to whole objects and by a prevalence of integration, ambivalence, depressive anxiety, and guilt. The way in which object relations are integrated in the depressive position remains the basis of the personality structure.

Paranoid and depressive anxieties always remain active within the personality, if the ego is sufficiently integrated and has established a relatively secure relationship to reality during the working-through of the depressive position; neurotic mechanisms gradually take over from the psychotic ones (the earlier ones).

The gradual development of the ego, with its integration, consciousness, intellectual capacities, and the relation to the external world, is steady. At the same time, the infant's sexual organisation is progressing: urethral, anal, and genital trends increase in strength, though the oral impulses and desires still predominate. The range of phantasies widen, and there are changes in the nature of the defences.

The conflict between love and hatred comes out in full force. Guilt increases. Ambivalence (love–hate) is experienced towards the whole person. The destructive impulses diminish but are felt to be a great danger to the loved object, now perceived as a person. Manic defences (denial, idealisation, splitting, and control of internal and external objects) can be used to counteract persecutory anxiety.

At this stage, the drive to make reparation to the injured object comes into full play, this is linked to feelings of guilt. Omnipotence decreases as the infant gradually gains a greater confidence in both his objects and his reparative powers. Here the foundation for normal development is laid.

Klein's conceptualisations of the foundation for normal development

Melanie Klein described what would be the basis for normal development in her paper "Some Theoretical Conclusions Regarding the Emotional Life of the Infant", by considering the infant's development through the first year of life.

In the process of normal development:

> the relations to people will develop, the persecutory anxiety relating to internal and external objects would diminish, the good internal objects become more firmly established, the child has feelings of greater security and the perception of reality should increase, therefore objects will appear in a more realistic light. There is also a change in the attitude towards frustration.

> (Klein, 1952b, p. 215)

All the developments mentioned above lead to a better adaptation to external and internal reality while also strengthening and enriching the ego.

When the infant's sense of reality in relation to his objects and his trust in them increases, he becomes more capable of differentiating between frustration imposed from without and his internal phantasised dangers.

Hatred and aggression become more closely related to the actual frustration derived from external factors. Therefore, persecutory fear, internal and external, is diminished. This leads to a greater capacity to re-establish the good relationship with the mother and to other people. When frustrating experience no longer operates, ambivalence and aggression diminish. The stronger and more coherent ego brings together and synthesises the split-off aspects of the objects and of the self.

Through this process, the infant deals with his own aggression, which rouses less guilt and enables the child to experience his aggression in a more ego-syntonic way, and he is also more able to sublimate. A growing adaptation to reality results in a more secure relation to the external and internal worlds. This leads to the lessening of ambivalence and aggression, which makes it possible for reparation to play its full part.

> If this process has been successful, in decreasing the persecutory anxiety and splitting processes leading to integration; the ego is able to introject and establish the complete object, and to go through the depressive position. If this process is not successful, the process of introjection of the complete object will strongly affect negativity the development during the first year of life and throughout childhood.
>
> (Klein, 1952b, p. 216)

Melanie Klein's conclusion in this paper was that there is a close link between the infantile depressive position and the phenomena of "Mourning and Melancholia".

During normal mourning, the individual succeeds in establishing the lost loved object within his ego. She added that this process does not occur for the first time but it is rather the reactivation of the lost love object from early development. Through the work of mourning, the object, as well as all his loved internal objects that he felt he had lost in the past, are reinstated into the ego.

Through feelings of guilt and persecutory anxiety, the infantile depressive position is reactivated in full strength. A successful reinstating of the external loved object who is being mourned, and whose introjection is intensified through the process of mourning, implies that the loved internal object is restored and regained.

(Klein, 1952b, p. 217)

Mourning involves a repetition of the emotional situation that the infant experienced during the depressive position in the first year of life.

If the child undergoes an abnormal mourning, it will be a failure to establish the lost person within the ego. When the cannibalistic impulses are excessive, the introjection of the lost loved object miscarries. This situation will lead to illness.

The process of mourning arises from the depressive position and is gradually worked through. The first three or four months of life establish the core of the ego. If this stage is successful, the ego is able to introject the complete object and go through the depressive position.

The first three to six months of life are a crucial phase. At this time, the infant is faced with the effects of conflicts, guilt, and sorrow inherent to the depressive position. If the ego is unable to deal with anxiety situations arising at this stage, it can regress to the paranoid-schizoid position. This compromise situation will affect the course of normal development.

The depressive position is bound up with fundamental changes in the infant's libidinal organisation. During this period, middle of the first year, the infant enters the early stages of the direct and inverted Oedipus complex. This early stage is characterised by the important role of the part-objects in the infant's mind while the relation to complete objects is being established. Here the oral libido is still leading. Powerful oral desires, increased by the frustration experienced in relation to the mother, are transferred from the mother's breast to the father's penis. Genital desires coalesce with the oral desires. Oral and genital desires coexist with desires for the father penis and towards the mother. Jealousy appears towards the mother with the phantasy that she contains the father's penis.

(Klein, 1952b, p. 218)

Another aspect of the early Oedipus stages is bound up with the essential part of the mother's inside and the infant. own inside. The infant has the urge to enter his mother's body and take possession of its contents. This is predominantly of an oral and anal nature. When the genital desires increases it is directed more towards the father's penis (equated to babies and faeces), which the infant feels, the mother's body contains. The early stages of the Oedipus are the quite complex: desires from various sources converge and are directed towards part-objects as well as whole objects; namely the father penis which both desired and hated. This exists towards a part of the father's body, also felt by the infant to be inside himself and inside the mother's body.

(Klein, 1952b, p. 219)

Envy appears connected with the oral greed first directed towards the feeding breast.

The infant's feeling in relation to both parents is described by Klein; she said that "when the infant is frustrated, father or mother enjoys the desired object of which he is deprived, mother's breast, father's penis—and enjoys it constantly" (Klein, 1952b, p. 219).

The infant experiences intense emotions and greed towards the parents due to the phantasy of their constant state of mutual gratification of an oral, anal, and genital nature.

These sexual theories are the foundation for the combined parent figures phantasy, the mother containing the father's penis or the whole father; the father containing the mother's breast o the whole mother; the parents fused inseparably in sexual intercourse. Phantasies of this nature contribute to the notion of the woman with a penis. Gradually a more realistic relation to the parents develops, the infant comes to consider them as separate individuals so the primitive combined parent figures lose in strength.

(Klein, 1952b, pp. 219–220)

These developments are interlinked with the depressive position. In both sexes, the fear of the loss of the mother, the primary loved object—depressive anxiety—contributes to the need for substitutes;

and the infant first turns to the father, who at this stage is also introjected as a complete person, to fulfill this need.

(Klein, 1952b, p. 220)

Envy, rivalry, and jealousy are experienced towards the two people who are both loved and hated. The working through of these conflicts is part of the modification of the anxiety from infancy into the first years of childhood. When infantile neurosis comes to an end at about five years of age, persecutory and depressive anxieties have undergone modification. During this period, persecutory and depressive anxiety are again and again activated. Infantile neurosis begins within the first year of life and ends with the onset of the latency period, when modification of early anxieties has been achieved.

Klein's considerations on mental health

In Klein's 1960 paper "On Mental Health", she considered the following factors in describing an *integrated personality*:

1. *Emotional maturity*: This is the capacity to substitute the lost infantile objects and infantile phantasies so as not to interfere with the mature emotional life, to enjoy our children, enjoy our memories of the past.
2. *Strength of character*: The internalisation of the good mother becomes the foundation of the strength of character. The internalisation of good parents and the identification with them is the basis of future solid relationships and the capacity to deal with conflicting emotions, to understand others, have compassion, sympathy, and tolerance. These enrich our experience in the world and makes us feel more secure in ourselves and less lonely.
3. *Balance between internal life and adaptation to reality*: It is important to have insight into contradictory impulses and feelings and to have the capacity to come to terms with these inner conflicts. It is not to avoid the conflict rather it is being able to cope with them and experience gratitude and generosity. This results in a successful welding into a whole of the different parts of the personality.
Klein concluded:

In a normal person, in spite of these conflicts, a considerable amount of integration can take place, and when it is disturbed for external or internal reasons a normal person can find his way back to it. Integration also has the effect of tolerance towards one's own impulses and therefore also towards other people's defects. My experience has shown me that complete integration never exists, but the nearer he reaches towards it, the more will the individual have insight into his anxieties and impulses, the stronger will be his character, and the greater will be his mental balance.

(Klein, 1975, p. 274)

Klein's ideas about genital trends

In her paper "Some Theoretical Conclusions Regarding the Emotional Life of the Infant" (1952b), Klein also addressed the concept of the ascendancy of genital trends. She said that there are important aspects in the personality that have to develop in order to achieve ascendancy of genital trends. These aspects are the following:

1. When libidinal and reparative desires take over the more infantile traits, this results in progress towards ego integration.
2. There has to be a synthesis between pregenital and genital reparative tendencies.
3. It is important the diminution of anxiety as well as the diminution of oral, urethral, and anal trends.
4. Good objects in the inner world have to be established and a stable relation to the parents has to be developed.
5. Love, desires (aggressive and libidinal), and anxieties are transferred from mother to other objects.
6. Development of the capacity of symbol formation and phantasy activity.
7. Sublimations: love for primary objects is a precondition for a successful sublimation process.

(Klein, 1952b, pp. 223–224)

Klein's ideas about the termination of treatment

In her 1950 paper "On the Criteria for the Termination of a Psycho-Analysis", Klein described that in order for a treatment to be finalised, *it is necessary to analyse the conflicts and anxieties of the first year of life*

(*Klein, 1975, p. 43*). Termination actives the mourning of loss of the object from early life and presuppose the analysis of the first experiences of mourning. The persecutory and depressive anxiety has to diminish and modified.

With the reduction of the anxiety, development leads to strength and heterosexuality, capacity of love, object relations, and work, and use of adequate defences. The result will be an increase in strength and depth of the ego versus shallowness, increase of wealth of phantasy and freely experience emotions.

Klein emphasised "It is only *by analysing the negative as well as the positive transference* that anxiety is reduced at the root" (Klein, 1950, p. 47). Analysis makes its way from adulthood to infancy, and through intermediate stages back to adulthood, in a recurrent to-and-fro movement according to the prevalent transference situation.

Modification of anxiety through child development

In her 1952 paper "Some Theoretical Conclusions Regarding the Emotional Life of the Infant", Klein also described the modification of the anxiety through child development. She described "Love, desires, and anxieties (aggressive and libidinal) are transferred from the first and unique object, the mother to other objects; and new interests develop which substitutes for the relation to the primary object" (Klein, 1952a, p. 224).

These processes are the basis for the sublimation throughout life. It is a precondition for a successful development of sublimations as well as of object relations, that love for the first objects can be maintained while desires and anxieties are deflected and distributed. If hatred towards the first object predominates, sublimation and the relation to substitute objects are endangered. "During the second year, obsessional trends come to the fore. They express and bind oral, urethral and anal anxieties" (Klein, 1952a, p. 226). "Obsessional mechanisms form an important part of ego-development (habits of cleanliness, control of the sphincter proves to him that he can control inner dangers and his internal objects)" (Klein, 1952a, p. 227).

A further step in the development of instinctual inhibitions comes about when the ego can make use of repression. With moderate repression, the unconscious and conscious are porous to one another and therefore impulses and their derivatives are allowed to come up from the unconscious. This depends of the capacity of the ego to accept the standards of the external objects.

This capacity is linked with the greater synthesis within the superego and the growing assimilation of the superego by the ego.

> In view of the vicissitudes of anxiety the changes characteristic of the onset of the latency period will be as follow: The relation with the parents is more secure, the introjected parents are close to the picture of the real parents, their standards, and prohibitions are accepted and internalised, and the repression of the Oedipus desires is more effective.

> (Klein, 1952b, p. 229)

If the anxiety is gradually modified, progression is bound to dominate over regression and, in the course of the infantile neurosis, the basis for mental stability is established. Klein said that libidinal fixations determine the genesis of neurosis and also of sublimation; for some time, the two, neurosis and sublimation, follow the same path. It is the force of repression that determines whether this path will lead to sublimation or turn aside to neurosis.

Klein's development of the child analysis technique

Melanie Klein based her technique on child's play. Playing with the child works through the painful reality and controls the child's fears of his own instinct projected on to objects, such as toys; through this technique, the projection of his own aggressive instinct to the object can be worked through.

Melanie Klein said that by playing, we get access to the child's most deeply repressed experiences and fixations. Through play analysis, we analyse the transference situation and the resistance, the removal of infantile amnesias, and the effects of repression. It is also possible to work through the primal scene phantasies. She believed that the child develops transference neurosis in the psychotherapeutic setting with the analyst. The toys allow the child to master the fear of both the external and internal objects. For her, the play is the bridge between phantasy and reality. Klein said that play analysis has shown that symbolism enabled the child to transfer not only interests, but also phantasies, anxieties, and guilt, to objects other than people.

She believed that children with severe inhibitions of the capacity to form and use symbols, along with inhibitions of developing phantasy life, would have signs of serious disturbances. She also considered not only play but also dreams and drawings. The function of the play is to work through excessive anxieties and traumatic situation of the ego to allow the child to make active what he experiences as passive.

Play develops in the setting of the office within time and space. The mobility of the child tells us about the child's relationship with space and his corporal perception. When she made an interpretation of the play, she considered:

- the representation of the space;
- the traumatic situation;
- why here and now.

In her 1932 book *The Psycho-Analysis of Children*, Melanie Klein developed her ideas about the play technique through considering the stage of the child's life, early analysis, latency period, and puberty.

In describing her method of early analysis, she advised the analyst to use small toys at the child's disposal. She put them on a low table in her analytic room; these toys are of a wide variety (wooden men and women, carts, carriages, trains, animals, brick and houses, as well as paper, scissors, and pencils). Their smallness, the number and variety gives the child a wide range of representational play, and the child can use the toys in different ways. These types of toys are well suited for the expression of phantasies and experiences.

She mentioned that it was important to have a wash basin with running water. The play with water give us insight into the pregenital fixations of the child, giving us the knowledge of the relationship between its sadistic fantasies and its reaction formations, also showing the direct connection between its pregenital and genital impulses. Klein believed that the furniture of the room had to be specially selected for the child's play office.

Regarding the child in the latency period, Klein said that they presented different from small children as they have a limited imaginative life, due to the repression of their sexual impulses. Their ego is underdeveloped, and they do not have a clear idea of their need for treatment, and also their general attitude is of reserve and distrust. This attitude is in part related to their preoccupation with masturbation.

Therefore, the angle of approach has to be different to the one with small children. She added that when dealing with children of the latency period, it is essential to establish contact with their unconscious phantasies through the interpretation of the symbolic content of their material in relation to their anxiety and feelings of guilt.

In considering the analysis of children at the age of puberty, she said that in this period the impulses of the child are more powerful, the activity of the phantasy greater, and the ego has other aims and another relations to reality. There are some similar points with the analysis of the small child, such as a greater dominance of the emotions and unconscious, and a much richer life of the imagination. On the other hand, there are more manifestations of anxiety and affect than in the latency period.

The fuller development of the ego at the age of puberty and its more grown-up interests demand a technique approximating to the adult analysis. She said that for this reason the analyst must fully understand the technique applied to the analysis of adults.

Comparison of the technical ideas of Melanie Klein and Anna Freud

Melanie Klein

Melanie Klein interpreted the negative and the positive transference immediately.

She believed that the child expresses his phantasy of illness and cure in the first diagnostic play hour.

When the analyst detected signs of negative transference, she gave the interpretation containing the original objects, original situations, and the destructive phantasies, in order to diminish the level of anxiety. The child established a transference neurosis with the therapist from the beginning of the analysis. For Melanie Klein, play is similar to the free association of the adult. It was her priority to analyse the sources of the child's anxiety.

According to Klein, the basis of the transference in children is real transference to the analyst, as the projection on to the analyst of internal parental figures. These figures belong to the internal world, and not to the real external parents.

Klein gave transference interpretation because she believed that the child projects on to the analyst the phantasies and feelings towards the internal objects. Melanie Klein did not underestimate the negative influence that the parents can have on the child, but she believed that as the child becomes less neurotic, he can influence the relationship with the parents. Klein believed that the therapist should not inhibit the child's aggressive fantasies but should not allow physical attacks on the analyst. She also thought that every child should have his own toys in a locked drawer or a box, as this becomes an important element of the private relationship between the analyst–patient, in the transference situation.

Anna Freud

Anna Freud created an alliance with the child, and worked with positive transference. According to Anna Freud, the child is not conscious of illness, and so she had to create awareness of the symptoms through a previous non-analytic work. The child expresses to the therapist the situation with the parents. The analyst is a new object for the child. She combined therapy and education. She calmed down the child and maintained the positive transference. Anna Freud believed that if negative transference appears, it has to be dissolved. She engaged the child again in a positive transference and encouraged the child to verbalise the content of the anger.

In the beginning, Anna Freud viewed transference as "transference reactions", without developing into transference neurosis. She later modified her former opinion, but never was convinced that transference neurosis in children was the same as that in adults.

Contemporary Kleinians

Melanie Klein's ideas had a profound impact in the child and adult psychoanalytic world. Her psychoanalytic theories formed the basis of her future explorations. Even though many of her initial propositions were later modified, they provided the basis for her followers to move forward, developing and expanding their own theories of the mind.

One of the concepts that was modified was that some of her followers did not emphasise bodily organs but rather focused more on *organ modes* and on *functions*. They more frequently used terms such as: *hope, despair, dependency, denial, idealisation*.

The relationship between the Oedipus conflict and the depressive position has been emphasised, together with its important link with *thinking, learning,* **and** *acknowledging reality.* They enhance the functions of *understanding, connection,* and *remembering.*

Modern Kleinians consider unconscious phantasies in the transference, "here and now". Betty Joseph addressed the issue of transference and said that it is not that the analyst is not concerned about the patient's external life and what happens with their other relationships, but if we can start with the current situation, the patient's feelings and ways of relating in the session, then it becomes possible to understand how this may be reflected in the outside world and in his external relationships, and the interpretations can fan out accordingly, or the patient himself may begin to make these connections, verbally or just as shifts in feelings towards and about people (Betty Joseph, 2009, personal communication).

Modern Kleinians take into account countertransference in terms of projective identification, and they place an emphasis on the analysis of the defences. The important terms in their work are *transference, countertransference, projective identification, enactment,* and *containment.*

Wilfred Bion, a well-known English psychoanalyst, added the latter concept, of *containment*, whereby the analyst is unconsciously the container of the patient's internal world. The therapist has to be patient, tolerant, and steadfast. Bion used Melanie Klein's concept of projective identification. He arrived at the concept of container and contained, mainly from his studies of psychotic patients, their mental functioning, and their peculiar thinking. His ideas on containment show us how the environment (for the infant, his environment is the mother) works through the maternal reverie in helping or hindering the baby's development. Similar to this concept, Donald Winnicott created the concept of *holding;* even though these are slightly different processes, they share similar experiences, in particular a view of a close mother–infant relationship.

With regard to the concept of death instinct, Ronald Britton, a well-known post-Kleinian psychoanalyst, prefers the term "destructive instinct", as he sees destructiveness as originally directed outwards and in the course of development internalised. In relation to the concept of envy, Britton believes that envy exists as a compound of various elements in the personality. He suggested that these elements are combined with a "powerful quota of innate hostility", and this creates a potentially pathological envious complex.

Britton wrote:

> Envy arises from the conjuction of a number of factors: the recognition of the separateness of self and object; the disappointed wish to have the same nature as the loved object and for worship to be reciprocal, meaning the disillusion that comes with the realisation that idealisation of the self does not make one the ego-ideal. Also envy arises where there is a persistence of the belief that someone possess this lost identity, that someone else may be the ego-ideal existing in mutual worship with the superego.
>
> (Britton, 2008, p. 134)

Furthermore, he believed that:

> envy arises as a three-person relationship, as do in all object relations of the depressive position, while Klein considered envy to be dyadic.
>
> (Britton, 2008, p. 134)

Other authors stated that through their clinical practice it became clear that early and sustained environmental difficulties intertwined with innate envy.

Hanna Segal opined that envy arises from primitive love and admiration, envy has less strong libidinal component than greed, and is suffused with the death instinct. Envy is seen as an ambivalent emotion in which libidinal or destructive forces may predominant.

Three stages in Klein's professional development according to Horacio Etchegoyen

According to Horacio Etchegoyen, an internationally respected Argentinian Kleinian analyst, in his paper *Biografía breve de Melanie Klein* (2011), Klein's scientific development can be divided into three stages.

First stage

The first stage starts in 1919 to 1932 with the publication of *The Psychoanalysis of Children*. At this time, Klein established the playing technique for the analysis of children, leading her to conceptualise the idea of the early Oedipus conflict and early appearance of the superego.

Second stage

The publication of *Psychoanalysis of Children* (1932) opened the second stage. This was the time when she started to organise her discoveries and conceptualised the theory of development during the first year of life. Furthermore, when she described the concept of the depressive position. This idea was organised in two papers, "A Contribution to the Psychogenesis of Manic-Depressive States", presented at the Congress in Lucerne in 1934; and "Mourning and Its Relation to Manic-Depressive States", presented at the Fifteenth International Congress in Paris. This stage ended when she studied the first months of the infant's life and explained the paranoid-schizoid position, in her 1946 paper about the "Schizoid Mechanisms".

Third stage

The third stage started with her studies about envy, which began in her paper presented at the Geneva Congress and was crystallised in her book *Envy and Gratitude*, published in 1957, four years before her death. This conceptual development separated her from two important followers, Donald Winnicott and Paula Heimann.

Publications by Melanie Klein

1921   "The Development of a Child", in *Contributions to Psycho-Analysis*
1922   "Inhibitions and Difficulties in Puberty"
1923   "The Role of the School in the Libidinal Development of the Child"
1925   "A Contribution to the Psychogenesis of Tics", in *Contributions to Psycho-Analysis*
1927   "Criminal Tendencies in Normal Children", in *Contributions to Psycho-Analysis*

1928 "Early Stages of the Oedipus Conflict", in *Contributions to Psycho-Analysis*

1929 "Personification in the Play of Children", in *Contributions to Psycho-Analysis*

"Infantile Anxiety Situations Reflected in a Work of Art and in the Creative Impulse", in *Contributions to Psycho-Analysis*

1930 "The Importance of Symbol Formation in the Development of the Ego", in *Contributions to Psycho-Analysis*

1931 "A Contribution to the Theory of Intellectual Inhibition", in *Contributions to Psycho-Analysis*

1932 *The Psycho-Analysis of Children*, first published by Hogarth

1933 "The Early Development of Conscience in the Child", in *Contributions to Psycho-Analysis*

1934 "On Criminality", in *Contributions to Psycho-Analysis*

1935 "A Contribution to the Psychogenesis of Manic-Depressive States", in *Contributions to Psycho-Analysis*

1936 "Weaning or the Bringing Up of Children"

1937 *Love, Guilt and Reparation*

Love, Hate and Reparation, with Joan Riviere

1940 "Mourning and Its Relation to Manic-Depressive States", in *Contributions to Psycho-Analysis*

1945 "The Oedipus Complex in the Light of Early Anxieties", in *Contributions to Psycho-Analysis*

1946 "Notes on Some Schizoid Mechanisms", in *Developments in Psycho-Analysis*

1948 *Contributions to Psycho-Analysis 1921–1954*, first published by Hogarth

"On the Theory of Anxiety and Guilt", in *Developments in Psycho-Analysis*

1950 "On the Criteria for Termination of a Psychoanalysis"

1952 "The Origins of Transference"

"The Mutual Influences in the Development of Ego and Id"

"On Observing the Behaviour of Young Infants", in *Developments in Psycho-Analysis*

"Some Theoretical Conclusions Regarding the Emotional Life of the Infant", in *Developments in Psycho-Analysis*

Developments in Psycho-Analysis, first published by Hogarth

1955 "The Psycho-Analytic Play Technique: Its History and Significance", in *New Directions in Psycho-Analysis*

"On Identification", in *New Directions in Psycho-Analysis*
1957 "Envy and Gratitude"
1958 "On the Development of Mental Functioning"
1959 "Our Adult World and Its Roots in Infancy"
1960 "A Note on Depression in the Schizophrenic"
1961 "Narrative of Child Psycho-Analysis"
1963 "Some Reflexions on the Oresteia"
       Our Adult World and Other Essays
       "On the Sense of Loneliness".

CHAPTER FIVE

Donald Woods Winnicott

Biography

Donald Woods Winnicott was born in Plymouth, England, on 7 April 1896. He died in London, England, on 28 January 1971, when he was seventy-five years old. In the last years of his life, he suffered from a lung and heart condition but continued working.

Donald was the younger child of three, he had two older sisters. His father was a successful merchant who became the mayor of Plymouth. Winnicott's mother died in 1925 when he was twenty-nine years old. His mother was described as a vivacious and highly intelligent woman with good judgement and a sense of humour.

Donald Winnicott's first marriage ended in divorce. The couple did not have children. Winnicott met his second wife, Clare Britton, a psychiatric social worker, when he was working at the Evacuation Project. They were married in 1951, and they had an excellent marriage. They always interacted with love and companionship, sharing work and ideas, but not children.

He attended medical school in Cambridge, England, and in 1918, at the end of the First World War, he finished his medical training at St Bartholomew Hospital in London. In 1920, he qualified as a paediatrician. When he was twenty-three, he became familiar with Freud's ideas. In 1923, Winnicott began his own psychoanalytic treatment with James Strachey (Freud's translator of the *Standard Edition*), which lasted ten years.

Winnicott's interest in children and in child developmental processes led him to train as a consultant in children's medicine. (At that time, there wasn't a formal specialty in paediatrics.) He joined the staff at Queens Hospital for Children and at Paddington Green Children's Hospital.

At the time of the Second World War, he was appointed consultant for the Evacuation Project, a programme developed in London to protect the children against the dangerous effects of war. Winnicott's career was shaped intensely by the events in wartime Britain. At the Evacuation Project, his main role was in the supervision of the workers at hostels used for children who manifested delinquency to prevent them from placement. It was there that he realised the important role environment played in delinquent behaviour (antisocial tendency), and how much deprivation was a source of this tendency. Winnicott felt that Freud's ideas did not quite explain many of his observations with young children, so when he met Melanie Klein in 1927 in London, he became fascinated with her ideas about early child development. Winnicott learned about Klein's work in 1927, one year after Melanie Klein gave her series of six lectures in London in 1926.

In 1935, one year after he finished his analysis with James Strachey, Winnicott wished to be in analysis with Klein. She perceived that Winnicott was intelligent and insightful, so she preferred that Donald Winnicott analyse her son Eric rather than accepting him as a patient. Klein proposed that she would supervise the analysis of her son. Winnicott refused this arrangement, but agreed to accept Eric in analysis without Klein's supervision. Eric was in analysis with him from 1935 until 1939. In spite of this situation, Melanie Klein agreed to supervise Donald Winnicott with his other cases. This supervision lasted six years. In 1936, Winnicott had his second analysis, with Joan Riviere, for five years. She was one of the original members of the Kleinian Group. Riviere had a strong interest in language and was one of Freud's official translators, working under Stratchey for a period of time.

Klein's ideas deeply influenced Winnicott's work, and he integrated these into his own theories. Yet he developed his own unique psychoanalytic thinking and philosophies, especially about envy and the death instinct. His different ideas irritated Klein, and after the war their relationship became strained.

This time was a turbulent era at the British Psychoanalytical Society. With Freud's arrival in London in 1938, Anna Freud's presence and her own development of theories and technique had a strong impact in the British Society. Anna Freud had her followers and Melanie Klein had hers. The Society did not want to split, but the discord between these two groups was clear. As suggested earlier, the solution was the development of two groups, the Anna Freud Group (B), who followed her father's theory and added her own concepts; and the Melanie Klein Group (A), known as the "object relations theory" group. Later, with the presence of Winnicott and others who had their own ideas, a third group was organised. This was the Middle Group which later became the Independent Group. Winnicott and Paula Heimann moved away from the Kleinian Group, and they joined the Middle Group.

Among the Independents, the four British psychoanalysts who had the biggest influence on psychoanalysis were Ronald Fairbain, Michael Balint, John Bowlby, and Donald Winnicott.

In November 1968, Winnicott went to New York and presented a paper, to both the Downstate Psychoanalytic Society and the New York Psychoanalytic Society. Winnicott chose to present a paper at the New York Psychoanalytic Society that is now considered one of his best and most influential, "The Use of an Object and Relating through Identifications" (1968). At that time, the paper was not very well received in New York.

Winnicott's and Klein's ideas

Melanie Klein's theory places an emphasis on libido and aggression coming from inside of the infant, according to Klein, the infant's destructiveness towards the mother is related to a death instinct. Winnicott believed that in the infant–mother relationship, the mother hates the child before the child hates the mother. Winnicott shared with Klein a fundamental belief in the decisive importance of the earliest stages of development.

According to Dr Grolnick, in his 1990 book *The Work and Play of Winnicott,*

> Winnicott was able to take the best from psychoanalytic ego
> psychology, the best from the object relations aspect of Kleinian
> psychoanalysis and the best from his own creative wellsprings, in a
> humanistic, existential, political, personal and professional life, he
> structured an original system of thinking about human develop-
> ment and the repair of its imperfections that is well worth mining.
>
> (Grolnick, 1990, p. 21)

Winnicott had different approaches to four of Melanie Klein's major
ideas:

1. the nature of the psychological development of the infant;
2. the idea of the death instinct and the nature of the aggression;
3. the concept of envy;
4. the role of the environment, especially the mother, in shaping the
   infant's inner life.

Winnicott's critiques of Klein

Winnicott considered Melanie Klein a genius but disagreed with some
of her theories. As Winnicott grew in experience through patient observation, research, and knowledge, he created his own theory about early
development. At a certain point, he needed to be accepted professionally for his own ideas. This situation created intense tension in the relationship between Klein and Winnicott.

Melanie Klein took Freud's theory of death instinct and developed
her own with the concept of envy and early infant destructive feelings
towards the mother. Winnicott did not agree with this concept. For
Winnicott, one can understand the baby's earliest psychological condition only by fully exploring not only the power of the instincts in shaping the inner experience, but also the set of conditions under which
the infant comes into a psychological existence under the care of the
mother.

In 1960, Winnicott called this mother–infant relationship, the "unit
status". Under this condition, the infant starts to psychologically metabolise its instinctual life—the beginning of the inner sense of *personal
going on being*. Winnicott challenged Klein's concept of early development. She believed that the infant needs to control aggression as a manifestation of the death instinct. On the contrary, Winnicott thought that

the infant exists at first in a state of *unintegration*. The infant needs first to be rooted in its body and this only can be achieved with adequate maternal care.

Winnicott thought that Klein did not fully approach this important issue. According to him, Klein did not take into account the inner experience of the mother. For Winnicott, aggression exists because of unintegration, and is primarily *oral erotism* that has an aggressive component. In early life, aggression is part of the primitive expression of love. The infant state is *unconcern or ruthlessness*. For him, in this stage, the aggression is not destructive, only when he has an early rudimentary form of ego integration does the infant experience anger. At this stage, aggressiveness is synonymous with activity. Also he used the term *spontaneity*.

Winnicott stressed external factors, and he considered the trauma of birth as critical. Aggression for him did not depend on biological factors. For Freud and Klein, the constitutional element was paramount. Winnicott challenged the concept of Sigmund Freud and Klein on the destructive power of aggression. For Winnicott, the aggression grows over time. For Klein, envy was innate and present from the beginning of the infant's life, but according to Winnicott envy appears later, when there is ego organisation and a sense of separateness from the caregiver.

In his 1953 paper "Transitional Object, Transitional Phenomena", Winnicott intended to create a bridge between the inner life of the infant and the life outside itself. He stressed the idea that the internal objects are affected by the quality of care that the mother provides. Melanie Klein was distressed with this concept because Winnicott distanced even more from her and her ideas.

The transitional object brings the infant closer to the depressive position, where its "love and hate" can be brought together in relation to the same person.

Winnicott stressed the role of the mother's technique in enabling the infant to tolerate the coexistence of love and hate. He challenged the term depressive position (sense of illness), and introduced the concept of "stage of concern," although he embraced the term "manic defences" to avoid "anxiety".

Winnicott believed that it is in the depressive phase, not earlier, that the infant experiences the beginning of the recognition of the existence of ideas, phantasy and imaginative elaboration of function. Klein's description of the paranoid-schizoid position was for Winnicott what happened in the depressive position. Winnicott placed an emphasis in the interaction with the mother, he believed that the infant becomes able to accept the responsibility for the total phantasy of the full instinctual impulse that was previously ruthless. The infant develops a sense of guilt as well as the capacity to give, due to the sorting out of the good and the bad within.

Winnicott did not acknowledge Freud's and Klein's ideas of eros and sexuality. Klein gave Winnicott credit about his ideas of the earliest days of the infant's life and the unintegrated form of the early ego. Winnicott believed that in the beginning of life what is registered are moments of raw sensation. For Klein, the early process of splitting, projection, and introjection are evident in the infant's early phantasy world.

Klein used Winnicott's idea of the importance of the environment in her concept of the primary good object, which is not only the result of instinctually rooted phantasy but also depends on external nurturing. Furthermore, Winnicott stated that it is the gratification by the external good object that helps to break through states of disintegration.

Between several discrepancies between Klein and Winnicott regarding the initial contact mother–infant, the following two are essential: the seeking for the object, and the aggression towards the mother.

Seeking for the object

According to Winnicott, from the beginning of the infant's life, the infant seeks contact with a person, not simply instinctual gratification from an object. The infant starts life as a *social being*, with the need for *intimacy and relatedness*. The instinctual gratification from the object is only possible in a context of relatedness to the mother. It is the maternal care that makes it possible for the infant self to be enriched. It is the mother's role to protect the self of her infant; it is the self that must precede the self's use of instinct.

Aggression towards the mother

Klein built her theory around the infant's destructiveness towards the mother. Winnicott proposed an opposite alternative, suggesting that the mother hates the baby before the baby hates the mother, and before the baby knows the mother hates him.

Winnicott said that at the beginning there is only *primitive love* and this ruthless demand must evoke the hatred of the mother. The mother's hatred turns against herself and not against the infant. Winnicott regards this process as the source of *female masochism*.

Klein placed the infant's capacity for depression at the centre of her work. Winnicott began to take seriously the effect of the mother's depression on the infant. He believed that the normal infant, by natural right, uses his mother unconditionally for his own growth. He said that in the beginning of life the mother has to be at the infant's disposal. The mother should see the baby as a person.

The mother is seen as an empathic being, as she wishes to provide pleasure to the child but also knows that the child needs boundaries, restrictions, and frustrations. The mother should be able to contain the aggressive affects of the child and step back and intervene if it is necessary.

Donald Woods *Winnicott's main theoretical concepts*

True and false self

In his 1960 paper "Ego Distortion in Terms of True and False Self", Donald Winnicott developed the concepts of the true self and false self. The true self appears as soon as there is any mental organisation of the individual, quickly developing complexity and relating to external reality by natural processes. Winnicott said that the true self is capable of the *spontaneous gesture* and that only the true self can be creative. The good-enough mother is able to implement the infant's omnipotence, and this allows the spontaneous gesture to grow, and therefore develop the true self. Winnicott divided the true self and false self, as Freud divided the self in one part central and related to the insticts (sexuality pregenital and genital), and the other part related to the world.

Through his own observation of infants and mothers, Winnicott concluded that when the unintegrated infant's needs are met by the mother, the ego becomes stronger through the id satisfaction. This is the source for the true self to emerge. If this it is not accomplished, the false self will appear as a defence to hide and protect the true self.

In order to fully understand this concept, it is important to centre our attention on the dyad of mother–infant development. Winnicott believed that the good-enough mother meets the omnipotence of the infant, this allow the infant to have the illusion of omnipotent creating and controlling, slowly starts to recognise the illusory element, the playing and imagining. This is the basis for the symbol, which in the beginning is both the infant's spontaneity or hallucination, and also the external object created and later cathected.

Characteristics of the true self

Winnicott said that:

> At the earliest stage, the true self is the theoretical position from which come the spontaneous gesture and the personal idea. The spontaneous gesture is the true self in action. Only the true self can be creative and feel real. It comes from the aliveness of the body tissues and the working of body-functions, including the heart's action and breathing.
>
> (Winnicott, 1965, p. 148)

In sum, the true self has spontaneity; creativity; body aliveness; inherited potential (that which is original about the person); and only the true self is very private.

According to Winnicott, the true self is in constant state of internal relatedness. Clinical evidence of hidden internal life manifests itself in rocking movements and other signs of primitive life.

The true self does not have degrees; it is what is distinctive and original about a person.

The infant is able to react to stimuli without trauma because the stimulus has a counterpart in the individual's inner psychic reality.

> If the True Self is not interrupted, the baby develops the sense of being real and with this goes a growing capacity on the part of the infant to tolerate two sets of phenomena: (1) Breaks in continuity, of True Self living, and (2) Reactive or False Self experiences, related to the environment on a basis of compliance.
>
> (Winnicott, 1965, p. 149)

Characteristic of the false self organisation

Winnicott said: "When the mother's adaptation to the infant is not good enough at the start, the infant remains isolated, becomes compliant and a compliant false self reacts to the environment demands, and the infant seems to accept them. Through this false self, the infant builds up a false set of relationships" (Winnicott, 1965, p. 146). Winnicott added: "The false self has one positive and very important function: to hide the true self, which it does by compliance to the external demands" (Winnicott, 1965, p. 146). He added that the aetiology of the false self is the stage of first object relationship and eventually the false self results in feeling unreal or a sense of *futility*.

The false self has different degrees

Winnicott said that the extremes in the aetiology of the false self is accepted, there is the existence of a low or high degree of the false self defence, ranging from the healthy polite aspect of the self to the truly split-off compliant false self which is mistaken for the whole child.

The following are the different degrees of false self:

1. compliance with imitation
2. false self replaces the true self
3. false self hides true self and the true self has a secret life
4. false self builds on identifications and copies others to protect the true self from recognition
5. false self represents an adaptive social manner; it is a healthy compromise of socialised politeness
6. the false self is an aspect of the true self it hides and protects the true self; the true self preserves a continuity of being and is not involved in reacting
7. the false self cannot experience life or feel real.

The false self, in normal development, can develop into a *social manner*, something which is adaptable. In health, this social manner represents a compromise. Then the true self is able to override the compliant self.

Winnicott observed that there are some psychoanalytic treatments which are centred on the false self and they do not accomplish anything. The false self can be seen as a defence against the exploitation of the true self, which would result in its annihilation. This is a compliant aspect of the true self in healthy living, an ability of the infant to comply in order to avoid being exposed. He described a **"healthy compliance"**, which is the ability to compromise. This is an achievement in the infant development. He concluded:

> The concept of the false self hiding the true self *along with the theory of its aetiology* is able to have an important effect on psycho-analytic work. As far as I can see it involves no important change in basic theory.
>
> (Winnicott, 1965, p. 152)

Good-enough mother—good-enough environment

Winnicott described the good-enough mother and the good-enough environment, saying that these elements are what enable the infant to begin to exist, to have experiences, to built the personal ego and to ride the instincts. All this feels real to the infant who becomes able to have a self that can eventually afford to sacrifice spontaneity.

Dr Simon Grolnick, in his book *The Work and Play of Winnicott*, thought that the concept of good-enough mother was very broad. Mothers begin to move from the phase of *primary maternal preoccupation* when they are almost totally involved with their newborns to the phase of recognition that the cry of the infant and the mother's response are no longer simultaneous. The sense of symbiosis passes, and give way to a phase called the *holding environment*. Winnicott pointed out that some amount of frustration would contribute to the infant's ego strength. Grolnick concluded:

> the good-enough mother gratifies and at the same time frustrates, to the degree that impingement and trauma do not occur. Without a good-enough environment the true self never develops, and the feeling of being real is absent. *Futility* appears in a form of false self that hides the true self.
>
> (Grolnick, 1990, p. 31)

As an example, one of my patients with history of depression, after a couple of years of analysis, said in one of her sessions, "I feel more myself, more spontaneous, I allow myself to have different feelings." The therapy allowed her to express her true self without fear in the setting of the psychotherapy.

Transitional phenomena and transitional object

In Winnicott's 1953 paper "Transitional Object and Transitional Phenomena", he described an intermediate area of experience between the thumb and the teddy bear, between the oral eroticism and true relationship, between primary creativity activity and projection of what has already been interjected and between primary awareness of indebtedness and the acknowledgement of indebtedness. The transitional object and phenomena belong to the "realm of illusion", which is at the basis of initiation of experience. It is an intermediate area of experiencing where in both inner and external life contribute. The early stage in development is made possible by the mother's special capacity for adapting to the needs of her infant, thus allowing the infant the illusion that what the infant creates really exists.

The "theoretical first feed" is represented in real life by the summation of the early experiences of many feeds. After the theoretical first feed, the baby begins to have material with which he can create in his imagination. We could say that the baby is ready to hallucinate and see the nipple at the time when the mother is ready with it.

Memories are built from innumerable sense-impressions associated with the activity of feeling and of finding the object. In the course of time, there comes a state in which the infant feels confident that the object of desire can be found and this means that the infant gradually tolerates the absence of the object. In this stage, the concept of external reality is a place in which objects appear and disappear.

Through the magic desire one can say that the baby has *the illusion of magic creative power and omnipotence*, but is a fact through the sensitive adaptation of the mother. So a *Third Illusory World* builds up, which is neither inner reality nor external fact. Different objects and activities develop in this illusionary world. These are the Transitional Objects and Phenomena. Their importance is reflected in their persistence, even crude persistence over the years. *An infant's transitional object becomes decathected, but stays in the child's memory.*

There is a wide variation to be found in sequence of events that starts with mouth activities, leads to attachment to teddy bear, doll, or soft/hard toy. Infant's bubbling or songs or tunes while preparing for sleep come within the intermediate area as Transitional Phenomena, along with objects not part of the body yet not fully recognised as belonging to external reality. Transitional phenomena are a series of behaviours related to an autoerotic experience such as thumb-sucking, then external objects such as a blanket, cloth, or suchlike, used in caressing and also babbling and other noises. The pattern of this phenomena shows at about four, six, eight, or twelve months. It may persist into childhood, when the object is needed especially at bedtime or times of distress.

For Winnicott, the object is for the infant a transition, from being merged with the mother to a stage to be in relationship with the mother, as outside and separate.

Qualities of the transitional object

Winnicott described special qualities in the relationship with the object:

1. The infant assumes rights over the object.
2. The object never changes unless changed by the infant.
3. The object must survive instinctual love and hate, is cuddled as well as mutilated.
4. The object is prescribed as having reality of its own and gives warmth.
5. There is no noticeable difference between boys and girls in their use of the original "not-me" possession.
6. The object comes from without from our point of view, but not so from the point of view of the baby.
7. The object fate is to be gradually decathected. It is decathected but not forgotten; it is not mourned. It loses meaning, it becomes spread out over the intermediate territory between inner psychic reality and the external world, the whole cultural field.

(Winnicott, 1971, p. 5)

The transitional object is not an internal object (which is a mental concept), it is a possession. It is not an external object either. The infant can employ a Transitional Object when the internal object is alive and real and good enough (not persecutory).

The mother's adaptation to the infant's needs, when good enough, gives the illusion that there is an external reality that corresponds to the infant's own capacity to create. There is an overlap between what the mother supplies and of which the child might conceive.

Winnicott gave further commentary about transitional objects on the basis of accepted psychoanalytic terms:

> The transitional object stands for the breast, or the object of the first relationship.
>
> The transitional object antedates established reality-testing.
>
> In relation to the transitional object the infant passes from (magical) omnipotent control to control by manipulation (involving muscle erotism and coordination pleasures).
>
> The transitional object may eventually develop into a fetish object and so persist as a characteristic of the adult sexual life.
>
> The transitional object may, because of anal erotic organisation, stand for faeces (but it is not for this reason that it may become smelly and remain unwashed).
>
> (Winnicott, 1971, p. 9)

Illusion–disillusionment

In his book *Playing and Reality* (1971), Winnicott developed the concept illusion-disillusionment, as related to the good-enough mother/good-enough environment and transitional object. With this concept, Winnicott explained how the infant proceeds from the pleasure principle to the reality principle, or towards primary identification. Winnicott said that only if the infant has a good-enough mother (not necessarily the infant's own mother) would this process be achieved. He added that the infant's own mother is more likely to be the good-enough mother than some other person. Success in infant care depends on the fact of devotion to the infant, not on cleverness or intellectual capacities.

From the beginning of the infant's life he is exposed to frustrations, and the good-enough mother attends to the infant's needs by providing satisfaction.

The infant's means of dealing with his not having his needs satisfied because of maternal failure include the following:

1. The infant experiences, often repeatedly, that there is a time-limit to frustration. At first this time limit to frustration must be short.
2. The infant is growing a sense of process in dealing with frustration.
3. This is the beginning of the infant's mental activity.
4. The infant has to be able to employ auto-erotic satisfactions.

5. The infant capacity in remembering, reliving, fantasying, dreaming, will help the integration *of* past, present, and future.

(Winnicott, 1971, p. 10)

If the good-enough mother is present, the infant will gain from the experience of frustration because once the mother attends to the infant's needs the infant will develop a capacity to experience a relationship with the external reality, or even to form a conception of external reality. This process of adaptation would then be smooth.

> In the beginning, and almost one hundred percent of the time, the mother offers the infant the *illusion* that her breast is part of the infant, that it is an external reality that corresponds to the infant's own capacity to create. The breast is created by the infant over and over again out of the infant's capacity to love out of necessity.

(Winnicott, 1971, p. 11)

If all goes well, the stage is set for the frustrations that we term "weaning", the process by which opportunity for illusion and gradual disillusionment is provided. If the mother's presence fails, this process is disturbed.

Winnicott said:

> In infancy this intermediate area is necessary for the initiation of a relationship between the child and the world, and is made possible by good-enough mothering at the early critical phase. Essential to this process is continuity of the external emotional environment and of particular elements in the physical environment such as the transitional object or objects.

(Winnicott, 1971, p. 13)

In the normal child, this process of illusion-disillusionment is carried through well. The infant transitions from a state of merger with the mother to a state of being in a relationship to the mother as something outside and separate. If the mother is away over a period of time which is beyond a certain limit measured in minutes, hours, or days, then the memory or the internal representation fades, the transitional phenomena become gradually meaningless and the infant is unable to experience them. The object can be decathected, and as a consequence pathology and symptoms may appear.

The mirror-role of the mother and family in child development

Winnicott was influenced by the Lacan's 1949 paper "Le Stade du Miroir" (The Mirror Stage). Though he gave his own interpretation when he described the concept of the mirror-role of mother. Lacan initially proposed that the mirror stage was part of an infant's development from six to eighteen months, based on his belief that infants can recognise themselves in a real mirror. This was outlined in his first and only official contribution to larger psychoanalytic theory at the Fourteenth International Psychoanalytical Congress at Marienbad in 1936. By the early 1950s, Lacan's concept of the mirror stage had evolved: he no longer considered the mirror stage as a moment in the life of the infant, but rather that it represented a permanent structure of subjectivity or as he suggested the paradigm of "an imaginary order".

Winnicott understood that the baby is looking at his mother was the beginning of a significant exchange with the world, a two-way process in which self-enrichment alternates with the discovery of meaning in the world of things seen. Winnicott thought that in this interaction the mother's role was to give back to the baby the baby's own self, which continued to be important in terms of the child and the family. The mirroring function of the mother was seen as essential for the establishment of the baby's self-representation.

Winnicott said:

> As the child develops and the maturational processes become sophisticated and identifications multiply, the child becomes less and less dependent on getting back the self from the mother's and the father's face and from the faces of others who are in parental or sibling relationships.

(Winnicott, 1971, p. 118)

He added that the child benefit from being able to see themselves in the attitude of the individual members of the family. He suggested that we can include the real mirrors in the house, and the opportunities that

130 PIONEERS OF CHILD PSYCHOANALYSIS

the child gets for seeing the parents and others looking at themselves, understanding that the actual mirror has significance mainly in its figurative sense.

The concept of antisocial tendency

Many children were evacuated from Europe at the time of the Second World War due to Nazi persecution. The famous Kinder Transports which left Germany to England between 1938 and 1939 were trains full of children of different ages who were separated them from their parents allowing children to live while the parents perished, murdered by The Nazi. These children were supported by placements in orphanages and psychotherapeutic clinics in order to fulfill all their needs given their disruptions.

Winnicott and others had the opportunity of observing these children and helping them, not only with material needs, but also with psychological intervention. At the same time, through observations, they were able to conceptualise and create valuable concepts in the field of child development and trauma.

I had the opportunity to meet one of those kinder transport children, at the time an older woman who described how the older children took care of the younger ones. They went to England where they were placed in family homes and orphanages and never saw their parents again.

Analysts residing in England were involved in the care of these children and observed their behaviour and emotions according to age and the kind of early relationship they had with their parents. Anna Freud, John Bowlby, and Winnicott were involved in the therapeutic assistance and placements.

The experience of evacuated children from Europe to Britain changed psychoanalytic thinking about childhood. The developmental problems of evacuation, for both, mother and child, marked a turning point in the work of Bowlby and Winnicott. In Winnicott's view, the child carried his instinctual life and also his early environment inside of him, the child would recreate it in the new situation. Although he did not disregard the impact of unconscious conflicts, Winnicott noted that environmental factors were significant for the expression of symptoms. Children with good early experiences were able to make better use of the environment. Winnicott said that the capacity to be spontaneous could only come out from an early experience of reliability. Winnicott thought that mostly the child's real parents are likely to give the baby all his needs.

He further explained that an antisocial tendency is the result of the reaction to deprivation, not a result of privation. He thought that by deprivation (the loss of people whom they loved), the child experiences the loss of security, then these children could be lead to antisocial behaviour. He referred to a true deprivation as a loss of something good that has been positive in the child's experience up to a certain date. The lost experience can be a pinpoint trauma plus a sustained traumatic condition.

In Winnicott 1956 paper "The Antisocial Tendency", he stated that the antisocial tendency can be found in normal, neurotic and psychotic individuals, it is not a diagnosis. "The antisocial tendency is not a diagnosis but rather a tendency that can be found in normal, neurotic, or psychotic people" (Winnicott, 1958, p. 308).

Winnicott described two trends of antisocial behaviour: stealing and lying, and destructiveness:

> *Stealing* is at the centre of the antisocial tendency, with the associated lying. The child who steals an object is not looking for *the object stolen but seeks the mother over whom he or she has rights.*
>
> (Winnicott, 1958, pp. 310–311)

For example, I treated a four-year-old boy, son of diplomats, who constantly stole objects from every store to which he went. From a very early age, he was exposed to multiple separations from the parents due to his father's work, and from early in life he lived in an unstable environment. He was not able to establish a sense of security and he developed the symptom of stealing.

Primary creativity

In his last book *Playing and Reality* (1971), in the chapter "Creativity and Its Origins", Winnicott said that "Creativity is a healthy state and compliance is a sick basis for life".

Creativity makes the individual feel that life is worth living. *Compliance* carries with it a sense of *futility* and is associated with the idea that nothing matters and life is not worth living. This feeling of futility is often seen in our patients. It is recognised as a symptom in psychiatric terms, for example in the symptoms of anhedonia, hopelessness, and helplessness.

Winnicott was fully aware of the biological and hereditary causes of illnesses such as schizophrenia, but he advised us to take into account the vital importance of the environmental issues at the beginning of the individual's life. He did a special study of the facilitating environment in human terms, and in terms of human growth, emphasising that dependence has meaning. Winnicott said that patients who suffer from psychiatric illness could still be able to have a satisfactory life and even work. He was concerned with the stage where the baby is "schizoid," using Klein's terms. When he talks about creativity he relates to everything, cooking, art, gardening, and so on. The creativity is universal, it belongs to being alive.

Creativity is independent of the level of intelligence. Winnicott believed that all human activity can be creative, and creativity is related to the connection between the person and the external environment. In the extreme cases of loss of creativity, there is a failure from the beginning of the infant's life to the establishment of the capacity for creative living. Instead, what is manifested is compliance and the establishment of a false personality, false self. All what is real, the original and creative of that human being, is hidden. The individual does not care if he is alive or dead.

Creativity is enjoyment in every stage of life, feeling that life is real and meaningful. *Enjoyment* is related to the true self while futility is related to the false self. Winnicott felt that Melanie Klein offered an important contribution in 1957 to the subject of creativity. This was related to the recognition of aggressive impulses and destructive phantasy dating from very early in the life of the baby. Klein also included the concept of reparation and restitution. The concept of guilt is another important concept in her theory.

Behind this is Freud's concept of ambivalence (love–hate) as an aspect of individual maturity. Health can be looked at in terms of fusion (erotic and destructive) and this makes more urgent the examination of the origin of aggression and destructive phantasy. Winnicott believed that the capacity to live creatively depends of the quality and quantity of environmental provision at the beginning of life.

In Winnicott's 1948 paper "Reparation in Respect of Mother's Organised Defence against Depression", he said:

> Reparation provides an important link between the creative impulse
> and the life the patient leads. The capacity for making reparation in

response to personal guilt is one of the most important steps in the development of the healthy human being. Guilt connected with the aggressive and destructive impulses and ideas will lead to the need of reparation.

(Winnicott, 1958, p. 91)

A significant point in this paper is the concept of false reparation, which comes from the patient's identification with the mother, the guilt comes from the mother's organised defence against depression and unconscious guilt but not from the patient.

Through his observation of depressed children, he concluded that the child's depression can be the mother's depression, as an escape from his or her own; this provides a false restitution and reparation in relation to the mother, which interferes with the development of a personal restitution capacity because the restitution does not relate to the child's own guilt sense. This leads one to think that the child lives within the circle of the parent's personality, and this circle has pathological features.

The infant has no control over his mother's mood and may get caught by the mother's contra-depressive defences. In other words, the individual's reparation will not come from his own sense of guilt but from the guilt sense or depressed mood of a parent.

Primary maternal preoccupation

Winnicott had the thesis that in the earliest phase of the infant's birth the mother is dealing with a very special state, a psychological condition which he felt deserved a name, that is 1956 paper "The Primary Maternal Preoccupation". Winnicott explained that the mother develops the state of primary maternal preoccupation providing an environment for the infant to begin to make itself evident. The infant's own line of life is disturbed very little by reactions to impingement.

If the mother is sensitive she will be able to meet the infant's needs. At first, these are the bodily needs, but as a psychology emerges out of the imaginative elaboration of physical experience, bodily needs gradually become ego needs.

According to this thesis, Winnicott added that a good-enough environmental gratification in the earliest phase enables the infant to begin to exist, to have experience, to built a personal ego, to ride instincts, and to meet with the difficulties inherent in life. All this feels real to the infant who becomes able to have a self that can eventually even afford to sacrifice spontaneity, even to die. This will lead to ego maturity—instinctual experiences strengthen the ego.

On the other hand, without the initial good-enough environmental gratification, the self that feels it can afford to die never develops. The inherent difficulties of life cannot be reached, let alone the satisfactions. If there is not chaos, there appears a false self that hides the true self, that complies with demands, that reacts to stimuli, that rids itself of instinctual experiences. When the mother develops a primary maternal preoccupation, allows the infant to express himself spontaneously allowing the child to be able to experience what is proper of this early phase of life.

Winnicott then closely examined the infant's corresponding state as well as the mother's response in the beginning of the infant's life. He said that in the beginning, the infant brings with him:

> A constitution
> Innate development tendencies (conflict-free area in the ego)
> Motility and sensitivity
> Instincts (involved in the developmental tendency, with changing zone-dominance)
> Body needs, which will become ego needs.

> (Winnicott, 1958, p. 303)

The mother who develops the state of primary maternal preoccupation responds to the infant in a following manner. Her sensitivity increases. This lasts for few weeks after birth. The maternal preoccupation, those few weeks of intense worry, will be easy to forget after recovery; the memory tends to become repressed.

Winnicott said that a good-enough environment in the earliest phase of life, allows the infant to begin to exist, if the infant does not have this good-enough environment his self never develops, furthermore, considering ego maturity, if the ego is mature, the instinctual experiences will strength the ego, if the ego is immature, the instinctual experiences will interfere with the strength of the ego.

The capacity for concern

The capacity for concern belongs to the period of six months to two years old. It is one of the most important concept that was derived directly from Melanie Klein's ideas. In 1954, Winnicott wrote the paper "The Depressive Position in Normal Emotional Development", in which he stated:

> The Oedipus complex characterises normal or healthy development in children, and the Depressive Position is a normal stage in the development of healthy infants, the same that absolute dependence and primary narcissism, a normal stage of the healthy infant at or near the start. The depressive position in the emotional development is an achievement, and belongs to the weaning age (six to twelve months old).
>
> (Winnicott, 1958, pp. 262–263)

Winnicott said that the relationship between the environment, the mother who helps the infant to satisfy his needs, and the infant who is held by the mother, will allow the working through of the consequences of instinctual experiences. Working through is comparable to a digestive process, in other words, being able to metabolise feelings and experiences. The mother allows the infant to contain the love and hate in a way that can be controlled in a healthy way (ambivalence). This occurs in the weaning age from five months to nine months. Winnicott gives the example of the baby who drops things, the "dropping game", as he called it, as an expression of separation.

Winnicott suggested that when the infant reaches the depressive position is when the baby becomes a whole person, and therefore is able to relate to people as whole persons—a whole baby related to a whole mother. As part of normal development Winnicott suggested calling this depressive position the "stage of concern" (the infant will have the capacity to feel guilty feelings).

This unconscious process leads to guilty feelings due to the destructive elements inherent in loving, and relates to the phantasy of the damage done to the loved person. He proposed another way to describe this developmental process. Winnicott said that in the beginning of life the infant is *ruthless*, not concerned yet as to results of instinctual love. He called this *pre-ruth*.

Winnicott said that the change from *ruthless to ruth* or *concern* happens slowly in the development under certain conditions of mothering during the period around five to twelve months, or even later.

Winnicott described the importance of the unit status, the environment–individual set-up, which depends on stability and reliable simplicity of the environment. He noted that the mother has to combine two functions in time and persist with them to allow the infant to recognise that special setting.

The two functions are: (1) mother has to adapt to the infant's needs by her technique of infant care, and the infant has to know this technique as part of the mother. The mother has been loved by the infant as the one who has offered him all this. Winnicott calls this *affection*. At the same time, (2) the mother is the object of assault during phases of instinctual tension. In sum, the mother has two functions, one with the quiet infant, and the other with the excited infant.

At the same time, a good-enough mother and good-enough environment allows the baby to have the perception of two objects (mother of quiet phases and mother at phases of instinctual climax). The child's mind must integrate the split between the child-care environment and the exciting environment (the two aspects of the mother). Gradually, over time, the baby recognises the difference between fact and phantasy and outer and inner reality.

With regard to the depressive anxiety, instinctual experience brings the baby two types of anxiety: anxiety about the object of instinctual love and anxiety of the infant's internal tension.

Winnicott takes the example of the feeding experience which can be a satisfactory experience or a frustrating experience. At this stage, the infant becomes a person, with an inside and an outside.

After feeding, the infant imagines a hole in the mother's body, struggling with what it is good and self-supportive and what is bad—the persecutory feelings of the self.

The supportive and persecutory aspects become interrelated until some equilibrium is reached. When the mother is there for the infant's needs, an adjustment takes place in the psyche of the infant. The infant is now in a position to do something about the hole in the breast or body. This is the time when reparation and restitution appear. Winnicott said that in health, the inner world, meaning feeding, mother, holding, nurturing, becomes the rich core of the self.

Winnicott described this process as a *benign circle*:

> A relationship between the infant and mother complicated by instinctual experience. (instinctual experience)

Perception of the effect. (hole in the mother breast or body)
An inner working through, the results of the experience being sorted out by the infant.
A capacity to give due to the sorting out of the good and the bad within.
The infant is able to use the mechanism of reparation of the hurt object.

(Winnicott, 1958, p. 270)

The daily reinforcement of the benign circle allows the infant to tolerate the hole (result of instinctual love). This is beginning of *guilt feelings*. Guilt is the result of joining the two mothers (quiet and excited love, love and hate). The healthy child has a personal sense of guilt. Without the sense of guilt, the child loses the capacity for affectionate feelings.
    Winnicott said:

It seems that after a time the individual can build up memories of experiences felt to be good, so that the experience of the mother holding the situation becomes part of the self, becomes assimilated into the ego. In this way the actual mother gradually becomes less and less necessary. The individual acquires an internal environment. The child becomes able to find new situation-holding experiences and is able in time to take over the function of being the situation-holding person for someone else, without resentment.

(Winnicott, 1958, p. 271)

In the depressive position, absolute dependence becomes a dependency of a high order when the child is allowed to give, a reparative and restitutive giving. The giving is expressed in play-constructive play with the loved person near him.
    The necessary conditions for the development of the capacity for concern are:

1. *Integration of the* ego: the presence of the whole person, with an inside and outside, who can contain anxiety within the self. "I am" becomes "I am responsible" (the ego is beginning to be independent of the mother's auxiliary *ego*).

2. *Object relationship*: I love you (love), I hate you (hate); tolerance of the ambivalence.
3. *The mother (object) seen as a whole person who survives destruction, can be used and is a reliable presence*: object (mother), object (environment).

Winnicott published *The Development of the Capacity for Concern* in 1963. He said that the sense of guilt is anxiety linked with the concept of ambivalence—love and hate towards the object. Concern implies further integration, a sense of responsibility. The individual cares, minds, feels, and accepts responsibility. He said that *maturity* is the ability of the person to compromise, to feel, to act responsibly (as part of the self), and to follow the morals of local society.

The origin of concern is in the early stages of the infant's life, when the mother is a continuous presence for the infant. Failure of the mother to provide this situation leads to the loss of the capacity for concern, and in its place will be crude anxieties and crude defences of splitting or disintegration.

Emotional ego development

In his 1962 paper "Ego Integration in Child Development", Winnicott described:

> In the very early stages of the development of a child ego-functioning needs to be taken as a concept that is inseparable from the existence of the infant as a person. Winnicott said that it is not id before ego. Ego appears before the self, and the self develops after the child has begun to use intellect, after he looks at what others see or feel or hear, and what they conceive of when they meet this infant body.
>
> (Winnicott, 1965, p. 56)

Winnicott wondered about the beginning of the ego and ego strength. The strength of the ego depends on the mother. The good-enough mother will be able to meet the needs of her infant at the beginning of life, and to meet these needs so well that the infant will be able to have a brief experience of omnipotence, which is positive for the future development of the child.

If the mother is not good enough, the baby will not be able to start with ego maturation. The baby is an immature being who is all the time on the brink of unthinkable anxiety. Love in this stage is only show in terms of body care.

Winnicott said: "Unthinkable anxiety has only a few varieties, each being the clue to one aspect of normal growth." In Winnicott's terms, the unthinkable anxiety will be experienced as:

> Going to pieces
> Falling forever
> Having no relationship to the body
> Having no orientation.

> (Winnicott, 1965, p. 58)

These are the psychotic anxieties found in schizophrenia or to the emergence of a schizoid element hidden in a non-psychotic personality.

If the baby does not have a good-enough mother, there are degrees and varieties of maternal failure, such as:

> Distortions of the ego-organisation leading to schizoid characteristics.
> Lead to a false personality, defence that is a new threat to the core of the self and as a consequence hides and protects this core of the self.

> (Winnicott, 1965, p. 58)

The consequences of defective ego supported by the mother can be severely crippling and lead to:

1. infantile schizophrenia or autism
2. latent schizophrenia
3. false self-defence
4. schizoid personality.

> (Winnicott, 1965, pp. 58–59)

This can be determine by various kinds and degrees of failure of holding, handling, and object-presenting at the earliest stage. Winnicott does not deny the existence of hereditary factors, but rather supplements them with these concepts.

Ego development is characterised by various trends:

1. The main trend in the maturation process can be condensed in the word integration.
2. The ego is based on a body ego, the baby starts to link body with the body functions. Winnicott uses the term "personalisation" to describe the process.
3. Finally, the ego initiates object-relating.

(Winnicott, 1965, p. 59)

Winnicott matched three phenomena of ego growth with three aspects of infant and child care. They are:

1. *Integration matches with holding*
   Winnicott called holding the mother's capacity to identify with her baby and to allow her to fulfil her function as a mother. Holding is the basis for what gradually becomes a self-experiencing being. Winnicott said that the establishment of integration and the development of ego-relatedness rely upon good-enough holding. He said that holding is essential of this stage of absolute dependence, but even the growing child, the adolescent, and, at times, the adults, need holding when there is a strain that threatens confusion.
2. *Personalisation matches with handling*
   Winnicott said that through adequate handling the infant comes to accept the body as part of the self, and to feel that the self dwells in it and throughout the body. The boundaries of the body provide the limiting membrane between *me* and *not-me*, which is what he called *personalisation*.
3. *Object-relating matches with object-presenting*
   The presence of the object is the initiation of interpersonal relationships and also the introduction of the whole world of shared reality to the baby and growing child. The most primitive of all relationships is when the baby and the mother are not yet separated out in the baby's rudimentary mind. It is through this relationship that the infant experiences a sense of being, or identity. The mother offers the baby a holding environment.

Winnicott said that even when the opposite of integration is disintegration, he choose the word "unintegration". "Integration is linked with the environmental function of holding" (Winnicott, 1965, p. 61). Unthinkable anxieties are not analysable in terms of psychoanalysis. In sum, Winnicott described his understanding of the beginning of the ego with the following concepts:

1. Ego integration is the initiation of emotional development of the child; the child is moving from absolute dependency towards independence.
2. The beginning of object-relating within the framework of a baby's experience and growth is very complex, only can take place if the environment provides the infant with the object or manipulation that meets the baby's needs, therefore the baby feels confident in being able to create objects and to create the actual world. The mother gives the baby a brief period in which omnipotence is a matter of experience, an ego-experience related to a satisfactory breast-feed, or a reaction to frustration.

Here again, Winnicott reinforced the concept of the importance of the actual environment at the earliest stage, before the baby has differentiated between the not-me and me. Winnicott remarked on a great difference between the baby who gets ego support from the mother's actual adaptive behaviour, and love (ego strength), with the baby who the environmental provision is defective at this early stage (ego weakness).

In his 1964 book *The Child, the Family and the Outside World*, Winnicott said that in their early years, children simultaneously undertake three psychological tasks. First, they are building a perception of themselves as a "self" with a relationship to reality as they begin to conceive it. Second, they are developing a capacity for a relationship with a person, the mother. Third, they develop the capacity for relationships which involves several people.

Adolescence

In his 1968 paper "Contemporary Concepts of Adolescent Development and Their Implications for Higher Education", Winnicott conceptualised the development of puberty and adolescence considering multiple aspects such as: the individual emotional developmental, the emotional characteristics of the child, the role of the mother and the parents, the family, the role of schools, and *the immaturity of the adolescent*, and the gradual process of maturity in their lives, the individual identification with social groups and with society without too great a loss of personal spontaneity, the structure of society, the abstractions of politics and economics and philosophy and culture are also factors in the culmination of natural growing processes.

The ability of an adolescent to grow from individual dependency to relative dependence towards independence, are determined by several factors: (1) genes and inherit tendencies, (2) the existence of the good-enough environment, and (3) society issues.

Winnicott said that when we consider the structure of society we include members who are psychiatrically healthy, but must remember that the world is also made up of the immature in age, the psychopathic who were deprived, the neurotic, the mood disordered, the schizoid, the schizophrenic, and the paranoid. Nevertheless, Winnicott choose to view society from the perspective of the psychiatrically healthy.

For Winnicott, the main thesis is related to the importance of good-enough mothering, which includes fathers. While he uses the word maternal, he does not do so to de-emphasise the important role of the father. Maternal is also referring to the mutual feeling of responsibility and pride that the mother and father feel towards the care of the child, and the feeling of accomplishment to bring a baby to this world.

Winnicott strongly believed that the continuity of care is a central feature to create a facilitating environment, and it is only with this approach that the baby will be able to mature. With regard to puberty and adolescence, he viewed the adolescent stage as a stage of trouble. Even when parents offered to the child a good-enough environment, they cannot count on a smooth passage in those years. Winnicott believed that growing up is inherently an aggressive act, and in that stage of puberty and adolescence an unconscious phantasy of *the death of someone* is present, connected with the process of maturation and the acquisition of adult status. They go through a life-and-death struggle. Immaturity is an essential element of health at adolescence. There is only one cure for immaturity and that is the *passage of time* and the growth into maturity that time may bring.

Winnicott pointed out to the adults that it is important to understand this process, and to avoid allowing an adolescent to attain a false maturity by handing over to them responsibility that is not yet theirs, even though they may fight for it. Understanding has become confrontation, meaning that the adult stands up and claims the right to have a personal point of view, one that may have the backing of other adults. With the passage of time and experience of living the adolescent gradually accepts responsibility for all that is happening in the world of personal phantasy. The most difficult of all is the pressure felt from the unconscious phantasy of sex and the rivalry that is associated with sexual object choice.

Winnicott explained that their idealism is based on the exciting feelings in adolescence. Adolescence implies growth and this growth takes time. While growing is in progress, responsibility must be taken by parent figures. Understanding has to be replaced by confrontation. Confrontation has its own strength but should not be confused with vindictiveness or retaliation.

Psychopathology

In his 1951 article "Transitional Objects and Phenomena", Winnicott described psychopathology related to the infant's transitional object. He wrote about addiction, fetishism, and *pseudologia fantastica* and thieving. He stated that even when the use of a transitional object in infancy is a healthy experience, this stage could give place to pathological behaviours.

Addiction

Winnicott said that addiction is related to a regression to early stages of development at which the transitional phenomena was unchallenged.

Fetishism (linked with the delusion of a maternal phallus)

He said: "Fetish can be described in terms of a persistence of a specific object or type of object dating from infantile experience in the transitional field, linked with the delusion of a maternal phallus" (Winnicott, 1958, p. 242). In other words, a specific object or type of object, dating from an experience during the period when the mother gradually pulls back as an immediate provider of satisfaction of the child's desires, persists in adult sexual life.

Before this transitional phase, the child believes that his own wish creates the object of his desire (specifically the qualities of his mother that fulfil his needs), which brings with it a sense of satisfaction. During this phase, the child gradually adapts to the (frustrating) realisation that the object cannot be controlled to serve the child's needs. The transitional object is always the result of a gratifying relationship with the mother, specifically with the maternal body. It stands for the satisfying qualities that the object (the mother/father) of the child's first relationship has.

The child adapts to the impact of the realisation that the mother is not always there to "bring the world to him" through phantasising about the object of his desire while attaching to an object (a teddy bear, a piece of cloth), he creates an illusion of the previous object.

The infant passes from magical, omnipotent control to control by manipulation (involving muscle eroticism and coordination pleasure). In opposition to this, the fetish represents the impossibility of pleasure with the body of the mother or the paternal body in the case of females.

Winnicott said that even when fetishism is less abundant in the female psyche, it is not only in men that occurs. The transitional object may eventually develop into a fetish object and can persist as a characteristic of the adult sexual life.

Normally, the child gains from the experience of frustration during the transitional phase, but the infant can be disturbed by a prolong use of the object and/or not being allowed the natural separation from it.

Pseudologia fantastica and thieving

Urge to bridge a gap in continuity of experience in respect to a transitional object. *Pseudologica fantastica* and thieving, or pathological lying and creating long untrue stories, can be described as an individual's unconscious motivation to bridge a gap in continuity of experience in respect of a transitional object.

The role of the father

In his paper "What about Father?", Winnicott included the importance of the father during infant or toddler child development by saying:

> Even when some fathers have difficulties relating to the infant, their participation, the acceptance of the responsibility for the

child's wellbeing, gives the basis for a good home. The presence of the father can help the mother, in feeling well in relationship with her body and her mind. The father is needed for the moral support and backing for her authority, he is needed because of his positive qualities and the qualities that distinguish him from other men, and the liveliness of his personality. The mother should include the father in the child's life, he thought that it is the mother's responsibility to encourage the father to have time alone with the child.

(Winnicott, 1964, pp. 114–115)

Winnicott believed that children are lucky when they can get to know their fathers, as knowing the father as a separate individual, known for what he is, the child can learn about relationships that include love and respect without idealisation. For Winnicott, the father opens a new world to the children, as they begin to understand and learn the details of his work, his interests and his views.

Winnicott gave importance to the family, the family protects the child from the world, but gradually the world begins to seep in. Furthermore, the extended family, other groups, teachers and neighbours, the gradual incorporation of the environmental will be the way in which a child can best come to terms with the wider world, and follow exactly the pattern of the introduction to external reality by the mother.

Winnicott's developmental lines

Winnicott proposed developmental lines involving the self and its functions.

The development of the subjective and the objective self-dependence

As part of his theory of development and in developing the concept of true self and false self, Winnicott wrote about the formation of the basic self from two points of view. In his 1963 paper "From Dependence toward Independence in the Development of the Individual", Winnicott stated that a mature individual can not develop in an immature or ill society, health means both health of the individual and health of society.

Dependence was described by Winnicott as being divided in three stages:

1. *Absolute dependence*
   In this stage, the infant does not know about maternal care, nor knows about bad or good care. He is only in the position to gain or suffer from the care he receives.
2. *Relative dependence*
   The infant starts to become aware of the need for the maternal care, aware of dependence. Winnicott said that this period last from six months to two years. At two years old a new development appears, and the child is now equipped to deal with loss.
3. *Towards independence*
   The infant develops means to manage without actual care. This is achieved through the accumulation of memories of care, the projection of personal needs and the introjection of care details, with the development of confidence in the environment, and intellectual understanding with its implications.

Winnicott said that independence was never absolute. The healthy individual does not become isolated, becomes related to the environment in a way that the individual and the environment can be said to be interdependent. Winnicott believed that the environment enabled the child to realise his potential. The more the mother is at the baby's disposal, the more a sense of continuity, and a core identity is laid down.

The holding of the mother and the security gained, protects the baby from the impingements of the environment. Winnicott's ideas of mirroring, the relationship between the baby and the caretaker are important. The baby looks and feels into this human mirror and sees himself, the need of the good-enough mother is a very important interaction.

Development of self constancy—object constancy

Winnicott said that in the development of self constancy, it is the process that is internalised, not the structure. There is a built-in maturational core of self that, when recognised and validated, can lead to the sense of self-continuity and therefore constancy. At the same time, this happens in the caretaker through a process of mirroring, therefore providing a self-stable self-system.

Development of a sense of security and self-control

Winnicott stated that in order to achieve a sense of security, the baby needs to build internally a belief that there is something good, reliable, and durable which would allow him to recover after being hurt.

He advised parents to protect the infant from the impingement and trauma that occurs from the environment and from drives or impulses. This protection is experienced early in the life of the infant in the form of safety and security. Winnicott advocated controls coming from a "living situation", a dialogue between the child and his parents.

Winnicott said that good conditions in the early stages lead to a sense of security, the sense of security leads to self-control, and a self-control leads to diminish the need for outside controls.

Development of self-assertiveness

Winnicott saw aggression as one of the necessary parts of the process of the infant's ability to place the object outside the projective world and into the sphere of reality. He considered aggression in the healthier developmental sense and referred to the positive values of destructiveness. Winnicott said that to be an assertive individual one must first feel that an effective self exists. One must feel real through the loving interplay of a relationship. Every aspect of the development of the self is involved in creating an individual who feels a sense of being, one who is able to impact the world, and to be able to be assertive.

Development of a sense of authenticity

Winnicott paid attention to authenticity, naturalness, spontaneity, freedom, and responsibility. He presumed a primal authenticity and innocence. Winnicott viewed each infant as having an individual core of variations, saying that when the caretaker is attuned to this core (meaning with care and empathy), the caretaker reflects back what she sees and feels, and thus the true self appears. The true self requires validation. After a while, attunement and mistuning appear simultaneously as well as consecutively. It is here that the false self appears. Winnicott stated that without a false self, a social self, and a true self, the person would not be able to survive in the world.

Development of the capacity to be alone

His 1958 paper "The Capacity To Be Alone" is one of the most compelling of Winnicott's papers. In this paper, he described how the capacity to be alone is one of the most important signs of maturity in emotional development. For Winnicott, being alone is at the same time being in the presence of someone else.

With the internalisation of the caretaker, the caretaker will have a self-evocative function. The mature adult is able to tolerate extended periods of time alone, being able to work, play and be productive while by themselves because there has been someone there, internalised, and now part of himself, who is watching over him and providing the sense of not being lonely during activity. Capacity to be alone involves the consideration of the internalised and externalised object as well as the self.

The psychotherapeutic process

With regard to the psychotherapeutic process, Winnicott described the psychoanalytic work as both an *interpretative* and a *holding environment*, analogous to maternal care. He added that psychotherapy is a form of play. Furthermore, Winnicott said that the interpretative work goes together with support and the ability to facilitate each other in the total life experience of the patient.

Psychotherapy has to do with two people playing together, children and adults. The setting is important; it has to be good enough and safe enough, which gives the patient the feeling that she can take risks in her experience of living and allow the true self to emerge.

In his 1971 book *Playing and Reality*, Winnicott said that psychotherapy takes place in two areas of playing, the one of the patient and the other one the therapist. If the patient does not play, the centre of the treatment should be concentrated to stimulate the patient to be able to play. This applies to children and adults. Adults mainly use verbal communication, for example, the choice of words, the inflections of the voice, and sense of humour.

Winnicott said that playing has a time and a place. Playing is universal and facilitates growth and therefore health and prepares for group relationships and problem solving. It is also a form of communication in psychotherapy; a specialised form of play in the service of communication with oneself and others that has been developed as a therapeutic method.

He postulated the term of a *potential space* between the baby and the mother so as to give a place for playing. This space varies according to the life experience of the baby in relation to the mother or mother figure. He explained that in order to control the outside world one has to do things, it is not enough to think or to wish, one has to take into consideration that doing things takes time, he added that for the child, playing is doing, in playing the child or the adult is free to be creative.

In Winnicott's paper "Mirror-Role of Mother and Family in Child Development", he said that he believes that in the process of therapy, our role is the give back to the patient what he/she brings. The patient then will find his or her own self, and in this way the patient will be able to exist and feel real. Feeling real is beyond existing, it is existing as oneself and relate to objects as oneself, this ability to have a self allows the person be able to retreat for relaxation. He added that even when some patients do not get cured they are grateful to us for seeing them as who they are, which is a gratifying feeling for the analyst.

In his 1954 paper "Metapsychological and Clinical Aspects of Regression within the Psycho-Analytic Set-Up", Winnicott said that the therapeutic work in analysis is similar to the one done by child care, by friendship, by enjoyment of poetry and cultural pursuits. Psychoanalysis can allow the patient to express and use the hate and anger belonging to the original failure.

Winnicott believed that Freud left us the task to research the role of regression in the service of the psychoanalytic process. He added that regression will depend of the patient, as each patient has his own pace and will follow his own course beyond the application of the technique.

He divided patients in three categories. First, the patient who operates as whole person with difficulties in the area of interpersonal relationships. Winnicott said that this patient would benefit from psychoanalysis. Second, the patient with incipient wholeness of the personality, ambivalence, and the dawning recognition of dependencies, Winnicott name this description, the stage of concern, also known as depressive position. These patients require the analysis of mood and feelings, similar to the previous category. In the third group are patients with whom the analyst has to deal with the early stages of emotional development before and up to the establishment of the personality as an entity, before the achievement of space–time unit status.

Winnicott considered that for a treatment to be successful the patient has to be able to achieve regression in search of the true self. He described the idea that there are two kinds of regressions in relation to instinctual development: one that returns to an early failure, and the other, to an early success.

Winnicott expressed the concern that not only does regression occur to good and bad points in the instinct experiences of the individual but also to good and bad points in the environmental adaptation to ego and id needs in the individual history. He suggested we pay more attention to ego development and to dependence. Therefore, when we talk about regression, we immediately speak of environmental adaptation with its successes and failures. Winnicott believed that is from psychosis that the patient can recover. He said that psychosis is related to health, through regression we reach past failure from the environment that will be emerging and be able to heal through the ordinary life.

Winnicott stated that the therapist has to have the capacity to contain the conflicts of the patient, to contain them and to wait for their resolution in the patient instead of anxiously looking around for a cure. There must be an absence of the tendency to retaliate under provocation. He believed that it is the individual who suffers who can most readily be helped.

He said that the elements in therapy can roughly be classified into four types: (1) external relationships, as between whole people, (2) samples of the inner world, (3) variation on the theme of a phantasy life placed either within or without one self, and (4) intellectualised material.

In Grolnick's 1990 book *The Work and Play of Winnicott*, he explained that, for Winnicott, the *mother* is seen as empathic and wishes to provide pleasure to the child, but also she knows that the child needs boundaries, restrictions, and frustrations. She is able to absorb the aggressive affects of the child, steps back and intervenes if necessary. During the therapeutic process, Winnicott would offer the patient a holding and constant environment, which allows her to play and express conflicts. Winnicott would offer himself as the constant therapist-mother who would be there for the patient, and give the interpretation she needs to have Winnicott as her constant mother who understands calmly and nurtures. "Mother should see the baby as a person. Analyst should see the patient as a person as well" (Grolnick, 1990, pp. 47–48). In the case of the therapist, if the aggression gets out of control, he should end the session if it is necessary.

Theory of play

Winnicott understood therapy as two people playing together, being a child or an adult. Winnicott postulated the theory of play to describe a sequence of relationships related to the developmental process of playing.

1. At first, the baby and object are merged. Baby's view of the object is subjective and the mother is oriented towards the making actual of what the baby is ready to find.
2. Later, the object is repudiated, re-accepted, and perceived objectively. This process is complex and depends on the mother's ability to participate and give back what is handed out. If the mother can do this well, the baby has an experience of omnipotent intrapsychic process and control. When the baby trust the mother, an intermediate playground appears; the playground is a potential space between the mother and the baby, joining mother and baby.
3. The next period is being able to be alone in the presence of someone. The child plays under the assumption that the person who he loves is available and continues to be available.
4. The child is getting ready for the next step, it will allow and enjoy two play areas. First it is the mother who plays with the baby and sooner or later she introduces her own playing and she finds that babies vary according to their capacity to like or dislike the introduction of ideas that are not their own. This is the playing together in a relationship.

Winnicott believed that playing is itself a therapy. He thought that while the child plays, it is important to have the presence and availability of responsible people around, though their inclusion in the children's play it is not necessary. As playing is a creative experience that occurs in a space-time continuum, it is an intense and real experience for the child patient; it is a basic form of living.

Furthermore, playing is outside the individual, not the external world. Play implies trust, is satisfying, and in playing, the child or the adult is free to be creative. Creative playing is allied to dreaming and to living but does not belong to phantasy.

In his book *The Child, the Family and the Outside World* (1964), Winnicott described that at an early age it is legitimate for the inner world to be outside as well as inside and we should enter into the imaginative world of the child when we play the child's games and take part in "other ways" in the child's imaginative experiences. He wrote: "Play can easily be seen to link the individual's relation to inner reality with the same individual's relation to external or shared reality" (Winnicott, 1964, p. 145). Winnicott compared the therapist–patient relationship to the mother–infant relationship. He gave extreme importance to reassurance in treatment.

In his 1962 paper "The Aims of Psychoanalytic Treatment", Winnicott said that in doing psychoanalysis his aim was: keeping alive, well and awake. "I am being myself and behaving myself" (Winnicott, 1965, p. 166). He stated that he did adapt to the individual expectations at the very beginning. The therapist represents the reality principle—time. Winnicott said that it is important to make interpretations; otherwise the patient will think that the therapist knows everything. One interpretation per session is enough, or it could be one interpretation divided in two or three parts.

In this paper, Winnicott revealed his thesis that psychotic illness is related to environmental failure at an early stage of the emotional development of the individual. As he described in his paper about the true self and false self, he reminded us that the sense of futility and unreality belongs to the development of a false self, considering that the false self will develop as a protection of the true self.

As the setting of analysis reproduces the earliest mothering techniques, the regression of a patient would be an organised return to early dependence or double dependence. The patient and the setting merge into the original success situation of primary narcissism, and the progress from primary narcissism starts anew, with the true self able to meet environmental failure situations without organisation of the defences that involve a false self protecting the true self. Furthermore, he added that to this extent psychotic illness could only be relieved by specialised environmental provision interlocked with the patient's regression. Progress from the new position, with the true self surrendered to the total ego, can now be studied in terms of the complex processes of individual growth.

Winnicott described that with our psychoanalytic interventions, we affect the patient's ego in three phases.

1. *Early phase*

   In the early phase of the child treatment, it is important to give the child the similar good treatment given by the mother, which provides ego support and therefore makes the infant's ego strong leading to ego strength.

2. *Long phase*

   During this phase, the patient develops confidence in the process, as it allows experimentation in terms of ego independence.

3. *Third phase—the independent ego*

   The independent ego of the patient begins to show through and to assert its own individual characteristics, the defences loosen up, the patient does not feel trapped in the illness, feels free, and growth and emotional development is seen.

Winnicott said that we now see the growth and emotional development that was restrained in the original situation.

In considering Winnicott's ideas about psychotherapeutic technique, it is important and helpful to include his two concepts of approach in psychotherapy. He introduced the idea and significance of the spatula game and the later technical innovation of the squiggle game.

Spatula game

In his 1941 paper "The Observation of Infants in a Set Situation", Winnicott described the early spatula game, he observed that a baby picked up a tongue depressor, a spatula, from his medical table, and he observed that the child would interact with it, by waving it about. At some point, the baby held the spatula quietly, unmoving, and pausing. Then suddenly, the spatula became a "something", perhaps an aeroplane, moved up and down by the child with the delight of discovery. This "moment of hesitation", in which the baby was given both the presence and the space to be in his quiet inner world, uninterrupted, was understood by Winnicott as important.

He said: "The spatula can stand for different things, the breast, the penis, people, can be a thing that the infant can takes or leaves, not connected with a human being, according with the infant' stage of development" (Winnicott, 1958, p. 64).

Winnicott concluded that it is important to give the child time to decide, even with regard to small things. Winnicott said that if a child is hurried or directed in its early reaching for an object and at the time he is not yet ready to deal with it, the object remains alien from the adult world. In this case, creativity will be interfered and will become passive compliance.

Squiggle game

In the later squiggle game, Winnicott's most famous technical innovation, he made a squiggle and asked the child to turn it into something. He felt this encouraged the creation of meaning. The child was then invited to make a squiggle in return, which kept the game going and gave the therapist more material with which to work. Winnicott thought that by responding to the demand and turning the squiggle into something recognisable and shareable, the child offered a sample of his internal world.

Continuing with his creative understanding and contribution in the area of psychoanalytic technique, Winnicott wrote his paper, "String: A Technique of Communication" (1960). In this paper, he gave the example of a seven-year-old boy whose mother suffered from depression, and who was away from her son several times—once for the birth of his younger sister when he was three years old, next for a surgical intervention, and then for a two-month hospitalisation for depression when the boy was four years, nine months.

Using the squiggle game, Winnicott was able to detect the boy's fear of separation. The complaint of the parents was that the boy developed an obsession with a string, which he was using constantly. On one occasion, the father found the boy hanging upside down on a rope shortly after his mother had another bout of depression. Winnicott's interpretation was that the boy had a maternal identification based on his own insecurity in relation to his mother, and added that this could develop into homosexuality. Winnicott concluded:

> the boy's compulsion to use the string was at first an attempt to communicate symbolically with his mother in spite of her withdrawal during depressive phases, and furthermore as a denial of the separation. As a symbol of the denial of separation, the string became a thing that was frightening and that had to be mastered, and as a consequence its use became perverted.

(Winnicott, 1965, p. 157)

Winnicott admired Melanie Klein and followed her in many of her theoretical and technical conceptualisations and contributions. In his

1962 paper "A Personal View of the Kleinian Contribution", Winnicott said that Melanie Klein's contributions in child psychotherapeutic technique were very valuable and important to take into account. In this paper, he summarised these aspects:

1. Her use of tiny toys in initial stages.
2. The application of the play technique to analysis of children of two- and a-half years old, and others of older ages.
3. The recognition of phantasy in the child or the adult, inside and outside the self.
4. The capacity to understand the internal benign and persecutory objects and their origin in satisfactory or unsatisfactory instinctual experiences, originally oral and oral-sadistic).
5. The importance of projection and introjection in relation to the child's experience of the body functions of incorporation and excretion.
6. Melanie Klein's emphasis on the importance of destructive elements in object relationships, besides anger and frustration, development of a theory of the individual's capacity for concern (the depressive position in Kleinian terms), relationship of constructive play, work, and potency and child-bearing to the depressive position.

Furthermore, Winnicott shared with Melanie Klein her idea of understanding denial, of depression (using manic defences), the understanding of threatened chaos in inner psychic reality, and defences related to this chaos (obsessional neurosis or depressive mood). He agreed with the idea that the analyst should be aware of infantile impulses, retaliative fears, and the splitting of the object prior to ambivalence.

Other contributions he welcomed were her theories of the life and death Instincts, and her attempts to organise infantile destructiveness in terms of hereditary and envy.

Publications by Donald Woods Winnicott

1931 *Clinical Notes on the Disorders of Childhood*
1941 "The Observation of Infants in a Set Situation"
1942 "Child Department Consultations"
      "Review of the Nursing Couple"
1945 "Primitive Emotional Development"
1949 "Hate in the Counter-Transference"
      The Ordinary Devoted Mother and Her Baby

1953 "Transitional Object and Transitional Phenomena"
1955 "Metapsychologic, Clinical Aspect Regression and the Psycho-analytic Situation"
1956 "On Transference"
1957 *Mother and Child: A Primer of First Relationship*
1958 *Collected Papers: Through Paediatrics to Psychoanalysis*
      "Review of the Doctor, His Patient and the Illness"
1960 "The Theory of the Parent–Child Relationship"
1962 "The Theory of the Parent–Infant Relationship: Further Remarks"
1963 "Dependence in the Infant Care, Child Care, Psychoanalytic Setting"
      "The Development of the Capacity for Concern"
      "Review of the Nonhuman Environment in Normal Development and in Schizophrenia"
1964 *The Child, the Family and the Outside World*
1965 *The Family and Individual Development*
      Maturational Processes and the Facilitating Environment
      "Failure of Expectable Environment on Child's Mental Functioning"
1966 "Correlation of a Childhood and Adult Neurosis"
      "Psychosomatic Illnesses in Their Positive and Negative Aspects"
1967 "The Location of Cultural Experience"
1968 "Playing: Its Theoretical Status in the Clinical Situation"
1969 "The Use of an Object"
1971 *Therapeutic Consultation in Child Psychiatry*
      Playing and Reality
1974 "Fear of Breakdown"
1977 *The Piggle: An Account of the Psychoanalytic Treatment of a Little Girl*
1984 *Deprivation and Delinquency*
1986 *Holding and Interpretation*
1987 *Babies and Their Mothers*
      The Spontaneous Gesture
1988 *Human Nature*
1989 *Psychoanalytic Explorations*
1993 *Talking to Parents*
1996 *Thinking about Children.*

CHAPTER SIX

Clinical case presentation: Melanie Klein, Anna Freud, and Donald Woods Winnicott in perspective

Alice

History

Alice was a five-year-old girl who lived with her parents and her ten-year-old brother. Her mother was a teacher and her father a civil engineer. Her father was frequently absent from home due to his work. Her older brother did not exhibit psychological problems at the time of the consultation.

Alice's parents consulted me for their five years old girl who was enuretic as returned wet daily from nursery school. She was shy, insecure, and not trusting. Alice was frequently sad and spent time by herself. She had difficulties with aggression and avoided contact with other children, she was afraid that she would attack and hurt other children. She did not have friends and avoided birthday parties.

Alice exhibited oppositional behaviour, especially with her mother, but she fought with her father as well. At times, she communicated using baby talk which was difficult to understand.

She was stubborn, had temper tantrums, sleeping disturbances, and she needed a night light because she was afraid of the dark.

She asked many questions about death and sex. Although she had good motor coordination, she frequently had the tendency to fall and hurt herself. She cried often and was very demanding.

Medically, she suffered from mild hypoacusia, transmission type. At the time of the consultation, her appetite was decreased at home but she ate better in other people's homes.

With regard to her developmental history, pregnancy and birth was within normal limits. At the time of her pregnancy parents had severe marital problems, they argue often and mother often screamed. The family went through a traumatic loss of a paternal uncle who "disappeared" for political reasons at the time of Alice's birth. Alice was breast fed till three months. At that time she consistently ate well. The family had moved to another home when she was two months old.

When she was two and half years old she was toilet trained but at three the enuresis began during the day and night, especially when she went to school. She talked at three years old. At four years old she was toilet trained during the night, after she was transferred from the bedroom that she shared with her brother to her own.

The severe arguments between the parents with frequent screaming and yelling continued through out her childhood. The children witnessed their parent's constant arguments. At five years old, two months previous to the consultation, she was bitten by their cat and needed vaccinations. She was deeply affected when she learned that the cat died ten days later.

First play session

Alice took all the toys from the basket and carefully placed everything on the table. Then she took the planes, the truck, and the cars. She placed everything on top of the truck. She took a little car in her hand, she lied down on the floor, she made the car go around her legs and parked it on her genital area and said: "It is parked". She took another small car, did the same, and placed it underneath the other one on the floor. She moved herself on the floor. She became agitated.

She took a plane and move it in circular movements around and around in the air. She took the car which was parked near her genital area and made it move around the furniture in the office. She found a pin; she used it to picked one of the tyres and said, "The tyre blew out".

Afterwards, she used the pin as an antenna for the car and said in a very babyish manner "the car has an antenna". I asked, "for what?". She said: "to be able to listen better".

Kleinian approach to Alice's case

The first year of the infant' life was very important for Melanie Klein. She stated that the transition from the breast to another source of oral gratification demands significant psychological work. Klein would be interested to know how Alice interacted with the breast while she was being fed, and later to know about her oral intake, how she responded to the changes of food, from breast, bottle and solids, as a pattern of future acceptance of losses and adaptation to reality.

According to Klein, Alice's hatred to her mother probably had a connection with the child's early frustration and development of sadistic-aggressive phantasies of attacking and destroying her mother's inside and depriving it of its contents.

Her understanding would be that the appearance of her symptoms of anger and fights with her parents could be related to the deep anxiety situation of paranoid quality, as well as fears of retaliation related to the mother's inability to modulate her aggression and her aggressive attacks.

The regressive behaviour of temper tantrums, baby talk, and putting her finger in her mouth could be a manifestation of her need to regress to an oral phase when the paranoid anxiety was the predominant.

Klein would add that Alice was afraid to be counter-attacked, she experienced the relationships as a mutual destruction, her own attack and the mother's retaliation, expressed with the symptoms of constant fighting. She would say that the sadistic aggressive phantasies were related to the idea that the excreta (urine-faeces) had a symbolic meaning of powerful weapons.

Sleeping with her brother stimulated her impulses and displaced onto him ambivalent feelings, which determined the expression of aggression and fear through the nocturnal enuresis which stopped when she no longer slept with her brother.

Let's review the first play hour: planes, trucks, and cars. Little car through her legs, bigger car underneath the small car. Plane in circular movements. A pin initially destroying the tyre, and then becoming an antenna to listen better. Alice identified herself with the truck and put all the other objects on the truck. In Kleinian terms, this could represent herself with her conflicts and anxieties that she had to endure due to her mother's inability to modulate Alice aggressivity (death instinct). Alice symbolically represented her psychosexual development with the car moving through her body and parking near genitalia. The two cars parked could express her preoccupation with her Oedipal phantasies towards mother and father. Klein would say that the urine was a symbolic representation of her aggression directed to her mother as a component of the sadistic aggressive impulses between her parents and herself.

The pin blew out one of the tyres, this could be a message to the therapist that there was something wrong inside of her that has to be repaired, the flat tyre (conflicts and phantasies) that does not allow her to move on. The pin became an antenna to be able to listen better. This can represent Alice symbolic wish of being able to be understood and the phantasy of cure by the therapist, who would help her repair what it was destroyed and to be able to be free of anxiety and move on without the pressure of severe anxiety of paranoid quality.

After the interview with the parents and the child, Klein would draw a treatment plan with the child. I would like to delineate some concepts related to her technical approach that is unique in her theory and clinical work.

The therapist understands and interprets the anxiety, defences, and phantasies from the beginning of the treatment. She interprets the positive and negative transference. Interpretations are given from the beginning of the treatment. The therapist does not soothe the child or calm down her anxieties. When Alice refused to listen, the interpretation of the negative transference is given. Klein would make conscious Alice's aggressive impulses, helping her reach the understanding of the phantasy linked with it, and helping her repair the attacked object, namely her mother.

For example, during one session she played "kiosk" with mother–daughter interaction, sometimes she was the mother and other times the daughter. The mother had everything and the daughter demanded everything leaving the mother empty. After this play, she became very agitated and aggressive. Klein would interpret her envy of her mother's contents and the attack towards the contents with the wish to possess the richness of the interior of her mother's body. This phantasy was linked to her fear of retaliation.

For Klein, the play of the child was like the dream in the adults, where it is a façade and we have to discover the latent content. Klein viewed the free play as an equivalent to free association in adults. Understanding and interpreting the child's phantasies determines future adult sexual life freedom. She gave extreme importance to the struggle between life and death instincts, as well as bad and good objects.

For Klein, the therapy of the child was not only therapeutic but also preventive of future illness, future neurosis. She believed that when the child changes her/his internal world, the child would make the parents change with her. Klein therefore had little contact with the child's parents. She expected cooperation and trust from them but they were not part of the active process of treatment.

Kleinian interpretation had to contain the transferential conflict, anxieties, and defences that she experienced with the primary objects, mother and father. The therapist, in the transference, represents the mother that the child rejects and attacks.

In one of the sessions, she covered her ears and did not want to listen to my interpretations. She said, "If you talk to me, I will not return". A Kleinian interpretation could be that she feared that my words were like urine that could attack her as she felt that she attacked me and the interior of her mother (when she wet herself during some of the sessions). Furthermore, she was afraid to be attacked and hurt by me (retaliation, counter-attack).

After ten months of treatment, Alice was able to control her enuresis, and she made a song "*Gracias a Beatriz no me hago mas pis*" (Thanks to Beatriz I do not pee any more). I would like to add that the modern Kleinians will no longer emphasise bodily organs but focus on organ modes and functions.

Anna Freud's approach to Alice's case

Anna Freud would describe the possible factors for the causation of Alice's disturbances, in this case the family turmoil at the time of her birth. She would focus on the parents inability to create an environment were Alice could develop, having the older brother a competitor for the love of her parents. Sharing the bedroom up to the age of four would also be an important factor. She would look at the favourable and stabilising influences of the intact family who was concerned and supportive when she had symptoms and pursued consultation.

Alice's parents appeared perceptive and insightful and willing to help. This has to be balanced against the excessive anxiety and intrusiveness, particularly on the mother's part. With regard to the drive development, the libidinal phase is the beginning of latency. Her unconscious fantasies interfered with the appearance of mature defence mechanisms. Some indication of oral and anal phase fixation were present.

Alice's aggressive manifestations were clear, she fought, she was oppositional, she was fearful of aggressive situations, afraid of hurting others, and at the same time she was frequently angry and had temper tantrums. Freud also comment that enuresis can be understood as the expression of sadistic-aggressive attacks through the urine.

The libidinal (narcissistic) and aggressive cathexis of self, was clearly disturbed. Alice hit herself, hurt herself frequently, and she did not like herself. With regard to libidinal and aggressive cathexis of objects, the material showed that she reached the Oedipal level with intermittent regression to earlier phases of development, such as the oral and urethral.

Alice experienced her mother as a threatening figure and she hated when her mother screamed. She said, "I want to die when you scream".

Anna Freud would look at the physical apparatus subservient ego development and say that it was damaged with hypoacusia. The mild body damage often potentiated the symptom of not wanting to hear. Alice did not want to listen or respond. Anna Freud would say that her ego identifications were with her brother, in her wish to be a boy, at time her mother who would scream and argue.

Alice's conflicts were internalised, although she experienced problems externally when confronted with her problems by her external objects, meaning parents, brother. Her internal conflicts was of Oedipal and oral nature.

With regard to her diagnosis, Anna Freud would say that Alice had a sufficient evidence of drive regression, particularly oral, phallic, and Oedipal fixation. She would say that she had a slow deterioration in her symptoms that would interfere with her future learning capacity.

In considering the treatment plan, Anna Freud would see the child three times a week and her parents once a week. She would establish an alliance with the child in friendly, warm way. She worked with the defences and ego strengths.

Anna Freud saw the child as incapable to establish free associations, because she would say that immature ego leads to ego dependency to the superego and therefore the inability to modulate the pressures coming from the id. *She did not interpret the negative transference.*

Anna Freud thought that it is necessary to prepare the child for the analytic work, by giving the child awareness of his problems, giving her confidence in the treatment and the therapist, and creating a positive transference to allow the child to wish the process of treatment. She wanted to create the alliance in order to assure the continuation of the treatment. She thought that the child had strong defences and resistances. The child does not ask for treatment, it is the parents who bring the child for treatment.

Anna Freud believed that the child did not have freedom of action, she did not believe in the play as a free association. The child could interfere with the analytic process with her aggressive behaviour and can endanger the safety of the therapist and herself. She thought that the child "acts out" more than freely associates, and sees the therapist as a new object and treats him as such, different from her parents. For Anna Freud, it is important to help the child to verbalise her feelings.

The therapist must become the representation of the patient's id, auxiliary ego to which the child clings for protection and is also treated as an external superego. She believed that the therapist "seduces" the child by tolerating freedom of thought, phantasy, and action, she directed the interpretations to help the child with her anxiety.

Her decision to include the parents was both a technical and theoretical consideration. Her opinion was that the simultaneous analysis of parents and children help then to understand the interaction between the child and the parents. Anna Freud thought that parents may also play a part in maintaining a child's disturbances. It is the task of the parents to help the child's ego overcome resistance and periods of negative transference without abandoning treatment.

She warned the therapist who interprets exclusively in terms of the inner world. She advised that research showed that pathogenic factors are operative on both sides, and once they are intertwined, pathology becomes ingrained in the structure of the personality and is removed only by therapeutic measures which affect the structure. Her interpretations were more from the ego, defensive, and adaptive standpoint, while Klein is more id-oriented and stressed the death instinct.

Winnicott's approach to Alice's case

For Winnicott, psychotherapeutic work was both interpretative but also holding environment, analogous to maternal care. He described psychotherapy as a form of playing, as it has to do with two people playing together. He would offer Alice a treatment, a setting which was good enough, to give her the feeling that the true self can emerge and accept the risks in the experience of living.

Winnicott is clear about the importance of giving interpretations, though one interpretation may be enough which could be divided in two or three parts through the session. He would offer Alice a holding and constant environment which could allow her to play and express her conflicts. He would offer himself as the constant therapist–mother who would be there for her and interpret Alice's needs to have him as her constant mother who understands her in a calm and nurturing way.

CHAPTER SEVEN

Margaret Mahler

Biography

Margaret Mahler (1897–1985) was born in Sopron, Hungary, she emigrated to New York in 1938, where she spend the rest of her of life. She died in New York City at eighty-eight years old.

Her father was a general practitioner, her mother was nineteen years old when she married Margaret's father. Margaret was the first-born child of an unhappy marriage. Her mother resented having a child at such a young age, so it was mainly her father who was her caretaker. She grew increasingly more distant from her mother. The definitive moment of rejection was when she overheard her mother telling her sister, four years her junior, that she was her favourite and that she loved and adored her more than anything.

Margaret's situation was a sad example of emotional devastation caused by parental favouritism. She compensated her loveless home atmosphere with an extraordinary success in school, where she excelled in mathematics and science. Margaret Mahler believed that the reason she became interested in paediatrics and psychoanalysis was because of her mother's rejection. She grew up unhappy, with low self-esteem, and deeply jealous of her sister. Her father was very supportive and encouraged her to excel in her intellectual growth. She was the second woman in Sopron to receive higher education, at sixteen years old she went to Budapest and lived with an unkind aunt.

Alice Kovacs (who became a psychoanalyst and later married Michel Balint, becoming Alice Balint), a classmate from high school, with whom she spent a lot of time together, shared with her a Sándor Ferenczi article. Ferenczi introduced psychoanalysis and the theory of the unconcious to Hungary, creating an important centre of psychoanalytic thought in Budapest. Alice's mother, Vilma Kovacs, was one of Ferenczi's first students and the leader of the Budapest psychoanalytic group, she was very social and frequently invited Margaret to social events. At one of her parties she met Michael Balint, and Sándor Ferenczi. Through Ferenczi, she became intrigued about Freud and the unconscious. Ferenczi was a great influence in Mahler professional future.

In 1916, she went to the University of Budapest where she studied art history and sculpture for one semester until she became interested in medicine. At the University she would find another source of unhappiness, she was discriminated as a woman and Jewish. In 1917, she enrolled in medical school in Budapest and after three semesters she transferred to the University of Munich for her clinical training, later she moved to Heidelberg, Germany, where she attended the University of Jena. Margaret went to the University of Jena to study with Ibrahim, a famous professor of paediatrics. Mahler began to understand the importance of play and love for mental and physical health in infancy.

Around 1920, she felt the pressure of Jewish hatred. Her sister went to live with her in Vienna to pursue studies in music. On one occasion, they were arrested by the local police, and thrown in jail for simply being Jewish. A family friend helped the two out of jail and advised them to leave the country. In 1921, she transferred to the University of Heidelberg for her final semester of medical school, due the anti-Jewish pressures in Vienna. She returned to Jena to take her exams and was one of two students to graduate Magna Cum Laude in 1922. She returned to Vienna to be licensed in medicine and be able to practise.

In 1922, she decided to change specialties from paediatrics to psychiatry. In 1926, she began her training analysis with Helene Deutsch. Deutsch was not welcoming of Mahler, but Ferenczi spoke on Mahler behalf and Helen Deutch agreed to continue her analysis until Mahler was certified as a psychoanalyst. Seven years later, in 1933, she was accepted as an analyst, the same year that she was grief stricken, when her long time friend and inspiration Sándor Ferenczi passed away.

She did not have a good psychoanalytic experience during her training. She was abruptly dismissed by Helen Deutch from treatment, she was rejected by Anna Freud who saw her work as deviation from the pure drive approach to the mind, nevertheless Mahler was active and attended seminars in the same circle as Anna Freud. In one of her seminars she met her future husband, Paul Mahler, who was a chemist. He was the only son of a successful business owner who eventually lost his fortune in an economic crisis. In 1936, Paul and Margaret married, when she was thirty-nine years old, their marriage ended in divorce in 1953. As the Nazi threat worsen, the couple moved to Britain for a few months. In 1938, the British Psychoanalytical Society lent them the money to move to United States. The Mahlers had very little money, and left their family and friends behind. The move was further anxiety provoking since neither of them were fluent in English. When they arrived to New York City, Margaret Mahler received her New York Medical licence. She set up her own private practice in the basement of a building and began to build her psychoanalytic practice.

In 1939, she met Dr Benjamin Spock, a famous paediatrician, and in 1940 gave a child analysis seminar, becoming the senior teacher of child analysis. She joined the Institute of Human Development and the Educational Institute along with the New York Psychoanalytic Society. In 1948, she was involved with clinical studies on benign and malignant cases in childhood psychosis.

In 1944, her sister left Vienna to Budapest escaping from the Nazis, her father died one month after the German invasion of Hungary, and her mother was murdered one year later in Auschwitz. In 1950, she joined the staff of the Albert Einstein School of Medicine and was the chairman of the child psychiatric programme, she held this position into the 1960s. She founded the Therapeutic Nursery for Psychotic Children at Einstein together with Manuel Furer, and the Masters Children's Center in New York.

Mahler was very interested in child development and, in 1955, she and Furer developed a research project they called the Natural History of Symbiotic Child Psychosis. In the earliest stages, the research was limited to the study of symbiotic psychotic children, and their mothers. They both saw the need to validate their findings with another parallel project in normal human development. For the most part, the research was carried out at the Masters Children's Center in New York. The product of this research would result in the development of her theory about the psychological birth of the human infant.

Margaret Mahler's main theoretical concepts

Mahler was very interested in mother–infant duality, and together with Fred Pine and Anni Bergman, carefully documented the impact of early separations of children from their mothers. They developed a crucial study of mother and child. Their observation lead them to conceptualise that the child is able to internalise the representation of the mother at thirty-six months old.

This gave the scientific basis to support mothers of being consistent in their nurture of their infant until they are ready for a healthy separation. From 1959 to 1962, the investigation of a control group of average mothers and their normal babies was begun at the Master Children Center in New York.

Mahler explained that the behaviour of the mother provokes the baby to establish a symbiotic dual-unity, necessary to develop the self-object differentiation and reciprocal object relations.

The documentation of *separation-individuation* was her most important contribution to the development of psychoanalysis. Her most important work was *The Psychological Birth of the Human Infant: Symbiosis and Individuation*, written in 1975 with Fred Pine and Anni Bergman.

Mahler developed her theory based on their studies with mothers and children. In the chapter "On Human Symbiosis and the Subphases of the Separation–Individuation Process", they described the different phases and subphases of this process.

The forerunners of the separation–individuation process

Normal autistic phase

This phase lasts the first few weeks of the infant's life. The infant is detached, self-absorbed, and spends most of the time sleeping. Later on, Mahler abandons this phase.

The beginning of the symbiotic phase

> From the second month on, dim awareness of the need-satisfying object marks the beginning of the phase of normal symbiosis,

in which the infant behaves and functions as though he and his mother were an omnipotent system, a dual unity within one common boundary.

(Mahler, 1975, p. 44)

The normal symbiotic phase

This phase lasts until four or five months of age. Here the child is aware of the mother but there is not a sense of individuality. The infant and mother are one. There is a barrier between them and the rest of the world.

The separation–individuation process

This process, named separation–individuation, is divided into subphases, each with its own onset, outcomes, and risks. There is a considerable overlap as well.

In the beginning of this phase, the normal symbiotic phase ends. Separation refers to the development of limits, the differentiation between the infant and the mother, and individuation refers to the development of the infant's ego, sense of identity, and cognitive abilities. Mahler described that the infant of few months breaks out of an autistic shell into the world with human connections.

Disruptions in the process of separation–individuation can result in a disturbance in the ability to maintain a reliable sense of individual identity in adulthood.

The first subphase: differentiation and the development of the body image—hatching (five to nine months)

Mahler wrote:

> The infant's attention, which during the first months of symbiosis was in part inwardly directed, or focused in a coenesthetic vague way within the symbiotic orbit, gradually expands through the coning into being of outwardly directed perceptual activity during the child's increasing periods of wakefulness.

(Mahler, Pine, & Bergman, 1975, p. 54)

Hatching lasts few months, the infant stops being ignorant of the differentiation between him and the mother. The shell rupture and there is increased alertness and interest of the outside world using the mother as a point of orientation.

The second subphase—practising (nine to ten to sixteen to eighteen months)

Mahler conceptualised this period in two parts: "1. The early practising phase, ushered in by the infant's earliest ability to move away physically from mother by crawling; and 2. The practising period proper, characterised by free, upright locomotion" (Mahler, 1975, p. 65). "The infant begins to actively explore and becomes more distant from the mother. The child experiences himself still as one with his mother" (Mahler, Pine, & Bergman, 1975, p. 65).

The third subphase—rapprochement (fifteen to eighteen to twenty-four months and beyond)

The infant once again becomes close to the mother. The child realises that his physical mobility demonstrates psychic separateness from his mother. The toddler may become tentative, wanting his mother to be in sight so that, through eye contact and action, he can explore his world. There is a risk that the mother will not understand and respond with impatience and unavailability. This can lead to an anxious fear of abandonment in the toddler.

Rapprochement is divided into further subphases: beginning, the desire to share discoveries with the mother; crisis (eighteen to twenty-one months), between staying with mother, being emotionally close, and being more independent and exploring; solution (twenty-one months and beyond), individual solutions are enabled by the development of language and the superego.

Mahler wrote:

> Disturbances during the rapprochement subphase are likely to reappear in much more definite and individually different forms during the final phase of that process in which a unified self-representation should become demarcated from a blended and integrate object representation.

(Mahler, Pine, & Bergman, 1975, p. 108)

The fourth subphase: consolidation of individuality
and the beginning of the emotional object constancy
(twenty-four to thirty-six months)

Mahler wrote that the main task of the fourth subphase is: "1. The achievement of a definite, in certain aspects lifelong, individuality, and 2. The attainment of a certain degree of object constancy" (Mahler, Pine, & Bergman, 1975, p. 109). The toddler understands that the mother has a separate identity and is a separate individual. This leads to internalisation, which is the internal representation that the child has formed of the mother.

> This internalisation provides the child with an image that helps supply them with an unconscious level of support and comfort from their mothers. Deficiencies in positive internalisation could possibly lead to a sense of insecurity and low self-esteem issues in adulthood.
>
> (Mahler, Pine, & Bergman, 1975, p. 109)

CHAPTER EIGHT

John Bowlby

Biography

Edward John Mostyn Bowlby was born in London, England, on 26 February 1907. He died on 2 September 1990 at his summer home on the Isle of Skye, Scotland, at eighty-three years old. The fourth of six children of an upper middle-class family, Edward John Mostyn Bowlby was raised by a nanny. John saw his mother only one hour a day after tea time, as she considered that parental attention and affection would lead to detrimental spoiling of children. When he was four years old, his nanny and primary caretaker left the family. Later, he described this loss as tragic and no different than losing a mother.

His father, Anthony Bowlby, was a surgeon to the king's household. At age seven, he was sent off to boarding school, as was common for boys of his social status. He later said that he wouldn't send a dog away to boarding school at age seven. Due to these traumatic childhood events he developed empathy for children's suffering.

In April 1938, he married Ursula Longstaff, also the daughter of a surgeon. They had four children. Mary, born 1939; Richard, born 1941; Pia, born 1945; and Robert, born 1948. After the Second World War

(1946–1947), Bowlby bought his house in Hampstead, London, where he lived the rest of his life.

Bowlby studied psychology at Trinity College, Cambridge, England. Later, he worked with maladjusted and delinquent children. At twenty-two years, he enrolled at the University College Hospital in London and graduated when he was twenty-six years old. While still in medical school, he applied to the Institute of Psychoanalysis. Following medical school, he trained in adult psychiatry at the Maudsley Hospital. When he was thirty years old, in 1937, he qualified as a psychoanalyst and he became a full member of the British Psychoanalytic Society in 1939.

His analyst was Joan Riviere, and one of his supervisors was Melanie Klein. During the Second World War, he was a Lieutenant Colonel in the Royal Army Medical Corps. After the war, he was director of the Tavistock Clinic, and from 1950, he was a mental health consultant to the World Health Organization. Bowlby began his career in classical psychoanalytic thinking but he walked away from the traditional metapsychology, instead basing his thinking in evolution and ethology. He did not participate in the turmoil at the British Society between the Kleinians and Anna Freudians, during 1940 to 1945, he belonged to the Independent group, which tried to find the origins of the psychopathology in actual interpersonal experiences.

Bowlby met Konrad Lorenz and read his book *The Rings of King Solomon* (1952), which led him to be interested in ethology. The studies of imprinting, especially the filial imprinting and its biological functions (protection and surviving) became important to his thinking. Furthermore, Harlow's studies about looking for contact in the monkey rhesus population added to his ideas. He concluded that the tendency of the child to establish a strong connection with the mother figure is part of a function of survival of the species as a protection against the predators in the context of adaptation, and this tendency is not only related to need of alimentation or oral needs. His ideas were highly criticised by the psychoanalysts of the time.

John Bowlby's main theoretical concepts

From the beginning of his career, Bowlby was interested in the consequences of children being separated from their parents during a child's hospitalisation, when the child is separated from his parents at early age. At this time in history, the parents were not permitted by the hospital to stay with their child during his hospitalisation.

During wartime, he worked with Anna Freud on evacuees, and with René Spitz on orphans. By the late 1950s, he had accumulated a body of observational and theoretical work which indicated to him the fundamental importance of attachment from birth for the infant development. He was interested in discovering the actual patterns of family interaction involved in both healthy and pathological development.

In his attachment theory, he proposed the idea that attachment behaviour was essentially an evolutionary survival strategy for protecting the infant from predators. Joyce and James Robertson worked with him at the Tavistock Clinic in London to study the brief separation between parents and children at the time of the child's hospital admission. Their focus was on children ages eighteen to forty-eight months.

Their work was documented in films in 1952 that showed the results of observing the child behaviour up to four years after the separation from the mother at the time of the hospitalisation. These observations had an impact on the field of paediatrics in England. These findings created changes in hospitals rules by allowing mothers to stay with their children during hospitalisation.

Mary Ainsworth, a student of Bowlby, further extended and tested his ideas and played an important role in suggesting that several attachment styles were observed. In 1956, Bowlby started to prepare the trilogy *Attachment and Loss*, Volume 1, published in 1969. Volume 2: *Separation, Anxiety and Anger* was published in 1972, and Volume 3, *Loss, Sadness and Depression* was published in 1980.

Before the publication of the trilogy, the main issues of attachment theory were based on concepts from ethology and developmental psychology. His three classic papers are *The Nature of the Child's Tie to His Mother* (1958), *Separation Anxiety* (1959), and *Grief and Mourning in Infancy and Early Childhood* (1960), which were presented at the British Psychoanalytical Society in London.

After the publication of *Maternal Care and Mental Health*, Bowlby developed a new understanding from the fields of evolutionary biology, ethology, developmental psychology, cognitive science, and control systems theory. The conceptualisation of his theory began with the publication of two papers in 1958, "The Nature of the Child's Tie to His

Mother", where the main concepts of attachment were introduced, and "The Nature of Love", by Harry Harlow with his studies with rhesus monkeys.

Attachment theory was finally presented in 1969 with his first volume *Attachment*. Bowlby modified psychoanalytic explanations for attachment, and in response, psychoanalysts rejected his theory. At about the same time, Bowlby's former colleague, Mary Ainsworth, was completing extensive observational studies on the nature of infant attachments in Uganda with Bowlby's ethological theories in mind. Her results in these studies greatly contributed to the subsequent evidence based of attachment theory as presented in *Attachment*. *Attachment* was revised in 1982 to incorporate more recent research. Bowlby's last book, *A Secure Base*, was published in 1988.

According to attachment theory, attachment in infants is primarily a process of *proximity-seeking* an identified *attachment figure* in situations of perceived distress or alarm for the purpose of survival. The biological aim is survival, and the psychological aim is security. "Attachment behaviour has been defined as seeking and maintaining proximity to another individual" (Bowlby, 1969, p. 195).

Bowlby said that infants become attached to adults who are sensitive and responsive in social interactions with the infant and who remain as consistent caregivers for some months during the period from about six months to two years of age. Parental responses lead to the development of patterns of attachment, which in turn, lead to "internal working models" that guide the individual's feelings, thoughts, and expectations in later relationships.

In Bowlby's approach, the human infant is considered to have a need for a secure relationship with adult caregivers from the beginning of their lives, without which normal social and emotional development will not occur. Bowlby wrote: "Children with a secure relationship to both parents were most confident and most competent; children who had a secure relationship to neither were least so; and those with a secure relationship to one parent but not to the other came in between" (Bowlby, 1988, p. 10).

Bowlby described that early experiences with caregivers slowly give place to a system of thoughts, memories, beliefs, expectations, emotions, and behaviours about the self and others. This system was called the *internal working model of social relationships*, which continues to develop with time and experience through life.

As the toddler grows, he uses his attachment figure or figures as a *secure base* from which to explore. Mary Ainsworth used this feature plus other features of attachment behaviour called "stranger wariness" and reunion behaviours to develop a research tool called the "strange situation procedure". This research tool was used for developing and classifying different attachment styles and to assess separation and reunion behaviour.

She introduced the concept of "secure base" and developed the theory that there are several attachment patterns in infants, which include: secure attachment, anxious-avoidant attachment, and anxious-ambivalent attachment, or resistant (insecure). Later, Mary Main and her colleagues identified the disorganised-disoriented attachment, for those children who lack of a coherent coping strategy, which is related to the severity of the separation. The type of attachment that the infants develop depends on the quality of care they received.

The attachment process is not gender-specific. Infants will form attachments to any consistent caregiver who is sensitive and responsive in social interactions. The quality of the social contact appears to be more influential than the amount of time spent.

Bowlby described attachment and adult pathology through numerous studies that concluded that severe disruption in the early attachment could lead to severe psychopathology, such as criminal behaviour, drug use, antisocial personality disorders, eating disorders, substance abuse and dependence, depression, anxiety, and borderline personality disorder.

Bowlby mentioned that disorganised attachment is associated with the presence of family risk factors, such as maltreatment, major depression, or bipolar disorder, and alcohol or other substance misuse by the parents. As a consequence of these risk factors, he found clinical problems in the child's development, such as childhood aggression, dissociation, and violence. This is also associated with disturbances in affect regulation and social cognitive skills, characteristic of dysfunctional groups with conduct problems. For example, problems of inattention and cognitive disturbances could appear, depending on the duration of the deprivation. On the contrary, he said, secure attachment leads to a general sense of competence and self-esteem.

His main contribution was to give significance to the infant's biological proclivity to form attachments—to initiate, maintain, and terminate interaction with the caregiver and use this person as a "secure base" for exploration and self-enhancement. For Bowlby, it was essential that the infant's needs were fulfilled by a secure, unbroken attachment to the mother. He thought that the child who does not have this safety would show signs of *partial deprivation* (development of excessive need for love or revenge, gross guilt, and depression) or *complete deprivation* (listlessness, quietness, unresponsiveness, and retardation of development, and later in development, signs of superficiality, lack of real feelings, lack of concentration, deceit, and compulsive thieving).

Separation

Robertson and Bowlby (1952) described three phases of separation response: "Protest related to separation anxiety, despair (related to grief and mourning) and detachment or denial (related to defence mechanisms, especially repression)" (Bowlby, 1988, p. 32).

Protest (related to separation anxiety):

This starts when the infant feels the threat of separation. The baby cries, feels anger, and searches for the parent.

Despair (related to grief and mourning):

Here, physical movement diminishes, crying becomes intermittent, sadness prevails, withdraw from contact occurs, and the child can show anger towards other children or a favourite toy.

Detachment or denial (related to defence):

Here, there is some return to sociability, accepting other adults who offer care. Abnormal behaviour at the reunion with the caregiver may occur. The detachment can persist following the reunion, and clingy behaviour as an expression of the fear of abandonment can occur.

In 1960, Bowlby believed that when a caregiver continues to be unavailable to the infant, the protest-despair responses will result in detachment and may affect the infant's ability to form interdependent and caring relationships in life.

Another important concept that Bowlby described was the behaviour reaction facing a significant loss, grieving. He categorised four phases in the experience of children and adults related to the grieving process.

The four phases during the grieving process are:

1. Phase of numbing that usually lasts from a few hours to a week and may be interrupted of extremely intense distress and/or anger.
2. Phase of yearning and searching for the lost figure lusting some months and sometimes years.
3. Phase of disorganisation and despair.
4. Phase of greater or less degree of reorganisation.

(Bowlby, 1980, p. 85)

Numbness

"Numbness occurs after the first reaction to the loss of a loved one, shock, distress, fear, and maybe anger, comes numbness" (Bowlby, 1980, p. 86).

Yearning and protest

Numbness is followed by protest. Protest can take the form of denial and last hours. Weeping is common as a form of protest as well as an attempt to recover what has been lost. In this initial phase of grief, anger and hostility can appear, towards the doctors and even towards the lost person. The world becomes empty and meaningless without the person, and searching and yearning can ensue. The predominant emotion is painful sadness. The process of transferring feelings of attachment for the person onto the memories of the person can occur, until gradually it reaches the internal realisation of the loss.

Disorganisation and despair

Throughout the process of mentally reliving the lost person, the bereaved starts to accept the permanent loss, and experiences restlessness and aimlessness. He can become withdrawn, introverted, and irritable. The world seems bleak and empty.

It is essential to recognise that contrary to the clinical depression, the person's self-esteem is intact. Somatic symptoms can appear such as loss of appetite, lack of energy, and digestive disturbances.

Repair and reorganisation

In this stage, the grief begins to recede and the person begins to establish new patterns and goals in their life. This process can take months or even years. Painful memories begin to fade and hurt is replace by good memories, pleasure, and affection. New activities and relationships begin. He wrote: "For mourning to have a favourable outcome it appears to be necessary for a bereaved person to endure this buffeting of emotion. It is important to accept that the loss is in truth permanent and that his life must be shaped anew" (Bowlby, 1980, p. 93). Bowlby emphasises that remembering and grieving losses that occurred in the past is a crucial part of any therapeutic process.

Anxiety according to Bowlby

Bowlby said that anxiety is related to the feeling of the risk of losing the mother. According to Bowlby, anxiety is the anticipation or unbearability of losing the attachment figure. "When the attachment figure is unavailable, the infant experiences separation distress. In infants, physical separation can cause anxiety and anger, followed by sadness and despair" (Bowlby, 1988, p. 30).

"A threat of loss creates anxiety, and actual loss sorrow; both are likely to arouse anger" (Bowlby, 1969, p. 209).

When the child is older, at three or four, physical separation is no longer such a threat to the child's bond with the attachment figure. The threat to security in older children and adults are produced by prolonged absence, lack of communication, emotional unavailability, or rejection or abandonment.

Phases in the development of attachment

In his book *Attachment*, Bowlby described several phases in the development of attachment, although there are not sharp boundaries between them (Bowlby, 1969, p. 265). Bowlby said: "the infant, at the time of birth, already has a number of behavioural systems ready to be activated, and each system is activated by stimuli, and terminated by other stimuli falling within broad ranges and is strengthened or weakened by stimuli of other kinds" (Bowlby, 1969, p. 265).

The system enables the infant to have a stable internal organisation. In the past, attachment behaviours were believed to be part of a behavioural system, but after continued observation and research, the consent is that the main component of attachment is a psychological mechanism.

For Bowlby, the goal that regulates the system is not the object, the mother as the object theory said, the goal that regulates the system is in the beginning a physical state, the need of the mother proximity, and later is supplanted by the more psychological goal of a feeling of closeness to the caregiver, so the goal is a state of being or feeling instead of object-related.

The phases in the development of attachment are:

Phase 1: Orientation and signals with limited discrimination of figure (from birth to about twelve weeks, although it may continue longer)

> The infant's ability to discriminate one person from another is limited to olfactory and auditory stimuli. The behaviour toward any person in his vicinity include: orientation towards that person, tracking movements of the eyes, grasping and reaching, smiling and babbling. Often the infant stops crying when he hears a voice or sees a face.

> (Bowlby, 1969, p. 266)

Phase 2: Orientation and signals directed towards one (or more) discriminated figure(s). (from twelve weeks to six months of age onwards)

The behaviour is the same as phase 1 as the infant behaves towards people in a friendly way, but in this phase he does so in a more marked fashion towards his mother figure than towards others.

Phase 3: Maintenance of proximity to a discriminated figure by means of locomotion as well as signals (from six or seven months of age to one year old until two or three years old)

> The infant increasingly discriminates people, and his repertoire of responses now includes following a departing mother, greeting her on her return, and using her as a base from which to explore.

Strangers become treated with increasing caution. His attachment to his mother-figure is evident for all to see.

(Bowlby, 1969, p. 267)

Phase 4: Formation of a goal-corrected partnership (from the middle of the third year)

The child is acquiring insight into his mother's feelings and motives. The groundwork is laid for the pair (mother–child) to develop a more complex relationship with each other, which Bowlby called partnership.

(Bowlby, 1969, p. 268)

Other concepts developed by Bowlby

The three behavioural systems: attachment—exploration—fear systems

Bowlby described three behavioural systems—attachment, exploration, and fear—which regulate the child's developmental adaptation. The exploratory behavioural system is connected with attachment. Bowlby stated that: "Attachment behaviour has been defined as seeing and maintaining proximity to another individual" (Bowlby, 1969, p. 195). Furthermore, he said: "The infant is attached to the mother when recognises her and behaves in a way that maintain his proximity to her" (Bowlby, 1969, p. 199).

The attachment figure gives the essential secure base from which the child can explore the world. The absence of the attachment figure interferes with the exploration. The successful attachment allows the development of social and cognitive capacities, and the secure attachment is established. On the contrary, if the child did not develop a secure attachment, the fear system aroused and the child's reaction to stimuli will be perceived as dangerous. "The three behavioural systems regulate the child's developmental adaptation" (Fonagy, 1991, pp. 8–9).

Affectional bonds or ties

Bowlby described affectional bonds or ties when one individual has more emotional significance than another, though it is interchangeable.

An affectional bond becomes an attachment bond when the individual seeks security from that specific relationship. During infancy and child-hood, bonds are with the parents (or parent substitutes) who are looked to for protection, comfort, and support.

> During healthy adolescence and adult life these bonds persist, but are complemented by new bonds, commonly of a heterosexual nature. Although food and sex sometimes play important roles in attachment relationship, the relationship exists in its own right and has a key survival function of its own, namely protection.
>
> (Bowlby, 1988, p. 121)

He also mentioned a complementary working model of the self, whereby a child with a working model of rejection from the caregiver will develop a working model of the self as unlovable, unworthy, and flawed. For him, cognitive and emotional characteristics are connected with attachment as a function of the nature of the past relationship between infant and caregiver.

In his book *Attachment Theory and Psychoanalysis*, Fonagy said,

> We believe that the parent's capacity to adopt the intentional stance towards a not-yet-intentional infant, to think about the infant in terms of thoughts, feelings, and desires in the infant's mind and in their own mind in relation to the infant and his or her mental state, is the key mediator of the transmission of attachment and accounts for classical observations concerning the influence of car-egiver sensitivity.
>
> (Fonagy, 1991, p. 27)

With regard to the prediction on the impact of early attachment on later development, Bowlby had no doubts that the differences in the secu-rity of infant-mother attachment would have long-term implications on later intimate relationships, self-understanding, and psychological disturbance.

Bowlby talks about the ego's capacity to create defences during the developmental process that organise characterological and symp-tomatic constructions. Attachment patterns could be seen as mecha-nisms of defence, used by the child to cope with the idiosyncratic styles of interaction of his caregivers. Attachment theory describes all the varieties of ways that involve behaviour or personality characteristics of the caregiver.

Integration between attachment theory and psychoanalysis

Bowlby and his attachment theory were very controversial among the psychoanalysts in the early 1960s. He was highly criticised for being mechanistic and non-dynamic. It was said that he did not accept the drive theory, unconscious processes, and unconscious phantasy concept.

There are authors, such as Peter Fonagy and Mario Marrone, who intended to integrate attachment theory and psychoanalysis understanding, which they agreed that it is a complex task. Fonagy said that there are many points of contact, some obvious, others more subtle, there are also points of significant divergence.

Fonagy tried to bring together attachment theory and psychoanalysis through cognitive science as mentalization, the theory of mind is the capacity of human beings to guess with some accuracy what thoughts, emotions, and intentions lie behind behaviours, such as facial expressions. The connection between theory of mind and the internal working model opens more areas of research in the future. Fonagy, in *Attachment Theory and Psychoanalysis*, said: "mentalisation, is a specific symbolic function central to both psychoanalytic and attachment theory, and appear in both theories of thinking" (Fonagy, 1991, p. 165). "Attachment security is a good predictor of metacognitive capacity in memory, comprehension, and communication" (Fonagy, 1991, p. 166).

"The secure infant feels safe in thinking about the mental state of the caregiver. In contrast the avoidant child shuns the mental state of the other, while the resistant child focuses on his own state of distress" (Fonagy, 1991, p. 167).

Fonagy said that there are concepts of mentalisation in psychoanalysis as well; Freud, in his concept of linking, refers from the physical (immediate) to the psychological (associative); Klein in describing the depressive position, stressed the recognition of hurt and suffering in the other, meaning, the awareness of mental states; and Winnicott in recognising the importance of the caregiver's psychological understanding of the infant in the emergence of the true self, and in acknowledging the dialectical aspect of this relationship (Fonagy, 1991, p. 167).

Bowlby's psychotherapeutic process

It is important to mention that in 1988 Bowlby published a series of lectures indicating how attachment theory and research could be used in understanding and treating the child and the family problems. His focus was trying to change the parents approaches, parenting behaviours, and the parents' relationship to the therapeutic intervention. One of the main goals was to lead to individual treatments, prevention, and intervention programmes, from individual therapy to public health programmes to interventions designed for foster carers. One of the main goals was to increase the responsiveness and sensitivity of the caregiver.

In his book *A Secure Base* (1988), Bowlby addressed the issue of applying the attachment theory to individual therapy. Bowlby advised to the therapists the need to explore the patient's representational models of himself and his attachments figures in the past, with the intention to review them in order to restructuring them in the light of the new understanding through the therapeutic relationship. In helping the patient with this task, he described five main ways to approach this goal.

Five therapeutic tasks during the process of treatment

1. The first is to provide the patient with a secure base where the patient feels safe to explore his past painful experiences. The therapist should provide support, encouragement, sympathy, and, on occasion, guidance.
2. A second is for the therapist to assist and has to help the patient to review and examine his current choices, considering the possibilities of unconscious bias when he selects a person with whom he expects an intimate relationship.
3. The third is the encouragement of the therapist to examine the relationship between both of them, the patient and the therapist. Taking into consideration that the patient can import in the therapeutic relationship perceptions, constructions, and expectations of how an attachment figure is likely to feel and behave towards him the way that his past working models of parents and self-dictate did.
4. A fourth task is for the therapist to encourage the patient to consider how his current perceptions and expectations, and the feelings and

action to which they give rise, may be the product of either the events and situations he encountered during his childhood and adolescence, especially with his parents, or as the products of what he may repeatedly have been told by them. This is often a painful and difficult process and not infrequently requires that the therapist allow his patient to consider as possibilities ideas and feelings about his parents that he has hitherto regarded as unimaginable and unthinkable. In doing so, a patient may find himself moved by strong emotions and urges to action, some directed towards his parents and some towards the therapist, and many of which he may find frightening and/or alien and unacceptable.

5. Fifth, it is important to enable his patient to recognise that his images (models) of himself and of others, derived either from past painful experiences, and maybe from misleading messages coming from a parent that may or may not be appropriate for his present and future.

Once the patient understands the nature of his governing images (models) and has traced their origins, he begins to see that what has led him to see the world and himself as he does and to feel, think, and to act in the ways he does. He will be in the position to reflect on the accuracy and adequacy of those images and on the ideas and actions to which they lead him in light of his current experiences of emotionally significant people, including the therapist as well as his parents, and of himself in relation to each. Through this process the therapist enables his patient to cease being a slave to old and unconscious stereotypes and to feel, think, and act in new ways (Bowlby, 1988, pp. 138–139).

Three important experiences in the development of Bowlby's work

It was described that there were three experiences during Bowlby work that lead him to the development of the attachment theory.

His experience with maladapted and delinquent children in 1944

When he was twenty-one years old, Bowlby worked in a home for maladjusted boys. A retrospective study he carried out ten years later, which examined the history of forty-four juvenile thieves (1944), formalised his view that the disruption of the early mother–child relationship should be seen as a key precursor of mental disorder. He observed that children who had been seriously deprived of maternal care tended to develop the same symptoms as he had identified in his "affectionless" young thieves.

During 1952, James Robertson, with Bowlby's encouragement, made the documentary film A Two-Year-Old Goes to the Hospital

James Robertson (1911–1988) was a psychiatric social worker and psychoanalyst who work at the Tavistock Clinic and Institute, in London. James joined Bowlby at the Tavistock Clinic in 1948 to make observations on children at the hospital or residential nurseries who were separated from their parents. James spent four years documenting the impact on the eighteen- to forty-eight-month-olds of these separations.

His supervision with Melanie Klein

Klein supervised Bowlby's treatment of a three-year-old boy, Klein stressed the role of the child's phantasies about his mother. Bowlby emphasised the actual history of the relationship of mother–child. His view was that children were responding to real life events and not unconscious phantasies. This point of view was rejected by the analysts of that time and he was ostracised by the psychoanalytic community.

Despite his being ostracised by the traditional psychoanalytic community, we considered very important to include the attachment theory due to the current relevance in the field of child development and its influence in the prevention of pathology in the future of the child.

CHAPTER NINE

Pioneers around the world

Hermine Hug-Hellmuth

Hermine Hug Hellmuth (1871–1924) was an Austrian Psychoanalyst who was considered the first child psychoanalyst in Vienna. From a Catholic background, she was the second daughter of Hugo Hug von Hugenstein, who served in the Austrian war as a military officer and civilian. Her mother, Ludovika Achelpohl, was a highly educated woman who mother tutored Hermine at home, but suffered from tuberculosis and died when Hermine was twelve.

Following her mother's death, Hermine attended public school and became a teacher. She taught in public and private schools before entering the University of Vienna in 1897, where she studied the physical sciences and in 1909 obtained a doctorate in physics. She became interested in psychoanalysis and started her own psychoanalytic treatment with the Viennese analyst Isidor Sadger. Her interest in psychoanalytic theory grew, and she decided to apply the new theory to children having problems. In 1910, she chose to concentrate in the field of child analysis and resigned her teaching position. The following year, Hermine published her first paper on psychoanalysis, "The Analysis of a Dream of a Five-Year-Old Boy", and in 1913 she published

"The Nature of the Child's Soul". That same year she was accepted as a member of the Wednesday Meetings, which later became the Vienna society. She was the third woman analyst to be accepted as a member of the Vienna Psychoanalytic Association. The first two women were Margarete Hilferding (1871–1942) and Sabina Spielrein (1885–1941). Freud respected Hermine's ideas and psychoanalytic contributions and gave her the official position of representing child psychoanalysis.

Hug-Hellmuth was the first analyst to write about the importance of the infant's emotional development in the first weeks of life and its earliest sexual feelings and masturbation. She also drew attention to the value of play in children as a method of observation of their development. She contributed to the idea of the importance of psychoanalysis in other pedagogical and educational dimensions. At the 1920 International Congress in the Hague, she reported on her early efforts to develop a psychoanalytic technique in her work with children, and also presented her paper, "On the Technique of the Analysis of Children".

In 1921, Hermine became director of the Educational Counselling Centre, a group associated with the Ambulatorium of the Vienna Psychoanalytic Society. There, her work was based on the observation and analysis of children's behaviour, with the idea of applying psychoanalytic theory to children's education and psychological health. However, her promising career was cut short on the night of 8 September 1924, shortly after the completion of her book, *New Ways to the Understanding of Youth*, when she was murdered by her eighteen-year-old nephew, whom she had protected after the death of her step-sister, the boy's mother, and she died at the age of fifty-three.

Sabina Spielrein

Sabina Spielrein (1885–1942) was a Russian psychoanalyst, and considered one of the first in the development of child analysis. Born in a wealthy Jewish family of Rostov on Don, where her father, Nikolai Spielrein, was a business man, and her mother, Eva Lublinskaya, practised as a dentist and was also pioneer of the role of women in society. Sabina was the oldest of five children, including a younger sister, Milotschka, who died young, and three brothers, Jascha, Isaak, and Emil. Her brother Isaac later became a Soviet psychologist and a pioneer of labour psychology.

Sabina's parents were strict and forced their children to endure a harsh upbringing. Her father tyrannised the household; her mother severely beat the children. At the same time her father was interested in his children's education and sent them to the best universities. He also encouraged all of them to learn languages, especially German and French. They employed a nursemaid, a music teacher, and a governess to prepare their children for high school.

Sabina was precocious, excelled in school, and studied piano. She enjoyed science, and from early age wanted to be a medical doctor. Sabina also experienced early losses. When she was fifteen her six-year-old sister died of typhoid, and her grandmother, with whom she was very close, died as well. Yet despite her depression and hysteric symptoms, she was able to complete the Russian gymnasium with honours. While she had suffered emotionally through the years of her early life these feelings worsened at age seventeen, when she became dysfunctional.

Sabina felt lost, as in those days being intelligent, Jewish, and a woman was placed her in a difficult and confusing position. She also had fears, for example about marriage. Her parents were not able to handle her pain and confusion so they sent her for treatment to the Heller Sanatorium in Switzerland, where she remained for one month. However, when the treatment did not have positive results, she was sent to a psychiatric hospital in Zurich, the Burgholzli, under the direction of Eugen Bleuler, where she was under the care of Carl G. Jung, one of Freud's early followers.

Carl Jung treated Spielrein with the psychoanalytic technique, after nine months of treatment she was discharged, although she continued her analysis with Jung on an outpatient basis. Spielrein was able to overcome her family issues and deep fears and felt strong enough to pursue her dream of becoming a medical doctor. Dr Bleuler then wrote a letter on her behalf and she enrolled in the Zurich Medical School.

The relationship with Jung grew into a romantic attraction, and Sabina fell in love with him during treatment. Jung had erotic feelings for Sabina, as they shared a passionate interest in psychoanalysis that bonded them. The relationship continued until 1909, when Jung ended the affair to save his marriage and career. Jung had already contacted Freud in 1906, asking his opinion about the challenging case of Sabina's treatment. She contacted Freud as well, and requested a consultation with him in 1909, which Freud declined, although he would eventually meet Sabina in Vienna in 1911.

This was a painful and at the same time a successful case. Sabina became scientifically productive and left valuable contributions in the field of child psychoanalysis. She published more than thirty papers, exchanged letters with Sigmund Freud, Otto Rank, Wilhelm Stekel, Pierre Bover, and other research people in the field. Furthermore, she reconnected with her family, exchanging letters with her parents, siblings, and friends.

Sabina was graduated from medical school in 1910–1911. Earlier, she had applied her experience with psychiatric patients during the time she was in Burgholzli, writing about schizophrenic patients. In her paper "Psychological Elements in a Case of Schizophrenia" (1911), she described a unique case of research in psychosis with a psychoanalytic orientation. This was the first time that a woman had written a paper of this nature.

Bleuler, Jung, and Freud were impressed with her paper, and it was immediately published. After the success of the paper, she left Zurich, went to Munich, and wrote another paper based on her self-observation. This 1912 paper, "Destruction as the Cause of Coming into Being", exhibited her experiences and personal frustrations. To her, the paper was the symbolic son that she fantasised about having with Jung, whom they called Siegfried.

Sabina did marry, a physician of Jewish Russian descent named Pavel Scheftel. They had two daughters, Renata, who was born in 1913, and Eva, born in 1926. When the First World War broke out in 1914, Pavel went into military service in Russia, while Sabina travelled to Geneva with her daughter. During Renata's early childhood, Sabina made many observations and transcriptions of the dialogues she had with her child, and later wrote papers using the material.

At the first International Congress, held in the Hague in 1920, she presented the paper "The Origin of the Words Mama and Papa", which was later published in *Imago* in 1922. In this paper, she described three phases of verbal development: *talk* with corporal expressions, the *magic state*, and the *verbal social stage*.

She then experienced some very productive years, taught classes and led conferences, and became a training analyst. At that time, she shared her theory about child development, including her thoughts on the origin of children's speech, and discussed the importance of suckling and the mother's breast. Her theory had a significant impact on Melanie Klein, who was present at the 1920 Congress.

At the same Congress, she met Jean Piaget and worked with him on themes that interested them both, including the evolution of language. Piaget's work was in the cognitive aspect of language, while Sabina was interested in both the cognitive and the emotional aspects. Spielrein also analysed Piaget for eight months, and they travelled together to the Congress in Berlin in 1922, which was the last time that Sabina met Freud.

In 1923, at a time when psychoanalysis was flourishing under the protection of Trotsky, Sabina returned to Russia with her daughter. It was a moment when the Psychoanalytic Society was founded in Moscow, as well as the State Psychoanalytic Institute, and Spielrein, who had studied with Freud and Jung, and remained very active academically, was the best-trained analyst in Russia.

She had been separated from her husband for several years, but after learning that he was having an affair and had fathered a child with another physician, Sabina returned to Rostov in 1924 to join her husband, and in 1926 Sabina had her second daughter, Eva.

In 1927, Pavel Sheftel was killed in Stalin's Great Purge, which marked the end of an era in Russia. In 1930, the political situation changed with the introduction of the Marxism-Leninism Dogma. However, Sabina stayed in Rostov and continued to be professionally active and involved in the school environment and in psychiatry, treating children and adults.

Sabina developed her own technique with children, using her concepts of the development of verbal communication and the influence of the abreaction of the repressed. However, in 1933, the practice of psychoanalysis was forbidden in Russia, and in 1936 the Communist Party signed a resolution that caused her to lose her job. In 1935, her father was sent to forced labour due to the political situation. Under Stalin (1937–1938), her three brothers were killed and sent to a common grave. Soon after this event, it is said that her father died of anguish.

Sabina and her two daughters survived the first occupation of the Nazis in Rostov, but in 1942, when the Germans took over the city, Sabina and her two daughters were killed by a German SS Death Squad. Sabina was fifty-seven years old.

Sabina Spielrein's first papers about child analysis

"Psychological Elements in a Case of Schizophrenia" (1911)
"Destruction as the Cause of Coming into Being" (1912)
"Contributions to the Knowledge of the Infantile Soul" (1912)

"Contributions to the Knowledge of the Infantile Soul" was Sabina's first child analytic paper. She was interested in Freud's 1909 paper about "Little Hans", and through the presentation of material from three clinical examples, she concluded that children had phantasies of birth and sexuality. She observed that the origin of infantile anxieties and phobias could be found in unconscious sexual phantasies.

Another of the themes she developed was that infantile development connected to thought and verbal communication, thus pointing the way to the application of psychoanalysis to education. She was also interested in the position of the mother, anxieties in the pregnant woman, feminine identity, and the role of empathy. Sabina addressed themes touching on the difference between the sexes, as well as the psychological differences—the differences in creativity in men and women. She concluded that these are neither biological or psychological, but social.

She established the concept of understanding the emotional development of the child, and her work deepened both Jung's and Freud's understanding of transference and countertransference. The relationship between Jung and Spielrein also forced Freud to think about the therapist's emotions and the human qualities of the relationship between the analyst and the patient.

Ultimately, even as one of the first psychoanalysts in the child field, Sabina's contributions unfortunately did not endure. For example, when Anna Freud presented her first paper in 1922, Sabina had already published twenty-five contributions ten years earlier. Her tragic death interrupted the transcendence of her work.

Phyllis Greenacre

Phyllis Greenacre (1894–1989), the daughter of Isaiah Thomas, who was a prominent lawyer in Chicago, and his wife, Emma Russell, was the fourth of seven children in her family. She graduated from Chicago's Rush Medical College in 1916, and moved to become an intern and resident at the Phipps Clinic at Johns Hopkins Hospital in Baltimore, where from 1916 to 1927 she worked in the Department of Psychiatry of the Johns Hopkins Hospital and Medical School. She was already involved in the psychiatry residency programme and was also on the teaching staff and engaged in research in neurosyphilis studies. From there, from 1927 to 1932, she was a psychiatric consultant to the child-care division of the Department of Public Welfare of Westchester County, New York.

For the following thirty years, Greenacre maintained an affiliation with the Department of Psychiatry of New York Hospital and

Cornell Medical College, beginning as an assistant professor and later becoming professor of clinical psychiatry. She had begun her psychoanalytic training at the New York Psychoanalytic Institute, graduated in 1937, and in 1942 was appointed as a training analyst. Greenacre died in at the age of ninety-five in Ossining, New York.

Phyllis Greenacre's main contributions

At about the same time that Greenacre was involved in the New York Psychoanalytic Institute, many European psychoanalysts had immigrated to New York to escape the Nazi death camps, and she was influenced by the ideas of the Viennese analysts Heinz Hartmann and Ernest Kris. Greenacre was devoted to psychoanalytic practice and made many contributions to psychoanalytic clinical research. Her interests were focused on studies of infantile development in relation to the genesis of later neurotic disorders. She was also interested in the connections between personal development and creativity, and wrote clinical papers on child development, psychoanalytic training, psychotherapy, and studies of creativity.

"The Predisposition to Anxiety" (1941) was her first paper; in it, she argued that the roots of anxiety might predate the existence of the ego. She explain her believe that

> The overload of anxiety of the severe neurotic can be divided in three forms:
>
> 1. The basic anxiety, blind or amorphous anxiety; which is always present in some degree through life.
> 2. The anxiety arising in response to these fresh experiences of danger and frustration.
> 3. The secondary anxiety, arising out of the inadequacy of the neurotic defence and the additional dangers, real or illusory, following the production of the symptoms.
>
> (Greenacre, 1952, p. 55)

In her paper "The Biological Economy of Birth", she wrote:

> The general effect of birth is by sensory stimulation, to organise and convert the foetal narcissism, producing or promoting a propulsive narcissistic drive over and above the type of more relaxed foetal

maturation process that has been existent *in utero*. There is ordinarily a patterning of the aggressive libidinisation of certain body parts according to the areas of special stimulation. Specially, birth stimulates the cerebrum to a degree promoting its development so that it may soon begin take effective control of body affairs; it contributes to the organisation of the anxiety pattern, increasing the defence of the infant, and it leaves unique individual traces that are superimposed on the genetically determined anxiety and libidinal patterns of the given infant.

(Greenacre, 1952, p. 25)

Greenacre wrote a paper about fetishism "Certain Relationships between Fetishism and the Faulty Development of the Body Image" (1953), observing that fetishists have a mutable body image, and went on to write several papers about creativity.

In volume one of her two-volume book *Emotional Growth: Psychoanalytic Studies of the Gifted and a Great Variety of Other Individuals* (1971), Greenacre described one of her main concepts regarding the development of the ego. She considered the impact and influence of early life experiences to be of extreme importance on later development, especially the preverbal months of life. She also considered the important role of aggression, and its interplay with the libidinal phase. She said that the anxiety response begins in intrauterine life and becomes organised at birth in the anxiety reaction. Variations in the birth process could be organic factors increasing the anxiety response, while increasing the anxiety potential and psychologically determining a more severe reaction to danger in later life.

Greenacre wrote that there are two special areas of process in ego development. The first is that of constitutional variation, following her belief that the core of the autonomous ego has its origin in the biological growth of the young infant, and that in addition to these, the patterns of physical growth and learning leave their mark on later patterns of mental functioning. She said that it is important to examine the individual differences in infant responses during the first year of life. The second area in the process of ego development has to do with the nature of the relationship between the infant and the mother, which she added, it will be displayed in the psychoanalytic treatment in relationship with the analyst.

In her 1958 article "Early Physical Determinants in the Development of the Sense of Identity", Greenacre said:

> At the beginning of life the sense of identity is present: in the development of the body's self-image, the awareness of the genitals, face, and the total body form. The core of identity lies in the structural organisation, but the awareness of identity, *the sense of identity*, is influenced by factors of external origin that affects awareness of external attributes.

(Greenacre, 1958, p. 126)

She concluded that identity has a stable core in both the body and its psychic structure and physical functioning.

> That stable core of the identity will face the changes throughout the child's development that are linked with different stages of the body as well as the child's maturational achievement and emotional problems.

(Greenacre, 1958, p. 126)

Furthermore, she wrote:

> Under most circumstances the sense of the own identity follows with the organisational structural identity but will always remain susceptible to the influence of changes in the individual's relationship to his environment-whether this be in this development within his adult family life, as a member of the community, or in other group relationships.

(Greenare, 1958, p. 126)

In Part II of the second volume of *Emotional Growth* (1971), Greenacre wrote about studies in creativity, and in Part III she addressed issues concerning psychoanalytic therapy and training.

She proposed a theory of aggression in her 1957 paper "The Childhood of the Artist", in which she noted that aggression is a positive response by the infant during both frustrating and gratifying experiences in early life. She connected aggression to the pressure of growth as expressed in the expansion and differentiation of the organism during what she called the *parasitic period* of foetal life. She added that in this stage the foetus is totally dependent on the mother for its existence, and its development is influenced by the same conditions affecting the mother. The force of growth would appear, from necessity, to be a non-hostile form of physical aggression; it will later contribute to the core of the autonomous ego, as the body ego develops into the psychic ego. Aggression becomes hostile, she said, at the beginning of object relationships.

She also noted that there is a transition from frustration leading to an undifferentiated form of suffering that can continue on to provide a potential for sadism and masochism. However, in this stage of transition from body ego to psychic ego, we have more knowledge regarding the somato-psychic and sadomasochistic disturbances.

In her book *Trauma, Growth, and Personality* (1952), Greenacre explored the way certain special or traumatic events impact the biogenetic development of the infant. She said that when we evaluate the effect of trauma, it is important to consider the maturational phase in which the trauma occurred, and whether the specific nature of the trauma will reinforce the libidinisation of the dominant phase, restate the dominant phase, or will lead to regression, depending on whether the phase is one closer to immaturity or maturity.

She suggested that:

> (1) The earlier in life severe traumata occur, the greater are the somatic components of their imprints. (2) Very severe or very prolonged (chronic) traumata may produce so massive a stimulation as to suffuse the organism. (3) The activation of libidinal zones prematurely may produce a precocious but vulnerable development. And (4) that excessive sexual stimulation early in life, whether massive or specific in origin, results in primitive erotisation and ultimately in some genital stimulation long before genitalisation, which is undeveloped before the phallic phase. She added that premature erotisation culminating in genital stimulation under strain might increase the pain component in the pleasure–pain amalgam, which is the nucleus of all satisfaction, here linked with genital arousal. The impact of the trauma will thus depend on the degree of prematurity and on the demand made by the special stimulus.

(Greenacre, 1952, p. 295)

Greenacre said that:

> it is a clinically observable fact that massive stimulation or severe
> frustration results in genital stirring, even in the very young infant,
> that is easily observable in the erection of the male. In these children
> there sometimes persist throughout the latency period a variety of
> autoerotic discharges and defences, with enuresis, thumb-sucking,
> special mannerisms, and masturbation occurring concurrently.
>
> (Greenacre, 1952, p. 298)

She noted further that all these cases show increased narcissism due to
traumatic stimulation in the first year or two of life, setting the groundwork for later bisexual identification, which may be appreciably intensified by the constant exposure to siblings of the opposite sex.

She said that examples of premature demands could be seen in early
masturbation long before the phallic phase, such as genital seduction,
as when mothers or nurses stimulate the baby boy's penis by daily pulling back the foreskin and swabbing it for the purpose of cleanliness.
Other examples can be force-feeding, the early giving of enemas, or
very early toilet training.

Furthermore, she added that

> the baby of eight to ten months of age begins to recognise people
> individually and responds to the face of the mother, and the infant
> at that age notices the presence or absence of external genitals, if
> there is a constant exposure and stimulation of this kind.
>
> (Greenacre, 1952, p. 299)

Greenacre's ideas about the psychoanalytic process

With regard to psychoanalytic treatment, Greenacre talked about *rap-
port* and *emotional engagement* between the patient and therapist, which
give some margin of real communication. This basic relationship is usually ambivalent in patients who have had serious disturbances in the
first two years of life, although hostile aggression may be concealed by
the patient, especially if he is anxious and needy.

Greenacre supported reconstruction in the analytic work, through
paying attention to screen memories and her belief that early preverbal
experiences can be traced through them.

She started the treatment only after several previous interviews in order to assess the level of the patient's functioning. She thought that early pathological experiences led to psycho-neurosis, especially if they happen in the first two years of life. Traumatic experiences could result in symptoms that could be masked by an overly positive transference, which can be seen as a defensive armour. Greenacre worked through this stage immediately and consistently until the hostility was uncovered. When the patient immediately expressed hostility, she worked with this aspect from the beginning, giving the patient relief in the fact that it would not threaten the treatment.

Sophie Morgenstern

Sophie Morgenstern (1875–1940) was a French psychoanalyst who came from a Jewish Polish family. She began studying medicine in Zurich in 1906, and by 1915 she was working in the Burgholzli clinic under Eugen Bleuler. She moved to France in 1924. She had begun her psychoanalytic treatment with Sigmund Freud and continued her analysis in France with Eugenie Sokolnicka, a student of Freud's who was considered to have introduced psychoanalysis to France. In 1925, she became a volunteer in the child clinic directed by the psychiatrist Georges Heuyer. She married Abraham Morgenstern, and the couple had one daughter, Laura, who died during a surgical intervention in 1937; the date of her husband's death is not known.

Between 1927 and 1939 Morgenstern published one book and fifteen articles, with her work based entirely in her experience with Sigmund Freud and reading his work, and at the time of the controversy between Anna Freud and Melanie Klein, Morgenstern aligned with Anna Freud's position.

In her 1927 paper "A Case of Psychogenic Mutism", she described her drawing technique, which she continued to investigate throughout her life. She studied children's stories, dreams, daydreams, games, modeling play, and their drawings, as well as their free associations when she worked with older children, in search of the latent content behind the manifest content.

In another paper, "Psychoanalysis Infantile", published in 1937, she described how she developed the concept of her drawing technique based on the drawing the children made. She was the first woman to practise psychoanalysis in France and the first analyst to use the technique of drawings. Advancing child psychoanalytic technique through the method of drawings was her major contribution.

Morgenstern believed that child neurosis shared the same structure and origins as adult neurosis, but that it showed greater malleability in the child when the superego could facilitate the resolution of conflict. She stressed the importance of caution in the formulation of interpretations regarding sexual curiosity, especially in the young patients.

Sophie Morgenstern killed herself in June of 1940 at the time of the German occupation in Paris, France in 1940; she was sixty-five years old.

René Spitz

The Austrian-American psychoanalyst René Spitz (1887–1974) came from in a wealthy Jewish family, and was born, in Vienna, although he spent most of his childhood in Hungary. He died in Denver, Colorado. Spitz discovered the work of Sigmund Freud following his graduation from medical school. In 1932, he left Austria and settled in Paris for six years, where he taught psychoanalysis at the École Normale Superieur. In 1939, he emigrated to the United States where he worked as a psychiatrist at Mount Sinai Hospital in New York City from 1940 to 1943.

It was in early 1935 that Spitz became interested the area of child development. He was one of the first researchers who investigated and used child observation observing both disturbed and normal child development, and he focused on the effects of maternal emotional deprivation.

Spitz developed the term *anaclitic depression* for partial emotional deprivation, as in the loss of a loved object. Spitz concluded that if the love object is returned to the infant within a period of three to five months, recovery is prompt; but if the child is deprived of a loved object for longer than five months, the child will show the symptoms of increasingly serious deterioration. He called this total deprivation *hospitalism*.

In 1945, he undertook research on hospitalisation and children in a foundling home, where he found that the developmental imbalance caused by the negative environmental conditions during the children's first year of life produced psychosomatic damage that could not be repaired by normal measures. His very important book, *The First Year of Life*, was published for the first time in 1965.

René Spitz has made many significant contributions in the area of ego development. Among these he described some specific markers in different periods of the child's life. These include:

1. The *smiling response*, which appears at about the age of three months in the presence of an unspecified person;
2. *Anxiety in the presence of a stranger*, which appears at about the eighth month; and
3. *Semantic communication* when the child develops obstinacy, which psychoanalysts may later connect to obsessional traits and neurosis.

Berta Bornstein

Born in Krakov, Berta Bornstein (1899–1971) was a Jewish-Polish American psychoanalyst, and by the 1920s was one of the early child analysts.

Bornstein's parents left Poland soon after Bertha's birth and settled in Berlin, where her father worked as an engineer. She was the eldest of four children, with one sister and two brothers. As a young woman, Bornstein became a teacher of handicapped children, and began her analytic training there with Hans Lampl and Edward Bibring when she was twenty. She participated in the child seminar directed by Otto Fenichel in 1924 at the Berlin Psychoanalytic Institute.

In 1929, Bertha left Berlin and went to Vienna, where she worked closely with Anna Freud; she then continued on to Prague and finally left Europe before War World II, landing in New York in 1938. She remained loyal to her teachers throughout her career. Her sister was also a child analyst but died at a young age in Prague in 1939.

Bornstein introduced a number of innovative techniques in the field of child psychoanalytic treatment, and was especially interested in those concerning the area of defences. She could detect the precocity of children and was able to get their confidence in a short time. In Bornstein's view, the analysis of children was based on the analysis of the defences. Her particular focus was on the child's defences against his unbearable affects of sadness and loneliness. Her goal was to help the child become consciously aware of his sadness before addressing his conflicts and anxieties over his aggression. It is important to note that Bronstein did not interpret unconscious wishes (for example, aggression against the mother), did not allow catharsis, and did not reassure the child, since she did not want the child to feel guilty, ashamed, or humiliated.

Bornstein was a pioneer in a new understanding of latency. She suggested that latency could be divided into two stages: from five-and-half to eight years of age, and from eight to ten, and suggested that the common factor in both is the development of the superego, which struggles against incestuous and pregenital wishes expressed through masturbation, believing that the first phase is more favourable for psychotherapy.

Bornstein was an admired teacher who taught at the New York Psychoanalytic Institute, Menninger Clinic, and Yale University. She died while vacationing at her summer home on the Island of Vinalhaven in Maine. As she was walking at the beachfront by her house she had a sudden cerebral accident, which led to her death at the age of seventy-two on 5 September 1971.

Edith Jacobson

Edith Jacobson (1897–1978) was a German-born Jewish psychoanalyst who emigrated to United States after escaping from the Nazi regime. The daughter of a physician father and musician mother, she attended medical school at Jena, Heidelberg, and Munich. She received her medical degree from Munich in 1922. From 1922 to 1925, she was a paediatric intern at University Hospital in Heidelberg, where she became interested in psychoanalysis, and in 1925 she began her training at the Berlin Psychoanalytic Institute. Her psychoanalyst was Dr Otto Fenichel.

In 1930, she became a member of the Berlin Psychoanalytic Society, and in 1934 she was chosen to be a training analyst at the Berlin Institute. In 1935, the Nazis imprisoned her because she refused to disclose information about a patient. In 1938, she became ill with Graves' disease and diabetes. She was hospitalised in Leipzig and, while there, escaped to Czechoslovakia with the help of her good friends Annie Reich and her husband, and shortly afterward she emigrated to the United States. After arriving in New York, Jacobson became a member of the New York Society and Institute. She later taught and became a training analyst.

Edith Jacobson's main contributions

Jacobson's theoretical and clinical work is centred on ego and super-ego functioning, the processes of identification underlying the development of the ego and superego, and the role of the ego and superego in depression. Together with Hartmann, she introduced the concept of *self-representation*.

She was the first theorist to attempt an integration of the drive theory with structural and object relation theory in a comprehensive developmental synthesis. She built on the contributions of Anna Freud, Heinz Hartmann, René Spitz, and Margaret Mahler. According to Jacobson, biology and experience mutually influence each other and interact throughout development, and she was interested in the early stages of child development.

Jacobson outlined the correlation of various stages of energic and structural differentiation to the constitution and cathexis of object and self representation, and to the corresponding ideational, affective and functional development (Jacobson, 1964, p. 52).

This is her process of structural and energic differentiation through the different infantile stages:

1. The primal (embryonal) condition of diffuse dispersion of undifferentiated drive energy in the unstructured "primal" self, the discharge is by silent physiological processes.
2. With birth, growing cathexis of the perception and memory systems of the motor apparatus and of the pregenital erogenous zones sets in. Discharge to the outside begins by way of primitive, biologically prepatterned (instinctive) reactions to internal and external stimuli.
3. In the stage of beginning structural differentiation and ego formation, pleasure principle and primary process prevail. There is the tendency to immediate drive discharge and signal affects begin to become effective.
    3a. When the child learns to walk and talk, and acquires urinary and bowel control, a more organised stage sets in. Object- and self-awareness grows, perception and organisation of memory traces expand. Object constancy develops.
4. Infantile sexuality reaches its climax; fusion and neutralisation of sexual and aggressive drives has set in. Thought processes are organised, functional motor activity and object relations develop rapidly. A concept of the self as an entity that has continuity and direction is formed. The reality principle and secondary process become more dominant. Signal anxiety (castration fear) exerts a drastic influence on repression and countercathectic formation.

5. Drive neutralisation is greatly enhanced by superego formation; the latency period begins. The superego establishes a lasting and dominant control over the cathexis of the self-representation. These changes and the establishment of physical, intellectual, and moral achievement standards enhance the experience of a consistent self that maintains its continuity despite changes.

(Jacobson, 1964, pp. 54–55)

She developed her own ideas based on psychoanalytic concepts. She believed that a balanced early experience would contribute to the harmonious development of the libido and aggressive drive. The libido will emerge from experiences of feeling good therefore will be less aggression. However, if the early experiences are frustrating, the aggressive drive might disturb the normal development.

As Jacobson conceptualised it, the libido helps integrate images of good and bad objects and good and bad self. She believed that the balance of good vs. bad experiences would shape the future growth of self and other representations, and especially the role of the child's aggression. This is because aggression facilitates separation and the establishment of different images of self and others. Libido and aggression cannot function without each other, libido promotes pulling together, and aggression promotes separation. They are both necessary to build a stable identity by integrating experiences from the environment.

She went on to speak of *affective matching* between mother and child, and several factors, like the baby's temperament, the fit or misfit between baby and mother, and the mother's capacity to respond adequately to the baby's needs, play an important role in this affective matching. Jacobson wrote: "Observation on infants leave little doubt that the child very early begins to perceive, to respond to, and to imitate the gestures, the inflections of voice, and other visible and audible affective manifestation of the mother" (Jacobson, 1964, p. 42).

She pointed out that only we could talk about ego identifications once the child developed ego attitudes and character traits taken over from the parents, and the child manifests true ego interests and practises meaningful ego functions guided by the parents' example and demands.

Jacobson believed that the early psychic state of a child is undifferentiated, with no clear boundaries between the inner self and the outer world. Here, libido and aggression are not experienced as distinct drives, just as, in Jacobson's view, a newborn cannot differentiate between self and others; it is only at six months that the baby is capable of making this differentiation. Gradually the aggressive and libidinal components become more differentiated, which leads to the development of new structural systems: the ego and the superego.

Jacobson observed that in the second year of life there is a gradual transition to individuation and ego autonomy in which the representations of the child become more realistic. The child discovers his own identity and learns to differentiate wishful self from realistic self and object images. She believed that the superego develops over a long time and only becomes consolidated during adolescence. Jacobson thought that in normal development there is a balance between libido and aggression that leads to a mature differentiation between self and others. A lack of balance between libido and aggression could lead to weak boundaries between self and others, as can be observed in psychotic patients.

She stressed the crucial role of parental influence with regard to the development of the ego and superego. She wrote:

> Parental love is the best guarantee for the development of the object and self constancy, of healthy social and love relations, and of lasting identifications, and hence for a normal ego and superego development. However the instinctual and emotional frustrations and prohibitions, combined with parental demands and stimulation of social and cultural pursuits, also make significant contributions to the development of an effective, independently functioning, and self-reliant ego.
>
> (Jacobson, 1964, p. 55)

In her 1951 paper "Contributions to the Metapsychology of Cyclothymic Depression", Jacobson extended her explanation of her concept of self-representation. She described the development of self-representation as follows:

> There are two sources for the formation of the self, first, from a direct awareness of our inner experiences and second, from indirect self-perception, that is from the perception of our bodily and our mental self as an object.
>
> (Jacobson, 1953, p. 56)

She added:

> The nuclei of the early infantile self-images are our first body-images and sensations. Like the primitive objet-images, our concept of the self is at first not a firm unit. It is fused and confused with the object-images and is composed of a constantly changing series of self-images, which reflect mainly the incessant fluctuations of our mental state.
>
> (Jacobson, 1953, p. 56)

She said that in normal development, the early infantile images of the self and its love objects develop in two directions; (1) part of them forming a consolidated, realistic ego and self-representation, while (2) another part forms the core of the superego and ego-ideal. She emphasised that an important step in development is when the child becomes aware of his helplessness and dependency.

When the child loses the belief in his own omnipotence, the child prefers security to pleasure, and thus learns to accept love-objects even if they do not give him pleasure; Jacobson believed this was a significant step in the development of masochism and depression.

With maturation, the capacity to differentiate truth from falsehood, the correct from the incorrect, reason from unreason, develops. This will lead the reality principle to supersede the pleasure principle, which allows the child to accept what is realistic and reasonable. Ideally, this process will bring the perception of the realistic object and self-representation together, along with the perception of the ego function and the capacity to evaluate the outside and the inside reality.

With regard to the concept of self-esteem, Jacobson said that part of the self is the emotional expression of self-evaluation and the parallel libidinal or aggressive cathexis of self-representation. She added that: "Self-esteem expresses the discrepancy between or accordance of the wishful concept of self and the self-representation" (Jacobson, 1953, p. 59).

She explained that pathology of self-esteem can occur in different circumstances, such as (1) pathology of the ego-ideal and the self-critical ego and superego functioning; (2) pathology of the ego functions and of the self-representations; (3) an increase in or inhibition of libidinous or aggressive discharges.

Libidinous impoverishment or enrichment of the self, whether from outside or inside, from somatic, psychosomatic, or psychological sources, may reduce or increase the libidinous or aggressive cathexes of the self-representations and lead to fluctuations of self-esteem, which will lead to states of elation or depression. She said: "Self-esteem is the emotional libidinous or aggressive cathexis of the self-representations. Self-esteem expresses the discrepancy between or accordance of the wishful concept of the self and the self-representation" (Jacobson, 1953, p. 59).

Another concept that Jacobson described is the idea that success affects the manic-depressive state (now known as bipolar disorder) in the same way as failure. She further explained that success or failure might arouse an initial hostile derogation of the love-object. This is not tolerated and will lead to a rapid reversal, an undoing and denial of the previous situation. With both failure and success an increase of aggression from the love-object to the self-image occurs. If the process is pathological, the patient will be emptied of libido and the object will be recathected, and as a consequence there will be a devaluation of the self and his love-object. This dynamic will result in pessimism, a feeling of worthlessness and emptiness, and self-esteem suffers.

Madeleine Rambert

Madeleine Rambert (1900–1979) was born in Lausanne, Switzerland. She trained as a teacher, and became interested in working with problem children. She opened a facility in Croix-sur-Romainmotier that was later transferred to Lausanne. She began her psychoanalytic training at the Institute Jean-Jacques Rousseau in Geneva. Later, in 1942, she became a member of the Swiss Psychoanalytic Society.

She was closely associated with the Vienna School and is best known for her use of puppet therapy. She used different characters, representing the family and other members of society, including doctors, priests, and so on. She said that through play with these characters the child expresses his conflicts in situations that are otherwise difficult to verbalise, in addition to allowing children to satisfy sadistic and masochistic fantasies that they could not express otherwise. In 1938, her book *Une Nouvelle Technique en Psychanalyse Infantile, Le Jeu des Guignole* (with its English translation, *Children in Conflict, Twelve Years of Psychoanalytic Practice* following in 1949) became an international success. In it, Rambert described three phases in the treatment of the child: (1) exteriorisation of the conflict; (2) conscious realisation and elimination of the neurotic conflict; and (3) re-education.

Erik Erikson

Erik Erikson (1902–1994) was a German-born psychoanalyst who emigrated to United States in 1933. His mother, Karla Abrahamsen, came from a prominent Jewish family in Copenhagen. At the time of Erik's birth in Germany, Karla had been separated for several years from her first husband, a Jewish stockbroker, Waldemar Isidor Salomonsen. Nonetheless the child was registered as Erik Salomonsen. His biological father is believed to be a Dane whose name was Erik, but Erik Erikson never met him, nor did he meet his mother's first husband, and the circumstances of his birth were kept secret from the boy for years.

After Erik's birth, his mother trained as a nurse and moved with him to Karlsruhe in southern Germany; there, in 1908, Erik was three years old when his mother married his paediatrician, Dr Theodor Homberger, his name was changed to Erik Homburger, and in 1911 Dr Homberger officially adopted him.

The development of identity was an issue of concern from his childhood on, as well as in his theory. He was a tall blond boy raised in Jewish traditions and was teased in elementary school for being Jewish and then in temple for being Nordic. These early experiences fueled his interest in identity formation and influenced his work throughout his life.

Erikson studied art and later became an art teacher. While teaching at a private school in Vienna, his friend Peter Blos, a German psychoanalyst who had emigrated to the United States to escape the Nazis, suggested to Erik that he might benefit from psychoanalytic treatment. Erikson then sought out Anna Freud and started analysis with her, going on to train in psychoanalysis at the Vienna Psychoanalytic Institute and become a psychoanalyst. He also studied the Montessori method of education, which led him to the field of child development, and took a teaching position at a school created by Dorothy Burlingham, a close friend of both Anna and Sigmund Freud, where Erikson stayed for several years.

Erikson met Canadian-born Joan Serson, who would become his wife in 1933. At the time of their marriage, Erikson converted to Christianity.

That same year, shortly after the Nazis came to power in Germany, Erikson graduated from the Vienna Institute, and the couple decided to emigrate with their children, leaving first for Denmark and then the United States. When he became an American citizen, Erikson officially changed his name to Erik Erikson. According to his son Kai Erikson, his father changed his name to define himself as a self-made man: Erik, son of Erik.

In the United States, he became the first child analyst in Boston, Massachusetts, teaching at Massachusetts General Hospital, the Baker Guidance Center, and Harvard's Medical School and Psychological Clinic, and establishing a solid reputation as an outstanding clinician. Later, he taught at the University of California at Berkeley, Yale, the San Francisco Psychoanalytic Institute, the Austen Riggs Center, and the Center for Advanced Studies of the Behavioral Sciences in Stanford, California.

His book *Childhood and Society* was published in 1950, and he spent ten years working and teaching at a clinic in Massachusetts and ten years more at Harvard. In 1960, he returned to Harvard as a professor of human development and remained at the university until his retirement in 1970. After his retirement, he continued to write and undertake research with his wife.

Erik Erikson's main contributions

Erikson is famous for his work in expanding Freud's theory of stages. Each stage involves certain developmental tasks that are psychosocial in nature at certain times. Erikson believed that every human being goes through eight stages in reaching his or her full development, from birth to death. He observed that each stage of psychosocial development is marked by a conflict that, when resolved successfully, will result in a favourable outcome, and described the eight developmental stages as follows:

1. Basic trust versus basic distrust: infancy—birth to eighteen months
   Erikson referred to infancy as the *oral sensory stage*, where the most important influence is the mother's love and care for the child, with emphasis on visual contact and touch. If this period is successful the baby develops a sense of trust, which becomes the basis for the development of the sense of identity. If the baby is constantly

frustrated it can develop feelings of worthlessness and a mistrust of the world.

2. Autonomy versus shame and doubt: early childhood—eighteen months to three years

This second stage is the anal-muscular stage of early childhood. The task is to achieve a degree of autonomy while minimising shame and doubt. During this stage, children learn to master skills for themselves. This is the time when the child learns to walk, talk, and self-feed; he also he also develops motor skills and toilet trains. Mastering all of these tasks gives the child a sense of autonomy and increased self-esteem. One of the important skills is the capacity to say "No" (the "terrible twos"). During this stage, children feel vulnerable and suffer shame and doubt of themselves if they have difficulties accomplishing these tasks smoothly.

The most important relationship is with the parents, who must reach a balance of allowing the child to expand and at the same time remain firm, as dependable limits are an important in avoiding the development of impulsiveness. If the child feels a little shame and doubt, it is beneficial. If the child feels too much shame and doubt because the parents exaggerate his restrictions compulsiveness can be a result. With a proper balance of shame and doubt the child develops the virtue of willpower and/or determination.

3. Initiative versus guilt: preschool—three to five–six years

This is the genital-locomotor stage or play age, and the task here is confronting the child with a learning initiative without too much guilt. Erikson here took into account Freud's classic Oedipal struggle, and said that it is resolved through social role identifications. The child copies the adults around him and takes initiative in creating play situations. Initiative means taking responsibilities, learning new skills, and feeling purposeful. Parents can encourage initiative by encouraging children to freely express their actions and ideas. In this stage, balance is necessary, as too much initiative and too little guilt can lead to a maladaptive tendency that Erikson calls *ruthlessness*. The extreme of ruthlessess is sociopathy. Too much guilt leads to inhibition. If it is a good balance, psychosocial strength of purpose results. In this stage, the most significant relationship is with the basic family.

4. Industry versus inferiority: school age—six to twelve years

This is the latency stage, and here the task is to develop a capacity for industry while avoiding a sense of inferiority. This is now a very social stage of development, because teachers and peers and other members of the community add to the parents' and other family members' influences. It is important to balance industry and inferiority (mostly industry) with a touch of inferiority because keeping the child humble leads to the virtue of *competency*.

If the child is not encouraged to succeed or is rejected by harsh teachers or peers, he can be lead to *inferiority* or *incompetence*. Too much industry leads to the maladaptive tendency of *narrow virtuosity*. These are children who are not allowed to be children, for example, a child actor or child athletes who are not allowed to have other interests.

5. Identity versus role confusion: adolescence—twelve to eighteen–twenty years

   In this stage, the task is to discover that the person is separate from the family of origin. This is needed to achieve *ego identity* and to avoid *role confusion*. Ego identity means knowing who you are and how you fit in society. The process in this stage is to take one's earlier experiences and establish a philosophy of life. Erikson suggested to adolescents that they might take a *psychosocial moratorium*, a time out, to do different things that lead to experimenting with life, like travelling or studying, until an ego identity is reached. Erikson called too much ego identity *fanaticism*, a maladaptive tendency to believe there is only one way. Similarly, by lack of identity, Erikson refers to the malignant tendency towards *repudiation*; the person repudiates their need for an identity. Alternatively, some adolescents fuse with a group and lose their own identity. The most significant relationships in this stage are with the peer groups.

6. Intimacy versus isolation: young adulthood—eighteen to thirty-five years

   This is the initial stage of being an adult, of seeking companions and love. The young adult relationship should be a matter of two independent egos wanting to create something larger than themselves. The task in this stage is to achieve some degree of *intimacy*, as opposed to remaining in *isolation*. This is the stage of finding satisfying relationships through marriage and friendship and also of beginning to start a family. In a successful experience, the person feels intimacy on a deep level. Unsuccessful experiences would end in isolation and distance from others. The more significant relationships in this stage are those among marital partners and friends.

7. Generativity versus stagnation: middle adulthood—thirty-five to fifty-five–sixty-five years

Erikson observed that in this stage, middle age is when the person tends to be occupied with creative and meaningful work and with issues surrounding the family. This is also a stage when one can feel they are in charge, a role that was always envied earlier. The task here is to cultivate the proper balance of generativity and stagnation. Generativity is an extension of love into the future, and Erikson added to the generativity of work and raising a family other activities such as teaching, writing, invention, arts, and science-anything that satisfies the "need to be needed". Stagnation, on the other hand, is self-absorption, caring for no one.

Erikson also talks about *overextension*, when people do not allow time to rest and relax, and mentions *rejectivity*, as state of too little generativity and too much stagnation, with the person no longer participating in or contributing to society. The significant relationships in this stage are within the workplace, the community, and the family.

8. Ego integrity versus despair: late adulthood: fifty-five–sixty-five to death

The task in this stage is to develop *ego integrity* with a minimal amount of *despair*. Erikson describes integrity as a feeling of fulfillment accompanied by a sense that life has a meaning and we have made a contribution to the world. On the other hand, adults may reach this stage and despair at their experiences and perceived failures, and they may fear death as they struggle to find a purpose to their lives. In this stage, the significant relationship is with all of mankind. Erikson further describes the maladaptive tendency in this stage as one of *presumption*, as taking place when a person presumes ego integrity without actually facing the difficulties of old age. He also included *disdain*, as when the person has contempt for life-one's own or anyone else's. Erikson describes the arrival of *wisdom* as occurring when the person has the strength to approach death without fear.

Arnaldo Rascovsky

Arnaldo Rascovsky (1907–1995) was an Argentinian psychoanalyst from a family of Jewish Russian immigrants. Rascovsky began his medical studies in 1924 at the Medical School of the University of Buenos Aires. In 1926, he attended the Childrens Hospital, pursuing his specialty in paediatrics until, towards the end of 1930, he became interested in psychoanalysis and finally left paediatrics to practise psychosomatic medicine.

In 1939, he met a number of analysts who had left Europe to escape the war and who had settled in Argentina; among them Angel Garma, Enrique Pichon-Riviere, and Marie Langer. By 1942 they had founded the Argentine Psychoanalytic Association, where Rascovsky held the presidency twice.

In 1943, Rascovsky founded the *Revista de Psicoanalisis* (Psychoanalytic Journal). Its first issue included Melanie Klein's article "Early Stages of the Oedipus Complex and the Formation of the Superego". Rascovsky also participated in the group that founded FEPAL (the Psychoanalytic Federation of Latin America) in 1960.

Even when Rascovsky was not yet a child psychoanalyst he developed a theory that is closely connected with our child psychoanalytic work, and published many books related to child psychoanalysis, among them *The Knowledge of the Son, The Foetal Psyche, The Killing of the Children*, and others. But his most relevant publication was the 1995 book *Filicide: The Murder, Humiliation, Mutilation, Denigration, and Abandonment of Children by Parents*.

Here, Rascovsky observed that direct filicide, or the murder of the offspring, as well as the diversity of its attenuated forms, such as neglect, abuse, denigration, mutilation, and abandonment, are increasing throughout our contemporary world, along with the progressive development of the sociocultural process. He explained that a parent's acts may be in accord with the suffering of her own inner child, and with what she was exposed to as a child herself. In response, the inner child passively suffers aggression from the superego, and tends to identify with the aggressor and to project and perpetuate the filicidal action on her own children.

It is to be noted that Rascovsky accumulated an enormous amount of material that confirms his theory, confirming his hypothesis of abuse and neglect by the parents, sometimes leading to the child's death.

On a larger scale, Rascovsky wrote that: "War is the institutionalisation of the primitive murder and denigration of children with the consequent denial of their persecutors through idealisation. It is social action that executes the compulsion to eliminate children" (Rascovsky,

1995, p. 256). For Rascovsky, this is the expression of parental aggression that still persists and preserves the dependent condition of children imposed by universal cultural models.

He added that one of the most damaging and covert forms of filial sacrifice is abandonment. He described how important the parents' presence is throughout infancy and childhood and until the child becomes independent. Moreover, he explained that parents should be the containers of the child's innate aggression, accepting and working through this aggression, because if they cannot do so this aggression will be pent up and become self-destructive in the child.

Rascovsky believed that the child's self-integration comes from the qualitative and quantitative presence of the parents and their substitutes, and must include a basic quantum of constancy; if this does not occur, abandonment equals filicide-becoming one of the ways that parents kill their children, simply by leaving them without the appropriate nurturing necessary for them to have healthy development from the beginning of life.

We agree with Rascovsky's statement in his book *Filicide*:

> Our hope for prevention and therapy resides in the total modification of the factors organising both the individual and the group so as to create a society in which today's antagonistic struggle between the generations is converted in a transcendent successions of generations.
>
> (Rascovsky, 1995, p. 264)

Raskovsky died in Buenos Aires at the age of eighty-eight.

Françoise Marrette Dolto

Françoise Marette Dolto (1908–1988), was the fourth of seven children of a French wealthy Catholic family of engineers. From birth, she was under the care of a nanny who was dismissed after six months due to her cocaine addiction, and during her childhood Dolto later said she felt that the adults never understood her and her feelings. However, she did have a personal teacher who trained her in the Fröbel method, based on motherly love and metaphysical and religious principles.

Friedrich Fröbel (1782–1852) was a German childhood education pioneer, who laid the foundation for modern education based on the recognition that children have unique capabilities and needs. He created the concept of the "Kindergarten", which extended to Europe and America. Fröbel thought that personal development comes from within. He proposed that the task of the teacher was to provide the conditions for growth without intervening too much in the learning process. He also emphasised play and created educational toys known as "Fröbel gifts".

Dolto developed a respect for the desire to learn. When she was eight years old, her wish was to become an "education doctor" to help parents educate and understand their children, but her mother never supported her wish. Dolto went through one especially painful episode when she was eleven years old. Her older sister had become very ill with bone cancer, and her mother asked her, on the eve of Dolto's first communion, to pray for her sister's health. It was clear to her that her sister was her mother's favourite. Her prayers failed to save her sister's life, and her mother's violent reaction proved to Françoise that her mother somehow blamed her for the death.

She began medical school at the age of twenty-three, where she met Marc Schlumberger, who became a psychoanalyst. He advised her younger brother to begin analysis with René Laforgue, the founder of the Société Psychoanalytique de Paris. A year later, Françoise began her own analysis with Laforgue, which lasted three years, later continuing her analysis with Jacques Lacan.

Dolto received her hospital training in a well-known department of child psychiatry and speech therapy run by Dr Georges Heuyer. There, she met Sophie Morgenstern, who was the principal pioneer of child psychoanalysis in France. In 1942, Françoise married Boris Dolto, an eminent physiotherapist. She became a member of the Société Psychoanalytique de Paris until the group split in 1953, after which she took part, with Lacan, Daniel Lagache, and Juliette Favez-Boutonier, in founding the Société Française de Psychanalyse. After this second group split in 1964, she remained with Lacan, the founder of the Freudian School in Paris, which she left in 1980, shortly before Lacan's death in 1981. She died in 1988 at the age of eighty.

Françoise Dolto's main contributions

Dolto, who had earlier studied philosophy, developed a theory around the key concepts of subject, language, desire, and body. Her theory of *the unconscious image of the body*, which she described in detail in 1984, is based on the belief that through our body, an image of the body is built up in the unconscious beginning in the foetal stage, a process she called *the unconscious symbolic incarnation of the desiring being*. This unconscious image of the body possesses several components: a basic image, a functional image, an image of the erogenous zones, and a dynamic image. Dolto concurred with Jacques Lacan when he said that this structuring is only possible once all these archaic experiences have been verbalised, that is, symbolised by language.

With regard to the ethics of education, Dolto recognised only one universal law, the taboo of incest. She said that the human being is not only the ego, but that there is also a lack of oneness of the human being. She talked to the infants she worked with, whatever their physical or mental health, without wondering if they could reason, and never intervened in an imperative manner, only indicatively.

She condemned any educational approach that controls the person or threatens them through obedience or imitation. She believed in providing support for the child, without regard for their age and ability, and said that in order for the child to have a normal development, the child must be regarded and trusted as one who will become a good adult.

In 1986, Dolto stated that the way to prevent deficient moral training demanded tolerance towards the different behaviour of each individual. She held that self-confidence must be always restored to every pupil, that everyone have the freedom to express themselves, with no store ever being set by imitation or rivalry, and that children should be taught daily the laws governing buying or selling and the sexuality of the country in which they live, and noted that any deficiency in these areas was far more dangerous for a society's future than poor performance at school.

The creation of the Maison Verte

The aim of the Maison Verte (the Green House), which opened in Paris in 1979, was to offer day care for children from birth to age three who would be accompanied by an adult and never left alone. Following Dolto's original plan for organising early prophylaxis, the goal at Maison Verte is to seek and limit the adverse effects of an unprepared separation. By involving both adults and children, a gradual separation can be implemented.

The leading element in the way in which the Maison Verte operates lies in the presence of parents reassuring children about an environment outside the family. Dolto described this early preparatory care as informing and dispelling misunderstandings. In 1985, she suggested that this preparatory care must, above all, enlighten the attitude of parents while the child is still in the foetal stage, in addressing the way the parents imagine their child and how they communicate with him, with a later follow-up at birth and in the early months of life.

Another basic purpose of the Maison Verte was to allow children to develop the security of being their individual selves. Dolto said that the child must be assured, first, that he is himself and that this himself is in a state of security, and with this assurance, no matter where he is, the child knows what the body needs and is able to be independent of what others say.

Judith Silberpfenning Kestenberg

Judith Kestenberg (1910–1998) was born in Tarnov, Poland, of Jewish parentage, and was trained in medicine, neurology, and psychiatry in Vienna. She came to New York in 1937 when she was twenty-seven years old, and completed her training at Bellevue Hospital when Dr Paul Schilder was the director of the programme there. She did her psychoanalytic training at the New York Psychoanalytic Institute, and graduated in 1943.

Her husband, Milton Kestenberg, was born in Lodz, Poland, and became a lawyer before coming to the United States in 1939. He managed real estate and, after the Second World War, he sued in the German courts to seek compensation for Holocaust victims and organised aid for their children. Milton and Judith were married in 1940, and they had two children, Howard and Janet, and later enjoyed four grandchildren.

The couple worked together in their pursuit of justice for victims of the Holocaust at the time when Milton began to represent victims, especially children. Together, they started the research centre's international study of the organised persecution of children, and she founded the Child Development Research organisation and the Holocaust Child Survivor Studies in Sands Point on Long Island, New York.

Kestenberg became a psychoanalyst specialising in child development, and was involved in the study of the emotional and psychological state of Holocaust survivors and their children. She published seven books and one hundred fifty articles. Her two areas of research were on Holocaust survivors and child development. She taught psychiatrists, psychologists, psychoanalysts, and other specialists in the fields of child development, mental health, and dance movement therapy. Beginning in 1972, she was also the founder and director of the Organization of Child Development Research (CDR), where she ran the Center for Parents in Long Island. It was there that her study of early development and methods of primary prevention evolved.

She began a pilot project in 1953 to observe the movements of the child, recording the non-verbal expressions of mothers and infants. The motor rhythms in gratification, frustration, random movement, and play were observed and recorded. Following the Anna Freud developmental profile and based on the Laban System of Movement Notation, with modifications adaptive to its psychological focus, Kestenberg developed a movement profile that helped to assess infants, children, and adults. This became known as the Kestenberg Movement Profile (KMP), whose goal was to understand typical developmental movements and psychological functioning. These techniques were developed to help prevent emotional disorders and help children avoid stress at vulnerable periods of development. The main goal of the centre was to optimise child care by using movement as the tool for both assessment and retraining techniques. Music, art, fine and gross motor activities, and play all contributed to the assessment and retraining procedures.

At the Center for Parents and Children, mothers and fathers accompanied their children from birth through age four in a developmentally attuned programme. Large numbers of KMP assessments were observed directly and also in film and video recordings. As a result of this research, the group discovered the existence of two more phases of development, the urethral and the inner-genital, adding to the original Freudian psychosexual developmental model, and demonstrating the basis of the maternality and paternality of all children. Correspondingly, by having both fathers and mothers attend, they discovered the feminine qualities in men and masculine qualities in women, which today are referred to as inner- and outer-genital phases of development. The group's findings have now linked the dominance of specific movement patterns with particular developmental phases and psychological functions. One of the main focuses of this research has been the development of techniques for the primary prevention of emotional disorders.

Kestenberg died in New York in 1998 at the age of eighty-eight.

Arminda Aberastury

Born in Buenos Aires, Arminda Aberastury (1910–1972) was an Argentinian psychoanalyst and the pioneer of child and adolescent psychoanalysis in Argentina, where she was considered Melanie Klein's ambassador. Aberastury first worked as a teacher, and later attended philosophy and education courses, becoming a professor in psychology at the University of Buenos Aires.

In 1937, she married the psychiatrist Enrique Pichon-Riviere, who, together with Angel Garma, Arnoldo Rascovsky, and others founded the Argentine Psychoanalytic Association in 1942. The couple had three children, Enrique, Joaquin, and Marcelo, but divorced in 1965.

Arminda Aberastury's interest in child analysis began in 1938. At the beginning of her career, she was influenced by the work of Anna Freud, as well as by Sophie Morgenstern's method, but later she began to correspond frequently with Melanie Klein and learned her theory and technical approach. The two finally met personally in 1952.

In 1953, Aberastury became a training analyst at the Argentine Psychoanalytic Association (APA), and taught for twenty years at the Teaching Institute, where she was the director. She introduced the teaching of child psychoanalysis as part of the curriculum in psychoanalytic training in 1948, and extended her teaching of child psychoanalytic ideas to paediatricians, child-care workers, teachers, doctors, and paediatric dentists.

Although Aberastury was strongly influenced by Melanie Klein's ideas, she nevertheless developed her own theoretical and technical thinking, especially in the area of intervention with parents. She was a prolific writer, producing numerous papers that were published in the journal of the Argentine Psychoanalytic Association, and wrote *Theory and Technique of Psychoanalysis of Children* and *Contributions in Child Psychoanalysis*. In her book *Theory and Technique of Psychoanalysis of Children*, published in 1962, she developed her ideas about play therapy, drawing, dreams, and play.

Aberastury suffered from a chronic skin illness that led her to take her own life at the age of sixty-two.

Arminda Aberastury's main contributions

In her paper "The Early Genital Phase", Aberastury explained that the appearance of teeth in the sadistic oral phase led to the phantasy of destruction, which dominates this stage. The phantasy causes the infant to abandon the oral relationship with the breast, and evokes the need to re-establish the relationship through another part of the body. In this period of life, the discovery of the vagina in the girl and the need of penetration by the boy lead to the early genital phase. The union penis-vagina replaces the union mouth-breast.

Aberastury wrote that as the child starts to walk, talk, wean from the breast, and experience early genital life, a fundamental change in the child's perception of the world occurs. The connection with the mother changes. The child separates from the mother and feels that as he does he is not destroying her, as he felt at the time of teething. This is the stage of working through the depressive anxiety. The child's first words also mean, for him, the reparation of the love-and-hate object, which is now rebuilt inside and projected to the outside world. Words place the baby in contact with the external world and this becomes their means of communication.

Aberastury held that walking and language have the same meaning ascribed to birth: separation and re-establishment, only in another form, and now offering a new contact with the lost object, the mother.

Freud described the phallic phase as occurring at the end of the Oedipus complex, whereas Aberastury said that the Oedipus complex marks the beginning of the phallic phase and early genital phase. With this theory, she modified the process of psychosexual development by suggesting that the anal phase appears after the oral and early genital phases. According to Aberastury, this helps to understand some of the pathology of early childhood that appears in the second half of the first year of life. The early genital life of the infant is very important during this stage and also has important consequences for adult genital life. The *primary genital stage*, as she described it, is situated between the sixth and eighth month of life. This course of development became a key theoretical concept in Aberastury's psychoanalytic theory.

In her paper "The Importance of the Genital Organisation of the Early Oedipus Complex", Aberastury further described an early genital organisation that takes place between the oral and the anal ones, usually covering the second half of the first year of life, heralded by the appearance of exhibitionism, voyeurism, body exploration, and culminating in masturbation and projective identification with the primal scene and in play activity. This finally gives way to the perverse-polymorphous phase. This concept led to a new formulation of the traditional description of the libidinal development made by Freud and his followers.

Aberastury noted that the same intensity one can observe in the infant who expects the appearance of the mother at the beginning of his life, also appears in relationship with the father around four months of age. The infant then begins the period of separation from the mother; this will be the end of the exclusive relationship with her. Moreover, Aberastury said that in order for this process to happen successfully, the father has to exist from the very beginning. Finding the father at this stage allows the infant to separate from the mother, and furthermore to be able to find the source of the masculine identification, which is necessary for both the boy and the girl. The bisexual condition of the human being needs the mother–father couple in order to achieve a harmonic development of the personality, while the displacement from the mother to the father correlates with the passage from the oral to the genital phase.

Aberastury explained that the same mechanisms that made possible the hallucination of the breast before the oral experience now appear with regard to the genital needs. The girl phantasies about something that can fill her vagina, and the boy about something that he can penetrate. Aberastury said that when the child begins with play activity at about four months of age, the objects function as symbols; between four and six months of age appears the ability to sit, and so the relationships with the objects change. The child plays hide-and-seek, which is the first play activity that is grounded in the anxiety of separation and mourning for the lost object. It appears that exploration of the genitals and their recognition, as well as the difference in the sexes, are apparent in their play activity as well.

In this paper, Aberastury pointed out the early genital phase in infants, the importance of weaning, and the stage of the beginning of the Oedipus complex. She added that the vicissitudes at this time of development explain much of the pathology seen at this age in the infant, including not only the points of fixation, but also the consequences of this fixation in future pathology, with phobias given as one example of this.

Aberastury's contributions in child psychoanalytic technique

Aberastury said that the understanding and interpretation of preverbal expressions leads to diagnostic methods based on play and drawings.

As Klein did, she gave parameters for the treatment of the small child, and noted that play develops in the office in limited space and time. She said that when we give an interpretation of play, we must take into account: (1) the representation in the space; (2) the traumatic situation involved; (3) why these appear here, now, and with me; and (4) what role humour has in the play. Aberastury added that play, like a dream, is an activity full of meaning and is at the base of learning and sublimation. She discovered that from a very early age the child understands interpretations and reacts to them with words, modifying the play or changing it completely. She also believed that it is important to give interpretations from the beginning of treatment in order to establish the analytic situation.

She clearly addressed transference in child analysis. Sigmund Freud discovered that the compulsion to repeat traumatic situations, and to elaborate them by repetition and action, is the basis of play activity. Melanie Klein had studied the child's tendency to play as a consequence of his acute anxiety, which drives him to continual symbolisation and personifications in order to test out in reality what is internal by projecting it, dividing it up, and repeating it. Aberastury agreed with Klein about the interpretation of negative transference through returning the affects to the original objects, alleviating the transferential anxiety, and continuing the psychoanalytic process. She said that the interpretation of transference by discovering the anxieties related to the original objects permits the modification of the primary terrifying images. On the other hand, the process of libido development facilitates the elaboration of tolerant images, and the synthesis between the different parts of the superego becomes possible according to the reduced splitting between the idealised and persecuting images.

Aberastury's ideas about child diagnosis interviews

In her paper "Interviews in Child Analysis", Aberastury described how she structured her diagnostic approach. The steps in this procedure proceed as follows: one or several interviews with the parents, a questionnaire for an extended developmental history, a description of one day of the child's life, and a description of birthday and holiday celebrations. She said that during this interview, it is important to take notes to permit a thorough evaluation of the child. After the evaluation, she scheduled an interview with the child. Her recommendation was not to take notes during the interview with the child in order to avoid inhibiting the child during the play. After the completion of the evaluation, the analyst discusses the contract with the parents and the child at separate times. With regard to interviews with the parents during the child's treatment, she recommended that these should be scheduled only when needed, and that the information given to the parents be shared with the child.

Serge Lebovici

Serge Lebovici (1915–2000) was a French psychoanalyst who came from a Jewish Romanian family. His father, a well-known physician specialising in dermatology, had emigrated from Romania to France in 1904 and his mother, Caroline Rosenfeld, was from an Alsacian Jewish family.

Lebovici began his medical training in 1933, and was admitted as an intern at the Hospitaux de Paris after his graduation. In 1938, he was forced to interrupt his studies due to the war. After his military service, he spent time as a prisoner of war in Nuremberg, but in 1941 was freed, along with his father. After they were both freed, his father was arrested by the Nazis in 1942, and was deported to Drancy and later to Auschwitz, where he was murdered.

Lebovici finished his doctoral dissertation in 1941, and in 1942 he married Ruth Roos. The couple had two daughters, Marianne (1943) and Elizabeth (1953). Lebovici specialised in child psychiatry, and helped train an entire generation of psychoanalytic-oriented child psychiatrists at the Salpêtrière Hospital. During the post-war period, he devoted his studies to understanding the socioeconomic origins of child disturbances. In 1949, he co-signed an anti-psychoanalytic manifesto, but soon renounced his signature and quit the French Communist Party to devote himself to psychoanalysis.

He became a member of the Paris Psychoanalytic Society the same year as René Diatkine, and they became close friends. In 1958, they worked together to establish the Centre Alfred Binet in Paris for child and adolescent psychiatry. At the centre, they taught therapists and evaluated and treated children and adolescents.

In 1952, its inaugural year, Lebovici was made secretary of the Paris Institute of Psychoanalysis, where he made it possible for non-medical doctors to become psychoanalysts. Lebovici refused to participate in the political arguments in the field of child analysis between the Anna Freud and Melanie Klein groups, but welcomed them all, Anna Freud,

Melanie Klein, René Spitz, and Donald Winnicott, whom he invited to Paris. In France, he became one of the principle initiators of the direct observation of early interactions between mother and child. He introduced the work of Bowlby (attachment theory), Brazelton (neonatal competence of the baby), and Stern (affective tuning) to French clinicians. Lebovici felt that an understanding of the process of parenthood required a psychological component that took into account the imaginary, phantasy, myths, and narcissistic representations of the developing child.

In his last work, he developed the concept of *enaction* to describe the analyst's emotional and physical trial in the presence of the mother and child during therapy. Another concept that Lebovici introduced was *metaphor-generating empathy* which he used to signify his ability to verbalise and represent the affects experienced during therapeutic sessions involving the parents and the child.

I had the opportunity to observe Dr Lebovici in 1974 at the Alfred Binet Center. I attended an evaluation of a family with a child, being able to view his office during the evaluation through a system of cameras that allowed the audience see the office via a screen. Levobici was dynamic in his approach to both the parents and the child. He made active interventions, stimulating the child to talk and draw. If he determined that the child needed affection, he embraced the child, taking the initiative to be physically close to the child. He read stories to the child and even rocked the child in his lap.

During the private interview with the parents, he took a thorough history of the couple's past and current functioning, including sexual issues and family dynamics. After the interview with the parents, and the one with the child alone, Lebovici interviewed the parents and the child together, letting only the parents talk about the child. After some time, the parents left the room, and Levobici had another interview with the child alone, and asked the child what he thought about what the parents had said about him.

Serge Levobici died in Paris in 2000 at the age of eighty-five.

René Diatkine

René Diatkine (1918–1997) was a French psychoanalyst born into a Jewish Russian family that had emigrated to France during the early part of the twentieth century.

Diatkine began his study of medicine in 1939 and continued through the Second World War, during which he was mobilised twice. In 1946, Diatkine became a physician and trained in psychiatry and psychoanalysis in Paris. He was an intern, then a senior psychiatrist at the Necker Children's Hospital and worked with sick children in Professor Heuyer's department. At that time he began his own analysis with Jacques Lacan. He became a member of the Psychoanalytic Society of Paris, directed by Lacan, in 1952, but later resumed his psychoanalytic treatment with Sacha Nacht.

In 1958, together with Serge Lebovici and Philippe Paumelle, he founded the Health Association and helped establish the Centre Alfred Binet, a psychoanalytic institution for teaching and treatment of children and adolescents. Diatkine became active in the creation of numerous institutions both in France and abroad, and was also an active writer about child psychoanalysis. He was particularly interested in his theory of the role of primal phantasies and expanded the application of psychoanalysis to individual psychodrama, techniques of language re-education, field work, and collaboration with teams of multidisciplinary caregivers, as well as coordinating programmes involving teachers and librarians.

Diatkine emphasised that the potential of latent mental material can lead to the possibility of psychic reorganisation, transmitting rather than teaching the richness and discipline of psychoanalytic thought. He always fought against reductionism.

He died in Paris in 1997, at the age of seventy-nine.

CONCLUSIONS

We widen our understanding of the mental dynamics of patients, children, and adults through reviewing several theories available to us. Through them we are given more tools to organise our ideas and give interpretations, and to better understand the developmental process of therapy in order to help our patients as well as our own children with their conflicts and anxieties.

Even now, after more than one hundred years of research, study, and development in the field of child psychoanalysis, we find parents who casually leave their young infants for extended vacations without giving a thought to the psychological consequences to the child.

The acclaimed thinkers we have addressed in this book, along with many other researchers and creative minds, have different thoughts, and have conceptualised their observations and research using differing terminology. Some of them emphasise the biological aspect, some of them focus more on the environment, while others place the emphasis on the object relations. Yet in all of them there is a major common denominator.

This common denominator is the great importance of the early experiences of the infant's life and the necessary physical and emotional quality of the mother–infant dyad that allows the child to develop a biologically and emotionally healthy life. Similarly, the importance of the father's participation from the beginning of the infant's life is recognised in all the theories, while the overarching relationship between the social environment and the development of the personality is crucially important.

Physical and emotional constancy is essential in the care of the infant through the period of its early development in order to achieve a healthy personality in the child, future adolescent, and adult.

The authors we have presented understood that it is difficult to be the ideal caregiver, yet it is important to consider the optimal emotional and physical consistency for the infant from the time of birth.

I believe that the goal of psychoanalytic treatment is to make conscious the unconscious, to decrease anxiety, to decrease superego severity, and to support the resolution of neurotic conflicts, with all elements leading to the resolution of symptoms.

As parents and therapists, we desire that our children experience healthy development and adjustment, and want them to continue to increase their capacity to learn and to experience enjoyment. Towards these ends, all of us have a major interest in the education of mothers and fathers, and in teaching them how to be good-enough mothers and fathers, so that they can understand the importance of their behaviour and their interactions with their babies. For the same reason, the parents' separation and its meaning for their infants should be more widely recognised.

Based on my own experience, I would like to illustrate some examples that show how important is the need for education in this area, in order to be able to prevent the kinds of events that make children vulnerable to future psychological symptoms that could interfere with a normal healthy emotional development.

I recently had the following experience with one of my students who was attending a psychoanalytic course. A new mother, she began feeling overwhelmed with life's demands. She and her husband decided to take a ten-day vacation, leaving their thirteen-month-old baby with her in-laws, who would be coming in from another state. On her return from the trip, she said to me: " Dr Reubins, you were right, I will not do it again."

Another interesting example occurred two years ago when the well-educated parents came to my office for a consultation on their twelve-year-old boy who had symptoms of depression, was crying a lot, had panic attacks, anxiety, somatic complains, social avoidance, and a history of poor school performance. The child had had several psychiatric treatments that slightly decreased some of his symptoms.

The family had undergone traumatic experiences when the mother attempted to have a second child. When I asked about the patient's first year of life, his parents reported that both of them had worked while the infant was under the care of five different caregivers during this period, until finally his mother stayed at home to take care of the child when the child was already sixteen months old.

And, most recently, I had an experience of this kind in my office when one of my patients mentioned that her sister would be taking a two-week trip with her husband, leaving their four-month-old baby with a newly hired nanny, all without taking into consideration the effects on the child of this premature separation from the mother.

Sigmund Freud first developed the concept of early deprivation. He said that anxiety is biologically triggered by external and internal experiences as well as the loss of the object.

Anna Freud guided us with her developmental lines and the description of the early and mature ego mechanisms of defence, contributing to our understanding of the need to offer the infant an environment where his development should be consistent both physically and emotionally. She paid much attention to the quality of caregiving, especially at the beginning of life. Melanie Klein's significant contribution was to identify the deep importance of early childhood, and especially of the first year of life, as constituting a fundamental period during which psychological processes occur, and as pointing to the future health or pathology of the human being. She also created an instrument, the play technique, for the analysis of children at a very young age, one by means of which we can explore the first year of life and study the transference, both positive and negative.

Donald Woods Winnicott enlightened us through his constant observation of babies and mothers. His legacy of the good-enough mother and a good-enough environment continues to play a strong role in raising babies and treating patients. He said that in the beginning of the infant's life, the mother has to be at the infant's disposal, and added that the holding environment provides the setting for the fusion of aggression and love, and, in enabling the tolerance of ambivalence and the emergence of concern, leads to the mature acceptance of responsibility.

Winnicott pointed to the evolution of the symbolic function in the transitional space between infant and caregiver, indicating that three conditions are needed to allow this to occur: a sense of safety in relation to the experience of the inner world, a limiting of the child's concern about external events, and opportunities to generate spontaneous creative gestures. Winnicott established that the mother's mirroring function is essential for the establishment of the baby's self-representation.

Margaret Mahler showed us through her research that the infant's psychological birth occurs at thirty-six months of age, a time she identified in her studies and observation. Again, it is the first years of life that provide the basis for the physical and emotional maturation that leads to the child's being able to reach the stage of separation-individuation at that time. Phyllis Greenacre also gave much attention to the growth of the infant and his relationship with the mother early in life.

John Bowlby was convinced that the differences in the security of infant–mother attachment would have long-term implications for later intimate relationships and self-understanding, as well as for psychological disturbance. Bowlby's theories differed from the Freudian psychoanalytic theory, as, for example, in Freud's setting the Oedipal period in the third and fourth years of life. Bowlby felt that Freud's view of development was mechanistic and linear, and, after extensive studies and research, concluded that what was particularly striking was the maternal sensitivity to the infant in the first year of life. Bowlby felt that when successfully established, this provided a secure base that would serve as an enduring template for the future wellbeing of the child.

Arnaldo Rascovsky boldly stated that:

> Humanity needs a central revolution with respect to the treatment of children. The country that wants good children must preserve the mother's assistance so that she can be with her child during the first years of the child's life. This is not respected in the contemporary world.

> (Rascovsky, 1995, p. 280)

Themes that are consistent through out all these theories include: the psychological consequences of significant early deprivation; the emotional constancy needed by the infant from the beginning of the infant's life; a good-enough mother; a secure base; the important quality of the unique mother–child relationship. All of the above serve as templates for later love relations. They also function as essential conditions for the child to grow into a healthy, secure, and independent adult.

Finally, these theories also address the issues of painful losses and separations at an early age, as well as discussing the environmental factors that both contribute to and facilitate the development of healthy defences.

It is my interest in these matters that leads me to hope that through continuing the transmission and understanding of these legacies, we can educate the future generation of psychiatrists, psychologists, psychotherapists, and, lastly but certainly not least, parents.

REFERENCES

Aberastury, A. (1952). *La Transferencia en el Analisis de niños, en especial en los analisis tempranos* (vol. 9, no. 3). Buenos Aires: Revista de Psicoanalisis.

Aberastury, A. (1957). *La inclusion de los padres en el cuadro de la situacion analitica y el manejo de esta situacion a traves de la interpretacion* (vol. 14, nos. 1–2). Buenos Aires: Revista de Psicoanalisis.

Aberastury, A. (1962). *Teoria y Tecnica del Psicoanalsisis de Niños*. Buenos Aires: Paidos.

Aberastury, A. (1964). *La Fase Genital Previa* (vol. 21, no. 3). Buenos Aires: Revista de Psicoanalisis.

Aberastury, A. (1970). *La Importancia de la Organizacion Genital en la Iniciacion del Complejo de Edipo Temprano* (vol. 27, no. 1). Buenos Aires: Revista de Psicoanalisis.

Aberastury, A. (1971). *Aportaciones al Psicoanalisis de Niños*. Buenos Aires: Paidos.

Aberastury, A. (1972). *Entrevistas en el Analisis de Niños* (vol. 29, no. 3). Buenos Aires: Revista de Psicoanalisis.

Aberastury, A. (1973). *La percepcion de la muerte en los niños* (vol. 30, nos. 3–4). Buenos Aires: Revista de Psicoanalsis.

Andreas-Salomé, L. (1987). *The Freud Journal*. London: Quartet Encounters.

Blum, H. (1994). *Reconstruction in Psychoanalysis*. Connecticut: International Universities Press.

Bowlby, J. (1969). Attachment. In: *Attachment and Loss*, Vol. 1. New York: Basic Books.

Bowlby, J. (1973). Separation anxiety and anger. In: *Attachment and Loss*, Vol. 2. New York: Basic Books.

Bowlby, J. (1980). Loss. In: *Attachment and Loss*, Vol. 3. New York: Basic Books.

Bowlby, J. (1988). *A Secure Base*. New York: Basic Books; London: Karnac.

Britton, R. (2008). He thinks himself impaired: the pathologically envious personality. In: *Envy and Gratitude Revisited* (Edited by P. Roth and A. Lemma). London: Karnac.

Dolto, F. (1971). *Psychanalyse et Pediatrie*. Paris: Éditions du Seil.

Dolto, F. (1981). *Au Jeu du desir*. Paris: Éditions du Seuil.

Dolto, F. (1985). *La Cause des Enfants*. Paris: Robert Laffont.

Dolto, F. (1988). *La Cause des Adolescents*. Paris: Robert Laffont.

Erikson, E. (1950). *Childhood and Society*. London: Karnac.

Erikson, E. (1959). *Identity and the Life Cycle*. New York: International Universities Press.

Etchegochen, R. H. (1981). *Biografia breve de Melanie Klein, vol. 2–3*. Buenos Aires: Revista psicoanalisis de Apdeba.

Fenichel, O. (1964). *Teoria Psyicoacnalitica de las Neurosis*. Buenos Aires: Paidos.

Fenichel, O. (1972). *The Psychoanalytic Theory of Neurosis*. New York: W. W. Norton.

Fonagy, P. (2001). *Attachment Theory and Psychoanalysis*. New York: Other Press.

Freud, A. (1926–1927). *The Psycho-Analytic Treatment of Children*. London: Imago.

Freud, A. (1936). *The Ego and the Mechanisms of Defence*. London: Hogarth; New York: International Universities Press, 1966; London: Karnac, 1992.

Freud, A. (1965). *Normality and Pathology in Childhood: Assessments of Development*. New York: International Universities Press; London: Karnac.

Freud, A. (1992). *The Harvard Lectures*. Connecticut: International Universities Press.

Freud, S. (1894a). *The Neuro-Psychosis of Defence. SE 3*. London: Hogarth.

Freud, S. (1896). *The aetiology of hysteria. SE 3*. London: Hogarth.

Freud, S. (1900). *The Unsconcious and Consciouness—reality. SE 5*. London: Hogarth.

Freud, S. (1900). *The primary and secondary process—repression. SE 5*. London: Hogarth.

Freud, S. (1900a). *The Interpretation of Dreams. SE 4–5*. London: Hogarth.

Freud, S. (1901). Symptomatic and chance actions. *Psychopathology of Everyday Life. SE 6.* London: Hogarth.

Freud, S. (1901b). *The Psychopathology of Everyday Life. SE 6.* London: Hogarth.

Freud, S. (1905c). *Jokes and Their Relation to the Unconscious. SE 5.* London: Hogarth.

Freud, S. (1905d). *Three Essays on the Theory of Sexuality. SE 7.* London: Hogarth.

Freud, S. (1909b). *Analysis of a Phobia in a Five-Year-Old Boy, Little Hans. SE 10.* London: Hogarth.

Freud, S. (1911b). *Formulations on the Two Principles of Mental Functioning. SE 12.* London: Hogarth.

Freud, S. (1913c). *On Beginning the Treatment. SE 12.* London: Hogarth.

Freud, S. (1914). *Children's dreams. SE 14.* London: Hogarth.

Freud, S. (1914c). *On Narcissism: An Introduction. SE 14.* London: Hogarth.

Freud, S. (1914f). *Some Reflections on Schoolboy Psychology. SE 13.* London: Hogarth.

Freud, S. (1914g). *Remembering, Repeating and Working Through. SE 12.* London: Hogarth.

Freud, S. (1915c). *Instincts and Their Vicissitudes. SE 14.* London: Hogarth.

Freud, S. (1915d). *Repression. SE 15.* London: Hogarth.

Freud, S. (1915e). *The Unconcious. SE 14.* London: Hogarth.

Freud, S. (1917e). *Mourning and melancholia. SE 14.* London: Hogarth.

Freud, S. (1918b). *From the History of an Infantile Neurosis. SE 17.* London: Hogarth.

Freud, S. (1920d). *Associations of a Four-Year-Old Child. SE 18.* London: Hogarth.

Freud, S. (1920g). *Beyond the Pleasure Principle. SE 18.* London: Hogarth.

Freud, S. (1921c). *Group Psychology and the Analysis of the Ego. SE 18.* London: Hogarth.

Freud, S. (1923b). *The Ego and the Id. SE 19.* London: Hogarth.

Freud, S. (1925j). *Some Psychical Consequences of the Anatomical Distinction between the Sexes. SE 19.* London: Hogarth.

Freud, S. (1926d). *Inhibitions, Symptoms and Anxiety. SE 20.* London: Hogarth.

Freud, S. (1930a). *Civilisation and Its Discontents. SE 21.* London: Hogarth.

Freud, S. (1931b). *Female Sexuality. SE 21.* London: Hogarth.

Freud, S. (1933a). *New Introductory Lectures on Psycho-Analysis. SE 22.* London: Hogarth.

Greenacre, P. (1952). *Trauma, Growth and Personality.* New York: Norton; London: Karnac.

Greenacre, P. (1953). *Affective Disorders: Psychoanalytic Contribution to Their Study*. New York: International Universities Press.

Greenacre, P. (1958). Early physical determinants in the development of the sense of identity. In: *Emotional Growth*. New York: International Universities Press, 1971.

Greenacre, P. (1963). *The Quest for the Father*. New York: International Universities Press.

Greenacre, P. (1971). *Emotional Growth* (volumes. 1 and 2). New York: International Universities Press.

Grolnick, S. (1990). *The Work and the Play of Winnicott*. New York: Jason Aronson.

Isaacs, S., with Klein, M., Heimann, P., Isaacs, S., & Riviere, J. (1943). The nature and function of phantasy. In: *Development in Psycho-Analysis*. London: Hogarth, 1952.

Jacobson, E. (1953). Contributions to the metapsychology of cyclothymic depression. In: P. Grenacre, *Affective Disorders*. New York: International Universities Press.

Jacobson, E. (1964). *The Self and the Object World*. New York: International Universities Press.

Jacobson, E. (1971). *Depression: Comparative Studies of Normal, Neurotic, and Psychotic Conditions*. New York: International Universities Press.

Jones, E. (1960a). *Vida y Obra de Sigmund Freud. Vol. I*. Buenos Aires: Ediciones Horme.

Jones, E. (1960b). *Vida y Obra de Sigmund Freud. Vol. II*. Buenos Aires: Editorial Nova.

Jones, E. (1960c). *Vida y Obra de Sigmund Freud. Vol. III*. Buenos Aires: Ediciones Horme, 1976.

Joseph, B. (1995). *Dialogos con Betty Joseph*. Buenos Aires: APdeBA.

Klein, M. (1921). The development of a child. In: *Contributions in Psycho-Analysis 1921–1945*. London: Hogarth, 1948.

Klein, M. (1923). Infant analysis. In: *Contributions in Psycho-Analysis 1921–1945*. London: Hogarth, 1948.

Klein, M. (1928). Early stages of the Oedipus conflict. In: *Contributions in Psycho-Analysis 1921–1945*. London: Hogarth, 1948.

Klein, M. (1930). The importance of symbol-formation in the development of the ego. In: *Contributions in Psycho-Analysis 1921–1945*. London: Hogarth, 1948.

Klein, M. (1931). A contribution to the theory of intellectual inhibition. In: *Contributions in Psycho-Analysis 1921–1945*. London: Hogarth, 1948.

Klein, M. (1932). *The Psycho-Analysis of Children*. In: *Collected Works*. London: Hogarth, 1975.

Klein, M. (1940). Mourning and its relation to manic-depressive states. In: *Contributions in Psycho-Analysis 1921–1945*. London: Hogarth, 1948.

Klein, M. (1945). The Oedipus complex in the light of early anxieties. In: *Contributions in Psycho-Analysis 1921–1945*. London: Hogarth, 1948.

Klein, M. (1946). Notes on some schizoid mechanisms. In: *Envy and Gratitude, and Other Works, 1946–1963*. New York: Free Press, 1975.

Klein, M. (1948). On the theory of anxiety and guilt. In: *Developments in Psycho–Analysis*. New York: Da Capo, 1983; London: Karnac, 1989.

Klein, M. (1950). On the criteria for the termination of a psycho-analysis. In: *Envy and Gratitude, and Other Works 1946–1963*. New York: Free Press, 1975.

Klein, M. (1952a). The origins of transference. In: *Envy and Gratitude, and Other Works 1946–1963*. New York: Free Press, 1975.

Klein, M. (1952b). Some theoretical conclusions regarding the emotional life of the infant. In: *Developments in Psycho-Analysis*. New York: Da Capo, 1983; London: Karnac, 1989.

Klein, M. (1955a). The psycho-analytic play technique: its history and significance. In: *New Directions in Psycho-Analysis*. London: Tavistock, 1955.

Klein, M. (1955b). On identification. In: *New Directions in Psycho-Analysis*. London: Tavistock, 1955.

Klein, M. (1957). Envy and gratitude. In: *Envy and Gratitude, and Other Works 1946–1963*. Vol. 3. New York: Free Press, 1975; London: Karnac, 1993.

Klein, M. (1960). On mental health. In: *Envy and Gratitude, and Other Works 1946–1963*. New York: Free Press, 1975; London: Karnac, 1993.

Klein, M. (1961a). *Narrative of a Child Analysis*. London: Delarte Press, 1975.

Klein, M. (1961b). A note on depression in the schizophrenic. *International Journal of Psychoanalysis, 41*: 509–511.

Klein, M. (1963). On the sense of loneliness. In: *Envy and Gratitude, and Other Works 1946–1963*. New York: Free Press, 1975; London: Karnac, 1993.

Mahler, M., Pine, F., & Bergman, A. (1975). *The Psychological Birth of the Human Infant: Separation and Individuation*. New York: Basic Books.

Marrone, M. (2001). *La Teoria del Apego*. Madrid: Psimatica.

Pine, F. (1985). *Developmental Theory and Clinical Process*. New Haven: Yale University Press.

Rascovsky, A. (1995). *Filicide*. New Jersey: Jason Aronson.

Segal, H. (1964). *Introduction to the Work of Melanie Klein*. New York: Basic Books, 1973.

Segal, H. (1979). *Melanie Klein*. New York: The Viking Press.

Spitz, R. (1945). Hospitalism: an inquiry into the genesis of psychiatric conditions in early childhood. In: *Psychoanalytic Study of the Child*. New York: International Universities Press.

Spitz, R. (1965). *The First Year of Life.* New York: International Universities Press, 1975.

Winnicott, D. W. (1948). Reparation in respect of mother's organised defense against depression. In: *Through Paediatrics to Psycho-Analysis.* New York: Basic Books, 1975.

Winnicott, D. W. (1953). Transitional objects and transitional phenomena. In: *Playing and Reality.* London: Tavistock, 1971.

Winnincott, D. W. (1954). Metapsychological and clinical aspects of regression within the psycho-analytic set-up. In: *Through Paediatrics to Psycho-Analysis.* New York: Basic Books, 1975.

Winnicott, D. W. (1956a). Mirror-role of mother and family in child development. In: *Playing and Reality.* London: Tavistock, 1971.

Winnicott, D. W. (1956b). Primary maternal preocupation. In: *Through Paediatrics to Psycho-Analysis.* New York: Basic Books, 1975.

Winnicott, D. W. (1958). The capacity to be alone. In: *The Maturational Processes and the Facilitating Environment.* New York: International Universities Press, 1965; London: Karnac, 1990.

Winnicott, D. W. (1960). Ego distortion in terms of true and false self. In: *Maturational Processes and the Facilitating Environment.* New York: International Universities Press, 1965; London: Karnac, 1990.

Winnicott, D. W. (1962a). Ego integration in child development. In: *The Maturational Processes and the Facilitating Environment.* New York: International Universities Press, 1965; London: Karnac, 1990.

Winnicott, D. W. (1962b). A personal view of the Kleinian contribution. In: *The Maturational Processes and the Facilitating Environment.* New York: International Universities Press, 1965; London: Karnac, 1990.

Winnicott, D. W. (1962c). The aims of psychoanalytic treatment. In: *The Maturational Processes and the Facilitating Environment.* New York: International Universities Press, 1965; London: Karnac, 1990.

Winnicott, D. W. (1962d). A personal view of the Kleinian contribution. In: *The Maturational Process and the Facilitating Environment.* New York: International Universities Press, 1965; London: Karnac, 1990.

Winnicott, D. W. (1963a). The development of the capacity for concern. In: *Maturational Processes and the Facilitating Environment.* New York: International Universities Press, 1965; London: Karnac, 1990.

Winnicott, D. W. (1963b). From dependence towards independence in the development of the individual. In: *Maturational Processes and the Facilitating Environment.* New York: International Universities Press, 1965; London: Karnac, 1990.

Winnicott, D. W. (1964a). What about the father? In: *The Child, the Family and the Outside World.* Massachusetts: Addison-Wesley, 1987.

Winnicott, D. W. (1964b). What do you mean by a normal child? In: *The Child, the Family and the Outside World*. Massachusetts: Addison-Wesley, 1987.

Winnicott, D. W. (1964c). The only child. In: *The Child, the Family and the Outside World*. Massachusetts: Addison-Wesley, 1987.

Winnicott, D. W. (1964d). Why children play. In: *The Child, the Family and the Outside World*. Massachusetts: Addison-Wesley, 1987.

Winnicott, D. W. (1964e). *The Piggle*. New York: International Universities Press, 1977.

Winnicott, D. W. (1964f). *Home Is Where We Start From*. New York: W. W. Norton, 1986.

Winnicott, D. W. (1965). On security. In: *The Family and Individual Development*. London; Tavistock,

Winnicott, D. W. (1971a). Creativity and its origins. In: *Playing and Reality*. London: Tavistock, 1971.

Winnicott, D. W. (1971b). Contemporary concepts of adolescent development and their implications for higher education. In: *Playing and Reality*. London: Tavistock, 1971.

Winnicott, D. W. (1984). *Deprivation and Delinquency*. London: Tavistock.

Winnicott, D. W. (1986). *Holding and Interpretation: Fragments of an Analysis*. New York: Grove Press.

Winnicott, D. W. (1987). *Babies and Mothers*. Massachusetts: Addison-Wesley.

Winnicott, D. W. (1988). *Human Nature*. New York: Schocken Books.

INDEX

Indexer: Dr Laurence Errington

Note: "Freud" in subentries etc. refers to Sigmund Freud.

241